Online Fashion

GIUSEPPE STIGLIANO / **PHILIP KOTLER** / RICCARDO POZZOLI

10 RULES FOR THE FUTURE OF HIGH-END FASHION

Published by
LID Publishing
An imprint of LID Business Media Ltd.
The Record Hall, Studio 304,
16-16a Baldwins Gardens,
London EC1N 7RJ, UK

info@lidpublishing.com
www.lidpublishing.com

A member of:

businesspublishersroundtable.com

Printed by Severn, Gloucester

ISBN: 978-1-911687-08-5
ISBN: 978-1-911687-09-2 (ebook)

Cover and page design: Caroline Li

Onlife Fashion

GIUSEPPE STIGLIANO / **PHILIP KOTLER** / RICCARDO POZZOLI

10 **RULES** FOR THE FUTURE OF HIGH-END FASHION

MADRID | MEXICO CITY | LONDON
NEW YORK | BUENOS AIRES
BOGOTA | SHANGHAI | NEW DELHI

Contents

CONTRIBUTORS

Acknowledgements

This book would not have come to be without the essential contribution of many people who, in various ways, supported us throughout its research and writing. We would like to thank some of them here, but we would also like to extend our gratitude to those whose names are not mentioned in these few lines.

Our heartfelt thanks go to all the managers we interviewed and their respective teams.

Without their valuable insights and the sharing of their experiences, this work would be decidedly less comprehensive.

Thanks to Francesca Airoldi, Francesco Bottigliero, Massimiliano Brunazzo, Stella Chirivi, Francesca Nardi, Ludivine Pont and Luca Zambrelli for facilitating contacts that led to a number of the interviews.

To Federico Capeci, Luigi Di Gregorio, Mauro Ferraresi, Chiara Magnaghi, Giuseppe Mayer, Giacomo Ovidi, Emanuela Prandelli, Francesca Romana Rinaldi and Marco Vezzani, for the valuable insights that emerged throughout numerous discussions.

To Alessandro Balossini Volpe for the accurate peer reviews, without which this book would not be the same.

To editor Marie Stafford and the entire Wunderman Thompson Intelligence team for sharing a wealth of research and insights with us. To Lynn Sproatt for her English translation, informed by her many years in advertising and marketing.

Finally, a special mention is due to our incomparable collaborators, Matteo Meneghetti and Andrea Panzeri, for the extraordinary support provided throughout the journey that led to this book.

Andrea Panzeri is Consultant at BIP, member of SIM – centre of excellence in Strategy, Innovation & Marketing. During his career, he worked as Brand & Business Development Strategist at VMLY&R (WPP group), Caffeina and OMD Italy. Matteo Meneghetti is co-founder and Chief Strategic Officer of Conic. Previously he held the role of Strategic Planner in RedCell (WPP group). Andrea and Matteo are lecturers at leading Italian universities and business schools on the issues of communication, marketing and digital transformation as applied to retail. They also collaborated in the drafting of the book *Retail 4.0 – 10 Rules for the Digital Era* by Philip Kotler and Giuseppe Stigliano.

Foreword

BY LUCIANO FLORIDI

In the past, when miners went down into the coal mine, they brought a canary with them. The bird was much more sensitive to poisonous gases than they were, and if it died in its cage, it meant they needed to escape: danger was imminent and there was no way to survive except by getting out. Today, the phrase "canary in the coal mine" is used metaphorically, referring to something that serves the task of sending an early warning signal.

I think the spirit of this book is well represented by this metaphor. Fashion is a sector that often represents the canary of a country's economy and culture. It is a precursor of change in society because more than other sectors it is sensitive to it, even if, unlike the metaphorical canary, it is often inclined to interpret it, if not also inspire it. This is why I believe that this book can aspire to speak to both insiders and anyone else curious to understand the direction in which consumer society is evolving. What is happening today in fashion will happen tomorrow in many other sectors of the economy, at least in the most advanced countries.

Having chosen fashion as our focal point, how can we now describe the context in which it moves and operates? We would tend to construct a scenario using two categories: where and when. However, space and time are no longer adequate to describe the society in which we live. Human experience is the lens we use to look at the world, and today that goes beyond presence (where I am) and localization (where I can take action). In the time of Homer's *Iliad*, even the gods were required, in person and at the right moment, to step onto the battlefield in order to influence events. Space/presence and place/interaction had to coincide to make sense. The acceleration that has occurred in recent years has crumbled these space-time categories, allowing us to live in a type of extended present, potentially detached from the ebb and flow of seasons and circadian rhythms, with all that this entails. But above all, we have become accustomed to operating in the infosphere, to being telepresent while we are in another location, from doing banking transactions without going to the branch, to online teaching without going to the classroom. Our temporality is increasingly marked not so much by the clock but by the latency of our connections.

The barriers between real and virtual have also collapsed between what, since the advent of digital technology, we have defined as 'online' and what has always been 'offline.' This new existence is increasingly an 'onlife' hybrid, much like the habitat of mangroves. These plants are able to flourish in brackish waters, given their innate ability to draw nourishment from both shallow and deep roots. For them, the dichotomy between fresh water and salt water, metaphorically corresponding to analogue and digital, simply does not exist. The sea and the river still exist, of course, but for the mangroves, everything takes place where they mix in brackish water. These are concepts (onlife, infosphere, mangrove society) made more evident by the COVID-19 pandemic, which has deprived us of offline experiences and forced us to temporarily transfer our lives online, migrating from biosphere to infosphere.

This book was written in a period of great suffering, profound changes and maximum uncertainty, anxiously awaiting the return to the free flow that characterizes onlife living. In moments of discontinuity like this, humans tend to make the mistake of prefiguring and then trying to build the future within the categories of the past. This is a trap to be avoided: we cannot interpret the 'new' with only the mental categories of the 'old.' The future is built *on* the past, not *with* the past. That is why looking at digital change only as a burden, an obligation and a cost is wrong today. This view leads people and organizations to resist rather than embrace the innovation and opportunities that digital offers. The quest for success cannot be limited to a reluctant adaptation to the context but must be based on the search for what can be done to make an impact in that context, to do better by innovating, not to do the same by resisting. Therefore, what is needed is a profound change in our interpretation of the reality surrounding us and that which we are constructing, of the operating models (including business and management models) that we want to implement, and of the strategies aimed at achieving these visions. In short, we need to change our attitude and be open to designing innovation.

Professor Kotler – to whom, together with Giuseppe Stigliano and Riccardo Pozzoli, I would like to express thanks for having given me the opportunity to introduce the reader to this work, whose title contains a neologism I coined some 20 years ago to decipher the contemporary world – has often maintained that, "If a company does not change its business model within five years, in five years it will have no business model." That is true. But beware: in a world that changes at the speed of an algorithm, that flows seamlessly between analogue and digital, between offline and online, and that the authors – not by chance – provocatively describe as 'without rules,' it would be a serious mistake if we did not take responsibility for finding new interpretive keys to establish new rules. It would mean giving in to the temptation of entrenching ourselves behind the **know-how** (the knowledge of how things are done) and in ceasing to confront the **know-that** (the knowledge of things and what things we should be addressing to accomplish them), setting aside that typically human characteristic of seeing the facts of the world from a selective perspective at a selective time. This is why, in other instances, I have suggested that our era is not so much the era of inventions or discoveries, but that of design, understood as the ability to identify the important problems to be addressed and the best solutions to solve them.

In my opinion, this work should be seen from this perspective. It reconciles the rigour of scientific research with the ability to popularize information, much like university settings that often address a diverse audience.

Readers who have the patience to peruse these pages will be left with a very clear picture of the phenomena that have changed the rules of fashion and a bouquet of guiding principles that can inspire the actions of those who work in this sector, and more generally in the market.

Enjoy the read.

Introduction

FASHION AND HIGH-END FASHION

In an era marked by sudden and profound change, the fashion world has also experienced significant transformations. Its boundaries, its rationale and its protagonists have all been redefined, with these changes continuing now and in the future. **The purpose of this book is to analyse this market with particular focus on the segment we'll define as 'high-end' and to provide entrepreneurs, professionals, workers in the sector, consultants and students an interpretive context to understand the latest and most up-to-date ideas and how to govern their growth.**

The starting point for our discussion begins with the title of the book, which emphasizes two important characteristics regarding its context: the increasingly blurred distinction between offline and online – hence the term 'onlife' – and the absence of rules, given the obvious outdatedness of those on which fashion companies have based their business strategies in recent decades. This has led us to propose a handbook of new rules, suitable for a world that increasingly appears to be lacking them.

To start, it is necessary to agree on a definition of **fashion**. Without forgetting its historical, cultural, social and psychological meanings, the focus here is the creative-industrial scope of fashion. For this writer, fashion is: "the clothing industry and that of related accessories (shoes, bags, jewellery, etc.), that being closely linked with the

1

sociocultural spirit of the times, markets products for which design, aesthetics and style are of primary importance for the consumer."

It is also necessary to clarify what we mean by high-end fashion. The following diagram is offered by way of explanation.

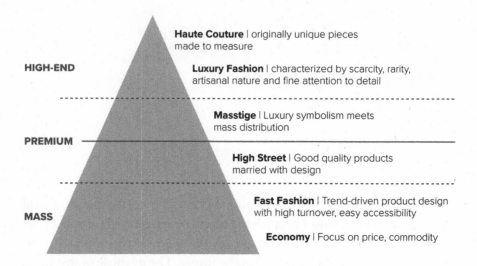

FIGURE 1.1: THE FASHION INDUSTRY PYRAMID

This pyramid represents the entire fashion industry. It is ideally divided into three levels defined by the titles **mass**, **premium** and **high-end**. The first level at the base consists of all the companies that use price as their only source of competitive advantage and those brands that we've come to call fast fashion. These latest players have rewritten many of the rules for the entire category and, for this reason, we'll discuss them in-depth in the pages that follow.

Moving to the middle level of the pyramid, we find brands that offer products of higher quality and sophisticated design, used to justify their price differential. Brands that can be defined as 'masstige' are in this segment. By adopting the communication codes of luxury, they aim to combine prestige with a wider market penetration.

At the top level of the pyramid, high-end can be found. We find the maisons that combine artisanship, scarcity and rarity in their DNA. Many high-end fashion players have their roots in what we can call 'original luxury' or haute couture. The apex of the pyramid, defined by the elitist production of unique and tailor-made pieces, can be considered as the origin of a segment that eventually expanded into what is now more commonly understood as 'luxury.' This fundamental concept, profoundly linked with the spirit of the times, will be discussed in several chapters. It is important to clarify now that when we speak of **luxury brands**, all the players in the top level will be identified as high-end, including both those properly belonging to 'luxury fashion' and the leaders within the small circle of haute couture.

This proposed diagram is useful for orienting oneself within the contents of the book. In our case, the construction of the pyramid is a combination of factors such as the production and distribution models, communication codes, price positioning, target audience and adherence to macro-trends.

We're also aware that markets change, by movement between the segments that can be caused by collaborations between players that are theoretically at opposite ends of the pyramid, or by external actors. Furthermore, people do not perceive segments, but instead relate to brands and real experiences. Therefore, it is even more useful to define the meaning of high-end in light of what it represents in people's minds. High-end refers to the concept of luxury.

This can be explained from the biological perspective, as it is possible to note how your brain perceives an external element imbued with scarcity to be 'luxurious.' We consider everything that is not readily available, or that is rare or difficult to find, or unique, to be precious. The principle of scarcity comes from the fact that humans have been genetically programmed to survive in difficult environments, where resources are scarce and therefore of high value. All of this, translated to the world of fashion, motivates customers to willingly spend what otherwise could hardly be rationally justified to own a particular asset. And it is precisely within this area of irrationality that the difference between premium and luxury plays out. High-end is not simply 'more premium.' The elements that denote premiumness are always technical and functional in character and as such are measurable and comparable. For this reason, brands occupying the middle segment of the pyramid must specifically improve if they want to be able to justify a higher price. The high-end, on the other hand, distances itself from this logic and instead allies itself to the dream dimension, using intangible aspects to establish uniqueness.

The high-end are not forced to compete on comparable characteristics. High-end players can follow rules, at times, diametrically opposed to those usually used by other segments, to create value and achieve success. Dream is the basis of luxury, and it is the high-end brands that can satisfy this desire.

THE BOOK

This book was written during one of the most extraordinary periods in contemporary history: the global COVID-19 pandemic. The virus has devastated the world economy and disrupted people's way of life, becoming a true watershed between what was and what will be. Fortunately, vaccines against COVID have arrived and at some point normal commerce will resume. We have set ourselves the task of capturing with rigour and objectivity the principal events in progress, and distilling these to 10 guiding principles that we hope will guide the decisions of those working within the field of high-end fashion in the coming years.

Even as it is clear to everyone that COVID-19 has changed the rules of the game in all market sectors, there are other **forces** that originated well before this event and that still influence fashion. We have identified five: **acceleration**, **hybridization**, **disintermediation**, **sustainability**, **democratization**.

We will focus on these in the initial part of the book. Their examination, and that of some of the most authoritative voices in the field, have led to the need to define new 'rules' for orientation in this increasingly volatile scenario, where the only constant seems to be change. These guiding Principles – **Be Inclusive, Be a Symphony, Be a Vibration, Be Timeless, Be Inspired, Be Relational, Be Purposeful, Be a Service, Be Collaborative, Be Antifragile** – form the backbone of the book.

Finally, in the last section, we have included transcripts from 16 interviews conducted with prominent leaders of high-end fashion who operate at an international level: Leo Rongone (**Bottega Veneta**), Brunello Cucinelli (**Brunello Cucinelli**), Alfonso Dolce (**Dolce & Gabbana**), Gildo Zegna (**Ermenegildo Zegna**), José Neves (**Farfetch**),

4

Marco Bizzarri (**Gucci**), Remo Ruffini (**Moncler**), Lorenzo Bertelli (**Prada**), Micaela Le Divelec Lemmi (**Salvatore Ferragamo**), Gabriele Maggio (**Stella McCartney**), Jacopo Venturini (**Valentino**), Jonathan Akeroyd (**Burberry**), Federico Marchetti (**YNAP**), Francesca Bellettini (**Yves Saint Laurent**), Davide De Giglio (**New Guards Group**) and Domenico De Sole (**Tom Ford International**).

These interviews serve the reader as a valid comparison with respect to the conclusions drawn within the book.

SOME QUESTIONS WE AIM TO ANSWER IN THIS BOOK:

- What events have most affected the fashion industry in recent years?
- What strategies should high-end players implement in response to these transformations?
- Which business models are still valid and which should be redesigned?
- What factors will determine the success of luxury fashion brands?
- What is the future of the high-end segment within the fashion industry?

The Five

Forces

ACCELERATION

"If everything seems under control,
you're just not going fast enough.**"**

———

MARIO GABRIELE ANDRETTI

Our world changes at the speed of an algorithm and the only constant is change itself. The marriage between the capitalist model and the consumer culture first triggered and then made constant acceleration essential. The very concept of time has changed, past and future are compressed, crushed into an eternal 'instantaneous' accelerated present, in which we are all frantically searching for significance and meaning. The result is a market in which supply is significantly higher than demand. Marketing must accelerate the semantic obsolescence of goods to speed their turnover. The very identity of individuals is defined and redefined through continuous consumption.

Fast fashion presents itself simultaneously as a result and as a contributing factor to the acceleration that has occurred in recent years throughout the fashion industry, affecting even the high-end segment. The pandemic then imposed a forced slowdown, leading prominent industry leaders to publicly admit that this pace is no longer sustainable and that the fashion system must actively develop an alternative model.

ACCELERATION AS A NECESSARY CONDITION

One of the salient features of the digital revolution is the spread of increasingly powerful, high-performing and therefore fast solutions and devices. Moore's law is at the base of this evolution. Intel co-founder and researcher Gordon Moore predicted back in 1965 that the computing power of computers would double every 18–24 months, and the halving of transistor sizes would occur. Over the years more powerful, smaller and cheaper processors have made new technologies accessible and practical for a vast number of users. We often talk about technical 'democratization.' Moore's law explains how it is possible that more than two thirds of today's population in the top 52 economies of the world have a smartphone in their hands that has more computing power than that of the entire Apollo space program in 1969, the year man first landed on the moon.

Many of us have devices capable of making our daily lives more productive and efficient, optimizing our time, a precious and increasingly scarce resource. One result was the rapid disappearance of many elements that had characterized people's lives for centuries. Email, for example, quickly made obsolete the system of letters, envelopes, postage stamps, post offices and employees, not to mention the wait between sending a message and getting a response. Another was the compression of audio files and images that have given rise to such formats as MP3, JPEG and MPEG making superfluous both the physical media and a great deal of the sector linked to the market of music, photography and home video. All of this has accelerated the dissemination of content on the web.

The capitalist system based on the flow of goods and information has drawn lifeblood from this scenario and in turn stimulated consumerism, the socioeconomic phenomenon typical in industrialized societies that encourages the purchasing of goods and services in ever-increasing quantities. In a global context, in which technological and digital evolution redefine the space-time dimension and further speed these flows, it becomes evident how ideal conditions can be created for a dizzying acceleration of the process.

On the supply side, companies have combined overproduction with marketing policies capable of constantly stimulating demand, working on 'hard' practices such as **planned obsolescence** (a strategy aimed at deliberately limiting the life cycle of a product) and 'soft' practices such as **semantic obsolescence** (a strategy that aims to speed up the social and cultural wear and tear of the product). People are encouraged to buy new products well before the old ones are actually worn out, thus generating value by artificially shortening the lifecycle of goods and services.

On the demand side, people realize that they can 'wear' different social identities by using goods to support them, which is ideal in a contemporary world where social position is no longer predetermined at birth and stable over a lifetime, but is the result of continuous negotiation. **In short, in pre-modern societies, evolution of the species took place in the material-biological context; in contemporary hypermodern society now, social life becomes the stage where it is played out.** Individuals define their 'social self' by constantly modifying and 'updating' their identity.

Often the acceleration of devices reaches such levels that companies have no way of meeting the timelines required for the process of ideation/testing/production/commercialization. They have to collaborate with third parties – industrial or commercial partners, with the same customers, or even competitors in cases of what is known as coopetition – to codesign and then cocreate the products they launch in the market. In some sectors, such intensity has been reached that the system needs a collective intelligence in which production and consumption merge in a kind of cross-fertilization in order to self-sustain itself. The thinking of Tapscott and Williams regarding **Wikinomics** must be considered: a 'fast' economy ('wiki' means 'fast' in Hawaiian), with a high rate of change, where several parts contribute in sequence or simultaneously for the creation of a certain result. User-generated content – the possibility for anyone to produce and distribute content through the network – and the sharing economy itself in which people prefer to temporarily 'access' goods and services, rather than 'own' them, must be looked at.

All this leads to feed and then perpetuate the vortex of acceleration, resulting in the present 'NOW' being the only relevant dimension, with past and future consigned to an ancillary one. It is not by chance that terms such as 'era of expectations' and 'culture of impatience' are often used to describe contemporary society. Or that the acronym IWWIWWIWI, which stands for "I want what I want when I want it," is used in relation to younger generations.

FAST = FASHION

The world of fashion – which is based on cyclical trends and is therefore driven by timelines – could certainly not remain free from this acceleration. Fashion is the driver of semantic obsolescence: what is not 'fashionable' is itself obsolete. In a world in which brand personality is a privileged vehicle for creating one's social identity, and where fostering it becomes an obligation, fashion inevitably plays a crucial role, in light of the fact that clothing and accessories have historically represented one of the most conspicuous modes of communication that people possess.

On the other hand, we must point out how traditional companies – in fashion as in other sectors – have struggled to embrace this paradigm shift, as it is in sharp contrast to business operating models and the time required to create, present, produce, distribute and market products. Furthermore, the adjective 'fast' also does not suit the high-end segment from the point of view of the products, which aspire to be long lasting, if not **timeless**. This is why the new model has not been interpreted effectively by the 'established companies' but rather by the new-generation companies that have been engineered to dismantle traditional creative, distribution and production processes.

The high-end fashion cycle typically consists of the following phases:

1. planning, design and product development;
2. sale;
3. production and delivery.

The duration of each stage varies according to each company, but can generally last from three to seven months. The longest and most important of these phases is clearly the first, as it determines the style of the collection and much of its success or failure. And it is precisely this stage that was targeted in the 1990s by the new generation of companies, designing a business model known as **fast fashion**.

Fast fashion aims to reproduce the runway styles presented by high-end brands on a mass industrial scale while reducing the time and costs of phase 1. The idea of quickly producing and marketing products inspired by the big fashion brands, and styles observed in the market, already existed in the DNA of some brands, such as Benetton in Italy. However, the term fast fashion was coined by *The New York Times* in the early 1990s to describe the methods of Amancio Ortega, founder of Zara, who at the time stated that it took 15 days, starting from a garment's design, until it was marketed in one of his stores. This is why fast fashion is inextricably linked to the name of the Spanish brand.

But many companies have been attracted to the idea of such an effective business model of reducing the gap between high-end and most mass-market segments in the name of acceleration and accessibility. Brands like H&M, C&A, Peacocks, Topshop, etc. come to mind. Technically, the oldest of these retailers is H&M,

which opened its first store in Sweden in 1947, followed by Zara in 1975. For both, 'speed' was the driving force behind their business model. This is an outside-in model, based on the idea that value is created from market cues, with the design, production and distribution of the collection proceeding in the shortest possible time. This vision is in contrast to the traditional inside-out model, based on the principle that value resides within the organization and is based on the talent and competence of its resources. For high-end companies, the competitive advantage is based on phase 1, while for fast-fashion players it becomes phases 2 and 3, which are inverted in order to pursue all possible optimizations.

This extreme quest for efficiency in the fashion system supply chain, of marketing products in the shortest possible time, had a side effect that first affected mainstream customers but soon also began influencing high-end followers too. This occurred when people, whose expectations had been conditioned by this speed, began to show some impatience in the wait between the time of the runway show and the moment when the products would become available in stores. To meet this demand, the **see now**, **buy now** model has spread, as it addresses the period between when the product is presented and when it is marketed.

In the face of the frenzied pace of fast fashion, traditional companies have been forced to increase the number of 'seasons' and to resort to numerous other moments for the releases of new lines, such as the **drop** or the production of **capsule collections** made ad hoc for certain occasions. In some cases, the acceleration has led to the expedience of **collaboration**, as companies working with partners that possess specific skills other than their own can reduce research and production time, and provide a shortcut to reach target markets other than their own. To satisfy increasingly demanding and impatient consumers and remain competitive, many high-end brands have been sucked into the vortex of consumerism, to the point that it has been provocatively stated that the market is now forced to deal with a calendar year of 52 seasons: one per week. If, in the past, fashion was conceived to make the consumer 'off-trend' after a season, in the recent past a dynamic has been created whereby the customer is likely to feel this in a much shorter period.

This system fully meets the need for the style surfing and instant gratification of the hypermodern global customer, who needs constant identity renewal in order to remain on the crest of the wave. As we have seen before, the main indicator of social fulfilment today is determined by material prosperity, and fashion is a very powerful indicator of this.

BACK TO THE FUTURE

Fashion is intrinsically linked to the concept of trends, so it is ephemeral by nature. Fashion has followed and contributed to economic and social evolution. On the other hand, even prior to the pandemic, many insiders were scrambling to declare the complete unsustainability of this model, especially for the high-end segment. We are clearly referring to both economic sustainability and to environmental and social sustainability. High-end brands have built their fortune on attributes such as innovative but long-lasting design – to the point, in many cases, of preferring the concept of 'style' over the more transitory one of 'fashion' – high-quality fabrics, workmanship and brand reliability. The risk is therefore that of diluting their own capital of credibility and jeopardizing the equity of the brand with obvious repercussions for both high-end and ready-to-wear. With the exception of rare examples where brands have literally reinvented themselves and managed to ride the wave of hypermodernity in an enviable way, the prospect of being sucked into the vortex is unfortunately quite real.

It will not escape the reader's notice that it is difficult to reconcile the need to meet such a fickle demand, attentive to 'fashion content' and rooted in instantaneousness, with operational models, the logic of production and commercial supply chains, the environmental impact, and all the attributes typical of high-end brands. This is a very common dilemma for established companies, which, faced with the paradigm shift triggered by the technological and digital revolution, find themselves in a delicate impasse, having to manage the transition along the entire value chain.

Therefore, it is essential to review the operating model (organizational and production); update professional skills (upskilling, reskilling, resource turnover); review marketing and sales strategies; and more generally to initiate an agile approach, open to experimentation. All this while taking care to preserve the crucial elements of the companies in question.

The pandemic has brought the market to an abrupt halt and amplified the voices of those calling for a slowdown to avoid breaking the system. They complain about the impossibility of going along with a model that seems more inclined to produce consumers who consume, rather than products to be consumed.

In April 2020, Giorgio Armani, a living fashion icon of the last 50 years, sent a letter to *WWD*, a magazine considered by many to be the 'Bible of fashion,' strongly denouncing the situation. According to the designer, it is necessary to limit the collections to the seasonal needs of customers and avoid overproduction in order to be more sustainable, and to desist in discounting products to follow the frantic pace. And, also, to reduce travel by management and buyers and to take advantage of the increased digital skills developed during the months of lockdown. Armani goes so far as to say that the decline of the high-end fashion system can be traced precisely to the efforts of trying to emulate the methods and pace of fast fashion, and in forgetting that **high-end products cannot and must not have anything to do with speed, as they require time to be produced and time to be appreciated.** He has defined a cycle, so accelerated that it makes a jacket obsolete after a few weeks in the store, to be immoral. In his words, "*I don't work like that, and I find it immoral to do so.*"

For him, the sector must strive for **timeless elegance** not only in aesthetic codes but also in design and manufacturing, which must work synergistically to make products long lasting because of their cultural relevance and intrinsic quality. 'Re Giorgio' (King George) as he is often called in the industry, also laments the absurdity of finding summer products in stores in the middle of winter (and vice versa), and that the priority should be the immediate satisfaction of the desire to buy a particular product in the corresponding season in progress. Needless to say, this letter has aroused interest and catalysed the views of numerous leading figures in the industry, who have sided in favour with this vision of authenticity and people centricity.

If, on the one hand, it is good to avoid an outright anti-modernist and nostalgic approach under the banner of "let's restore everything as it once was," on the other, it is imperative to come to terms with a social context in which the 'simplification' of experience has become an absolute value. People have become addicted to models devoted to **convenience** and optimizing the expenditure of time, money and energy, tending to refuse the burden of making efforts to access the value of things. We have everything just a click away, we are constantly connected, and in the coming years we will also connect billions of objects to ourselves and to each other. Space and time will increasingly appear to be subservient to our demands, needs and desires, and acceleration may continue *ad infinitum.*

The restart after COVID-19 will undoubtedly offer a unique opportunity to take action against the 'irrationality of rationality' that has occurred in the frantic search for productive and logistical efficiencies and in the desire to indulge in the dizzying acceleration of the last 20 years. **We have the responsibility, in fashion as in all sectors, to safeguard the ability of capitalism to generate value, freeing it from the exaggerations of the consumerist tendencies of recent decades.** We must promote a new idea of prosperity that is capable of simultaneously complying with the principles of what has been called the triple bottom line: people, planet and profit.

As for the acceleration, it is plain that in such a fast-paced world, time has become a luxury. But it will be a mistake to assume that its flow is always a waste to be made more efficient. Furthermore, in the high-end segment, waiting has historically contributed to increasing the perception of the prestige of the asset. Value is not defined by the formula, costs *divided* by benefits, but on the contrary, costs *multiplied* by benefits. This equation can still be relevant if the value perceived by the customer is of undeniable significance; otherwise, the wait will be poorly tolerated or even considered unacceptable.

HYBRIDIZATION

"Computing is not about computers any more. It is about living."

NICHOLAS NEGROPONTE

The overwhelming advance of digital technologies has blurred the boundaries between what happens **onland** and what happens in the digital sphere **online**. Increasingly large segments of the world's population are moving smoothly between physical and digital channels, forcing traditional companies to adapt their supply models in a complex attempt to meet the new demands required while preserving short-, medium- and long-term objectives.

The extent of this technological revolution is such that it has produced a cultural revolution: a different conception of reality in which technological mediation represents both the cause and effect of any innovation process. In a world where the processes of identity building transpire through consumption, hybridization gives rise to an 'augmented' humanity in which each of us is defined by the sum of our physical and digital presences. And this definition is necessarily fluid, allowing us to continue 'surfing.'

FROM TABLE FOOTBALL TO VIDEO GAMES

In *The Game*, Alessandro Baricco creates a picture of how the bit and pixel have burst into the analogue world with the metaphor of the transition from table football, through pinball machines, to video games. Table football definitely belonged to the world of the senses in the most literal way: there was no mediation by a screen: sounds, noises, smells and interactions were mechanical, physical, 'real.' The transition to pinball brought the first injection of hybridization: the game is put under glass, the sounds are mainly reproduced, the interaction is restricted to two buttons and physical intervention is very limited. With the arrival of Space Invaders, the first video game to achieve planetary success, the hybridization was complete: we remain onland with the body, but we are immersed in the digital dimension – though not yet online. Everything has become immaterial, sounds and movements are artificially reproduced, the intensity with which we move knobs and press buttons is irrelevant to the dynamics of the game. Furthermore, in some video games today the fusion of the two worlds is often even more pronounced as scenarios are simulated with extraordinary realism and the supporting hardware makes the activity even more immersive.

This metaphor is useful to grasp the scope and characteristics of the phenomenon we are about to describe and demonstrates how large portions of experience have migrated beyond a screen in recent years. The three key steps of the digital revolution that we are interested in focusing on at this stage are:

- dematerialization (digitalization) of texts, sounds, images, experiences;
- production of personal technological devices, first fixed and then mobile, to access that intangible content;
- creation of the internet and the World Wide Web to allow people around the world to exchange data in real time through their devices connected to the network.

THE EVOLUTION OF
THE CUSTOMER JOURNEY

The hybridization between physical and digital has primarily involved the younger generations, who have proven to be more naturally inclined to embrace the opportunities offered by digitalization. However, now this change progressively involves large segments of the population in the most economically advanced societies. In particular, during lockdown periods there has been a noticeable acceleration in the migration toward the use of online services. This has led this sector to review the user experience of their sites and applications in order to better respond to the needs of a wave of novice customers with less digital literacy. We are increasingly witnessing hybrid purchasing and consumption behaviours, in which people are browsing on their smartphones while visiting a physical store or entrusting entire stages of the **customer journey** to digital only to then pop into the store to try on a piece of clothing and check the quality of the fabric. Digital and physical merge and fertilize each other in a hybrid that has been defined as **onlife**, in which it seems less and less sensible to try to find a seamless solution.

On the supply side, the situation is quite complex. Traditional companies have been struggling with **digital transformation** for over a decade, with all the complexities of having to initiate a cultural change even before a technological and operational change.

All under the pressure of a plethora of new digitally native players who do not have the same burden of having to update the skills of their employees, review operating models, rethink the supply chain, acquire the latest technology or even take action to address the mindset of their employees.

Electronic commerce has spread over the last 25 years, thanks to the initiative of companies such as Amazon and Ebay, followed progressively by countless others. Established companies first viewed e-commerce as a timid rival, nothing to worry about too much, then as a competitor to be monitored because of its ability to erode market share, and then finally as a threat to take measures against. Traditional companies have only fully grasped the scope of the phenomenon in its recent stage of maturity and are now struggling to seamlessly integrate it into their value chain, in order to align all the touchpoints around the needs of the end customer, under the banner of what is known as **omnichannel**.

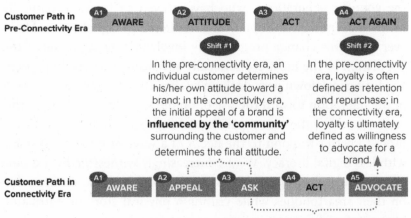

The shifting customer path in a connected world (Marketing 4.0: Moving from Traditional to Digital, Philip Kotler, Hermawan Kartajaya and Iwan Setiawan)

FIGURE 1.2: **THE EVOLUTION OF THE CUSTOMER JOURNEY IN THE DIGITAL ERA, MARKETING 4.0**

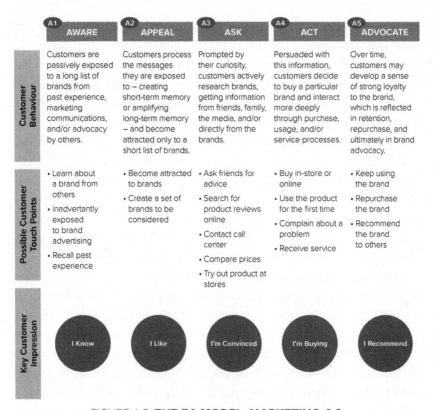

FIGURE 1.3: **THE 5A MODEL, MARKETING 4.0**

THE HYBRIDIZATION OF THE FASHION SYSTEM

In the fashion world and even more so in the high-end segment, the advent of digital was initially viewed with a mixture of snobbery and disinterest. Undoubtedly, one of the reasons for this attitude was the notion that the intrinsic characteristics of the products, the high price, the emotional involvement of the customer and the consequent importance of the sales ritual within the boutique, could preserve the sector from the impact of the digital revolution. This was largely true, at least until the advent of portals such as YOOX and Luisaviaroma in 2000. Until then, e- commerce sites that wished to sell fashion products were decidedly inadequate. In some cases, the user experience was poor in comparison to the brand's exclusivity or to the range of the products they aimed to sell, and for others, on the contrary, because the sites were too sophisticated compared to the technical capabilities of most potential buyers (and the same maisons). Furthermore, **in the initial phase the commercial aggressiveness of those selling online frightened high-end fashion brands because they risked trivializing the brands and products and impoverishing their semantic value, along with creating negative repercussions on the brick-and-mortar boutiques.** An implementation of an online sales channel would have involved a string of investments from an organizational and logistical viewpoint. All this did not make an attractive option when the cost-benefit ratio was still rather uncertain, given the low sales volumes e-commerce sites generated at the time.

This scenario has certainly changed in recent years. Digital literacy of the global population has increased as a result of the impact of COVID-19. The increased maturity of high-end customers and the influx of new potential buyers who have developed familiarity with e-commerce purchases has helped considerably in sectors that are in many ways related, such as design or luxury travel. It is important to note that in the migration between sectors, platforms and brands, people bring with them a specific set of expectations with respect to countless factors, such as quality standards for the user experience, content quality, ease of navigation, integration with traditional sales channels, availability and support capability of customer service, flexibility of payment methods, delivery and returns. These very high **experiential benchmarks** require specific skills, adequate technological equipment, an efficient organizational system and a complete review of the customer journey for the different client segments. All this is even more so in high-end clothing as the intrinsic characteristics and semantic value of the products make satisfying these standards a decidedly difficult task.

Some customers will seek online inspiration and reassurance regarding the quality of products and their ability to enhance their 'personal brand equity' and then will want to go onland for the final stages of the purchase process. On the other hand, others will prefer to begin the journey in a department store, then explore the websites of individual brands and perhaps complete the purchase on the site of a multi-brand e-tailer after reading reviews and making comparisons. It becomes crucial for brands to be present and relevant at all points along the customer journey, albeit with different methods and degrees of intensity depending on their capabilities and the strategic priorities of the business.

This scenario has become even more complicated during the pandemic, as significantly more high-end customers have suddenly shown interest in solutions such as live-streaming fashion shows, video chat shopping support and social shopping. Operators in the sector were rather lukewarm toward these methods until recently, but have since benefited from the socio-economic situation and they are gaining in importance.

It is now also necessary to redefine **human touch**, given the increased weight assumed by the technological component in customer interactions. What is the role of store sales staff in a world where relationships are often intermediated by a screen, and where conversational interfaces enabled by artificial intelligence (AI) play an increasing role? What human skills are worth investing in, to build new sources of competitive advantage in an environment that will experience increasing digitalization? Does it still make sense to refer to boutiques as 'point of sale' given that transactions will increasingly take place on websites and social media too? These are just some of the important questions for which we will try to provide critical insights, and hopefully, some useful answers in the following pages.

We were talking about the investments needed to adapt to the new expectations of customers and changing market characteristics. Well, another instance of particular importance for high-end brands is the decision of whether to directly manage their business presence online or through outsourcing. On the one hand, balanced against the cost of adapting the organization, the typical benefits of vertical integration are gained, in particular a range of important data and insights that can be vital for business strategies. On the other hand, there is a huge saving in financial resources, which can be an indispensable lifeline in historical moments such as the one we are going through, but with a resulting loss of opportunity in developing real business intelligence.

How to decide then? It would be advised to proceed with a careful analysis of the required investment, the benefits that may accrue, and the time frame within which the company expects certain returns. **Often in such a volatile, uncertain, ambiguous and complex situation, managers are required to base their decisions on the short-term horizon and to ensure turnover. This is ill-suited for an investment that involves an important reorganization such as the one needed to internalize the e-commerce function**, integrating it with the other business divisions.

All the indicators for the next few years point toward an even more decisive hybridization between online and onland. A further decline in the number of physical sales outlets can also be expected, due to both the ongoing financial crisis and to the increased digital literacy of the world's population and the spillover effect described previously. Depending on the latitudes and the degree of maturity of economies in various parts of the world, this phenomenon will assume different proportions and proceed at different speeds (in all cases, quite quickly). The onus is on industry brands to carefully calibrate the scope and extent of digital transformation, finding the most acceptable compromise between short-, medium- and long-term results.

The ambition of this book is to give an overall picture of the situation and define guiding principles rather than hazarding answers that claim to be valid for everyone. We recommend that all companies in the industry give due importance to these dynamics, and to avoid relegating digital technology to yet another company silo and instead embrace the idea that it is an enabler of innovation capable of revolutionizing the company's *modus operandi* and the rules of the market. **We are convinced that the pandemic has sounded the latest wake-up call for high-end fashion companies: computing is definitely not about computers any more – it's about life.**

DISINTERMEDIATION

"You can try to change people's minds,
but you're just wasting your time.
Change the tools in their hands and
you'll change the world.**"**

———

STEWART BRAND

As Luciano Floridi notes, one of the first effects of the digital revolution was the decoupling of presence and location, often making it unnecessary to be located in a given physical environment in order to be present there. We no longer need to write a letter, buy an envelope and a stamp, go to a post office and then wait for it to be delivered; we can do this in real time from anywhere. If we combine this with the possibility of purchasing goods and services through digital sales channels, we will have a sufficiently clear picture of how **the disintermediation of entire business supply chains has occurred**, along with the related adverse effects on all the intermediary players involved in the process. The phenomenon has affected, and is affecting, incredibly diverse sectors, giving rise to new concentrations of power and is likely to create the conditions for new business ecosystems based on communication, even before the product and distribution network.

THE DREAM OF PIONEERS

One of the dreams of the handful of Californian pioneers led by Tim Berners-Lee, who gave birth to the World Wide Web in the 1990s, was to redistribute power within society, removing the intermediation of the 'elite' to allow people around the world to communicate freely and share ideas, as well as to have access to unfiltered information that for centuries had been the prerogative of small groups of individuals. It is not surprising that the progressive spread of the internet and e-commerce has given rise over the years to a considerable amount of disintermediation. This has literally wiped out some supply segments and forced numerous companies to quickly review their business models to avoid going under. Thanks to the possibilities offered by the technological and digital revolution, from increasingly fast and powerful connections to the spread of computers and smartphones and the consequent proliferation of various types of sites and applications, we've witnessed the progressive and inexorable elimination of intermediaries from many distribution chains and from various acquisition processes of goods and services. The phenomenon has primarily affected the markets for services and intangible or easily 'dematerialized' goods in which physical distribution infrastructures soon proved to be nonessential.

Consider, for example, what has happened in tourism, publishing, music, home video and finance. In these industries, the commercial supply chains have been dramatically shortened, pursuing the aim of minimizing the distance between supply and demand. The dematerialization made possible by technological progress has thus given further impetus to the act of disintermediation.

The digital portals that combine a huge range of products, services and content accessible in real time (or in a short time) have based their competitive advantage on the absence of constraints related to the breadth, range and depth of the selection, as they need not submit to any physical limits. And they have also offered brands the chance to reach a vast audience at the same time, with the only requirement being a network connection.

One cannot fail to notice that **today these aggregators of supply represent such a concentration of power on a global scale that they are, in fact, new-generation intermediaries.** With all due respect to the web's creators, it must be noted that in the face of the goal to simplify supply chains, we're witnessing the birth of new elites who have given life to a form of **neo-intermediation**. This tendency raises important questions about both competitiveness and user data management. Shoshana Zuboff coined the concept of 'surveillance capitalism,' in which human experience becomes raw material to be transformed into data regarding behaviour. A part of this data is used to refine the actual products and services, while the remaining data is transformed into predictive elements that aim to anticipate the purchasing and consumption behaviour of current and potential customers. It is hoped that antitrust authorities, who are monitoring these dynamics, can find a constructive mediation between the growing opposition to large technology corporations and a healthy 'tech-realism' that aims to combine the benefits offered by technological innovation with the necessary regulations. The concept of disintermediation is not limited to the distribution realm, but also embraces that of marketing and, in particular, communication.

THE DYNAMICS OF
INTERMEDIATION IN FASHION

In the fashion world, the main points of focus have historically been the designers, creative directors and merchandisers. Over time, brands have also assumed a very important role, particularly during globalization due to the process of consolidation into a few large global holdings. Today the powerful multi-brand e-tailers, that are often the first point of contact between potential customers and that of the brand, must also be counted among the most influential actors. But in ranking the players that we could define as neo-intermediaries (rather than simple 'disintermediaries') in the relationship between the public and high-end brands, a place of honour undoubtedly belongs to **influencers**, as they have the ability to channel enormous volumes of sales and, in some cases, even to become brands themselves.

Back in 1992, Giampaolo Fabris made a distinction between 'testimonials' and 'influencers.' The former involved characters, known or not, whom the public acknowledged to have specific competence in a given field; hence the ploy of using an actor to portray a dentist while advertising toothpaste or of associating a famous athlete with a sportswear brand. Instead, in the view of the sociologist, the influencers were star celebrities able to extend a 'halo effect' to the brands and products they were associated with. **The use of these figures, particularly in the second case, has always been a sort of semantic shortcut to increase the public's goodwill and stimulate the propensity to purchase.**

The key to success in these affairs typically resides in the delicate alchemy that leads to the credibility of the source, which in turn is a function of the authoritativeness (derived from a recognized expertise) and the attractiveness of the figure (plainly connected to their fame and importance in the social context of reference). The public is driven to action if a dynamic is triggered that can stimulate both rational and emotional states, and this happens to varying degrees depending on variables such as: coherence between the brand/product and the figure, degree of transparency and importance of the product's objective benefits, relevance of intangible aspects compared to tangible ones, complexity of the decision-making process leading to purchase, specifics of the customer journey, etc. In the last 20 years the phenomenon of fashion influencers has literally exploded, in conjunction with the spread of smartphones and social media such as Facebook, Instagram, Pinterest and YouTube, which, due to their distinctive visual language, are well suited to emphasize the attributes of the sponsor companies' products.

At first, influencers operated within their respective blogs and struggled to find ways to monetize their work. Over time, these columns for enthusiasts have become sophisticated marketing tools capable of influencing trends and affecting the turnover for the companies that own the brands and products being promoted. Social media have allowed these personalities, who have gradually absorbed many of the characteristics of competent testimonials as well as those of influential public faces, to establish a very close relationship with their respective audiences. This suggests a further hybridization: their private and public lives are staged, often without any continuity. **Backstage and onstage apparently no longer have any boundaries, except for the realization that, in many cases, these are actually formulas designed to show off the backstage, making it part of the show.**

This clever mix has transformed them into an indispensable promotional vehicle on a global scale, both in the fashion sector and in others such as food, travel, sports and technology products. The greater the number of followers on the various social platforms, the more value they can potentially generate, provided they maintain high credibility.

This last aspect focuses attention on particularly topical issues: how far is it permissible to roam between different brands, products and services without diluting one's ability to influence the audience? How to make it unequivocally clear that this is sponsored content (and not the product of personal opinions on the part of the influencer)? It is evident that for a knowledgeable user the risk of misunderstanding is minimal, even when the protagonist of the post or video does not respect the rule of clearly indicating the nature of the collaboration with the sponsoring brands. But the issue becomes delicate, for example, with very young or those less discerning users who could be more easily swayed by the persuasive message from a source that is authoritative for them. **Many professionals claim to accept offers exclusively from brands that they identify with and would also recommend in private.**

Influencers represent, for all intents and purposes, the most modern form of disintermediation – or more properly neo-intermediation – in the fashion supply chain, to the point that some influencers have chosen to create their own brands and product lines to capitalize on the fan base they have earned, thanks to collaborations with well-known companies. The process is not dissimilar to the one undertaken in the past by brand names, with private labels used in the commercial distribution of consumer goods. The premise is, in many ways, the same: to benefit their audience, steering the fan base toward their own products from which they obviously gain more profit. The ability to checkout directly through social media is a further boost to the business of fashion influencers, as it simplifies the purchase path and consequently encourages more impulse purchases.

Fashion shows represent another interesting variation of intermediation. At one time, these all-important shows were primarily aimed at trade agents, distribution buyers and communication mediators, i.e. journalists from the sector's principal publications. They constituted a true 'monopolistic cartel' that had absolute power in shaping the evolution of the collections and in determining the success or failure of the maisons. This dynamic was also very much linked to the basic mechanics of the fashion system, which, as we have seen, categorically established a rather long period of time between the fashion show itself and the moment in which the products were actually available in the store to clientele.

Today the scenario looks very different. On the one hand, fashion shows – live or streaming – are now also open to influencers, thereby guaranteeing immediate access to a very large global audience. And in cases where they are broadcast live, sometimes the companies even make them 'shoppable,' allowing products presented on the runway to be immediately purchased. On the other hand, many designers and creative directors have become influencers themselves, establishing a constant flow of communication between the fan base and the company. It's clear that in this further hybridization,

the boundary between those who influence and those who are influenced is becoming very blurred. For many brands, these methods constitute portals for direct access to the final client, enabling that very interesting form of disintermediation known as **direct-to-consumer**, which we will deal with later in these pages.

With this in mind, the phenomenon of high-end brands that tend to become actual **broadcasters**, thus aiming to further disintermediate their dependence on official communication channels, should also be considered. The international consulting firm Bain & Company reported that companies have set aside the product-centric approach that has marked the success of fashion houses in recent decades, and instead are now placing interaction with their various target audiences at the centre of their business ecosystem. Everything else, including the product itself, becomes a potential vehicle to stimulate interaction with the audience, in a two-way flow that ideally also allows valuable insights to be gained that can inspire strategies for the company.

In this manner, **the brand is not just limited to disseminating and promoting proprietary content in a top-down logic but can instead embrace the principles of open innovation in order to exponentially increase its value proposition.** This takes the form of collaborating with other brands to develop joint communication initiatives, offering their own communication channels as a sounding board for third-party initiatives that can foster the brand's equity, proposing selective content in line with the brand's value system, ongoing partnerships with content creators and producers in order to constantly enhance the symbolic universe of the brand with original aspects. We believe this strategy to be particularly apt given the characteristics of the **hyperconnected infosphere** in which we live, the necessity of keeping the audience continuously engaged through the various channels of communication and the ways in which purchase and consumption decisions are made today.

As a testament to the potential of this strategy, note how it also applies to new-generation brands conceived and launched through careful marketing strategy before having even developed a full-fledged distribution channel. If successful, the management will evaluate whether to limit the sale to e-commerce or access the more traditional onland channels such as multi-brand stores, shop-in-shops, temporary stores and perhaps even single-brand stores.

In conclusion, the disintermediations enabled by digital transformation have disrupted a number of established balances, democratizing access to information and dematerializing several links in commercial supply chains. All this has created a new ecosystem in turn characterized by new intermediaries, polarizations of power and complex business logic. The market volatility is such that further developments can be expected in the near future, also in light of changing consumer habits brought about by the pandemic.

SUSTAINABILITY

"*Fashion is what goes out of style.***"**

———

SALVADOR DALÍ

The global fashion industry has a very high environmental, economic and social impact. The reasons can be found in both the current production models and in the dynamics of the sector itself. There are growing calls, from many quarters, for a new paradigm based on the creation of shared value and circularity. But is it actually possible to embrace this new way of thinking and operating? Is this also really a sustainable choice from the point of view of the companies in the industry? The impression is that it is indeed a necessary choice, but of such magnitude that it requires companies to implement a precise combination of endogenous and exogenous variables. This turns out to be particularly complex and tricky in a global and hyperconnected scenario, even more so following a systemic shock like the one induced by COVID-19.

THE ORIGINAL SIN

Fashion is ephemeral by its very nature, constantly evolving, perpetually in the making. Since its origin, it has been based on innovation and the rapid succession of trends. It feeds on the tension between two opposing forces in the human soul: the act of imitation, which leads to a reassuring validation from the group being imitated, and the need for differentiation, which lets us express our individuality. It thrives on the cyclical repetition of a ritual that is based on the semantic obsolescence of products. In other words, the system induces customers first to buy a product in order to participate in a kind of collective ritual, and shortly thereafter to feel the need to set it aside and buy something else that can renew their identity and enhance their image. The point is that this happens not when the products are actually worn out but when they have exhausted their 'communicative capacity.' The speed with which these cycles occur has greatly intensified in recent decades, and this makes the management of the production cycle and the disposal of unsold and no longer useful products even more complex.

Furthermore, the situation is aggravated by the more prevalent approach to production. The **industrial economy** has historically been based on a linear model of resource consumption: raw materials are transformed into increasingly sophisticated by-products until they become a product that is sold to a final consumer, who then is in charge of its disposal. There are many intermediaries along the value chain, and at each step value is created, but there is an environmental, social or economic impact that occurs at the same time. This impact is typically viewed as an inevitable negative consequence, inherent in the production process. If this dynamic occurs in a sector where product attrition is artificially accelerated to stimulate the rapid succession of cycles as described above, the impact becomes considerable. Therefore, it will not seem strange that this model has been called **cradle to grave**.

Over the years, globalization has further complicated the position of the fashion industry with regard to its impact on the economy, society and the environment. In a world where distances are shortened and communication happens in real time, companies the world over have seen tremendous opportunities in the fragmentation of the supply chain and in relocating production to countries where costs could be significantly reduced due, in particular, to lower labour costs, less stringent regulation, and closer proximity to the raw materials' origins. Fragmentation and delocalization have helped create a value chain that is far from transparent and also difficult to trace. In terms of environmental impact alone, the United Nations Economic Commission for Europe (UNECE) estimates that the fashion industry is the second most polluting industry in the world, after that of oil.

International public opinion, nongovernmental organizations and the strategic positioning of some companies – conceived in opposition to the aforementioned dominant model – have put the glaring unsustainability of this approach under the microscope, prompting the sector to examine its conscience. This has given birth to **Corporate Social Responsibility (CSR), that is the idea that the company, while pursuing legitimate profit, must explicitly take into account a series of internal and external instances, inescapably connected to its activities, and assume responsibility for them.**

This is certainly a notable and significant approach, which is an important first step in the search for a sustainable model. But it cannot be considered sufficient. In concrete terms, CSR translates into practices aimed at **compensation** for – and in the most virtuous cases also at limiting – one's own environmental, economic and social impact. This is certainly a very good start, but all the indicators lead us to think that if we want a long-term plan, we cannot be content with compensating for, or reducing, the negative consequences of the current model. We must also move decisively toward a complete overhaul of this model, in search of a new scenario in which all phases are truly sustainable. To continue with the metaphor that headlines this section, we could say that it is time to move on from the 'sale of indulgences' (the practice within the Roman Catholic Church of making a donation in exchange for receiving forgiveness of a sin), to a complete change of behaviour, with the goal of no longer sinning.

THE CIRCULAR ECONOMY AND THE CREATION OF SHARED VALUE

In 2002, Michael Braungart and William McDonough published a significant book entitled *Cradle to Cradle: Remaking the Way We Make Things*. As the title makes obvious, the authors propose changing the dominant model, **cradle to grave**, to that of a circular model of cradle to cradle. The basic concept is the transition from a linear process to a circular one in which considerable attention is paid to the sustainable management of all stages: conception, production, distribution and consumption. The ambition is to transform the entire process into a zero-sum game, using all waste as technical or biological fuel to power other processes. The company might find itself marketing what previously it had to dispose of and incur costs from. An economic system can be defined as circular when products and services are marketed in a closed circuit, which triggers a virtuous circle that potentially eliminates waste and the passive disposal of waste. This is why every link in the value chain needs to be reviewed, abandoning the previous linear view.

Designing a product with this approach means, for example, taking into account from the beginning of the process the ways in which it is possible to recycle a product in order to give it a new life after its first cycle of use, both through an **upcycling** method (increasing the quality and economic value of the original product) and through **downcycling** (decreasing the quality and economic value). Ideally, in this way obsolescence, either real or perceived, is no longer a problem as nothing is in fact actually wasted.

This approach clearly resonates with what Michael Porter and Mark Kramer argued in 2011 in the famous *HBR* article: "Creating Shared Value, How to Reinvent Capitalism and Unleash a Wave of Innovation and Growth." In line with the previous reasoning, the authors argue that companies must definitely set aside the idea of pursuing value creation exclusively for shareholders in order to systematically seek the creation of **shared value** for all the players in the value chain: employees, suppliers, business partners, external collaborators, customers and also society and the environment in the broadest sense.

Paying attention to the creation of value for all the stakeholders will, over time, become a source of competitive advantage and consequently result in value for shareholders. Obviously this preserves the main reason the company is in the market, but at the same time it includes a number of requirements that can no longer be ignored. **This represents CSV (Corporate Shared Value) surpassing CSR in terms of importance given that it is broader in scope, exceeding the limits related to compensation and reduction as described above.**

As noted by Francesca Romana Rinaldi and Salvo Testa in their numerous writings on the topic, companies operating in the fashion industry that intend to embrace a new paradigm of circularity with shared value creation must be willing to engage in the following activities:

- respect the environment by preferring raw materials that have the least impact on the land and on the workers (for example, by using organic cotton, linen and hemp instead of traditional cotton) and optimizing the consumption of other resources used in the production and distribution (energy, water);
- protect the social territory, workers and consumers, in accordance with the principles of the International Labour Organization (ILO) and guarantee a quality product;

- increase consumer involvement through communication
  and convey a positive message with authenticity and transparency in order to influence consumer behaviour,
  for example, by educating them on how to take care of the
  product and making them more aware of the importance
  of their own actions;
- support the culture, surroundings and territory in question
  through specific and lasting initiatives;
- comply with environmental and social protection regulations
  and voluntarily adopt a proactive attitude toward the most
  advanced standards, such as certifications;
- adopt an ethical attitude toward employees through fair
  remuneration, respect the human dignity of collaborators and
  consumers, respect codes of conduct, contribute to collective
  social and civil progress and to that of the community in
  question, ensure that aesthetics convey positive values,
  initiate an accountability mechanism in the value chain;
- invest in responsible innovation by leveraging transparency
  and supply chain traceability to rethink production processes
  in implementing the principle of the three Rs (Reduce, Reuse,
  Recycle), extend the life of the product as much as possible,
  including through the active involvement of the consumer.

But is it really possible to embrace this new paradigm? And is it
really a sustainable choice from the viewpoint of the companies in
the sector?

THE RESISTANCE FROM COMPANIES IN THE SECTOR

In order to effectively adhere to the principles described above,
companies in the sector must work to reduce the opacity that
characterizes the current fragmented and geographically dispersed
production system. They must also increase transparency and the
level of control over the supply chain, invest in the traceability
of raw materials and semi-finished products and, when possible,
promote collaborative consumption. It is clear that this represents

a profound change from the current model, with an inevitable and significant increase in costs for companies. This threatens to quash any attempt to move in this direction, especially in an historical moment like the present one in which budgets are burdened by the financial crisis resulting from the pandemic and consumer spending power has been considerably reduced. In fact, products in this sector are a result of the interaction of an intricate network of economic players located in different areas of the world. Therefore, it is very complicated to guarantee the transparency and traceability required by the market, and to adhere to the standards of circularity and shared value.

The alternative could lie in reversing the trend that has dominated recent decades, investing in the vertical integration of the supply chain and in **nearshoring** practices (contracting out some production phases to companies that are geographically less distant than is currently the case with **farshoring** to developing countries) and even **onshoring** (contracting out to companies located in the same country, but in areas where the labour force is less expensive or where other advantageous conditions exist). This would undoubtedly bring benefits in terms of monitoring and control, would certainly result in greater traceability and transparency, and would likely lead to an increase in product quality. In many cases, it would also reduce the environmental and social impact, by optimizing logistics and because more stringent regulatory standards would have to be observed.

On the other hand, such an approach would generate a substantial increase in costs for fashion companies, which could only be sustained with strong incentives and regulations aimed at preserving competitiveness on a global scale. **These costs should be viewed more as investments, since no company will be able to operate in the market, in the medium- to long-term, unless it adapts to these new rules of conduct.**

But for this to happen, massive international coordination is essential, requiring companies around the world to adhere to new standard protocols. Many international nongovernmental organizations are working toward this and, although some progress has definitely been made, it remains clear that the road ahead is still quite long and winding. The UN's 2030 Agenda features a list of 17 interconnected goals for a better and more sustainable future for all: themes intended to safeguard human welfare and the health of natural ecosystems. The Sustainable Development Goals aim to address a wide range of economic and social development issues including poverty, hunger, the right to health and education, access to water and energy, employment, inclusive and sustainable economic growth, change and environmental protection, urbanization, production and consumption patterns, social and gender equality, justice and peace.

FIGURE 1.4: **17 SUSTAINABLE DEVELOPMENT GOALS, UN DEPARTMENT OF ECONOMIC AND SOCIAL AFFAIRS**

At the G7 summit held in Biarritz (France) in 2019, 32 of the world's leading fashion houses signed a document known as the 'Fashion Pact' with the aim of aligning the industry with the United Nations' goals. For example, it states that 20% of companies are committed to zero emissions of CO_2 by 2050, to use 100% renewable energy in all directly managed production stages by 2030, and to eliminate the use of single-use plastics in B2B and B2C packaging by 2030.

That is considerable progress, but the feeling remains that it is not enough. Technology will certainly play a decisive role in this area, especially AI, big data and, of course, blockchain, but once again its proper use implies investments to develop the necessary skills and acquire the appropriate tools.

Ultimately the only way to reconcile the growing demand for sustainability and transparency from the market with the interests of businesses and the future of our planet lies in the decisive stance by governments around the world – in line with the provisions of the United Nations – that on the one hand impose compliance with new standards and on the other support economic players in the reorganization of the value chain into a circular one. **We need to explore alternative ways to ensure that the capitalist system, the real engine of prosperity that we enjoy in many countries today, is freed from its consumerist tendencies,** based on the continuous acceleration of the semantic obsolescence of goods, and expresses itself in new forms that are capable of creating shared value for all the players within the various supply chains. The global pandemic has imposed a moment of reflection upon the world. Hopefully this is the point in history when a new paradigm will be embraced, one that views the 'cradle' as not just as a point of departure but also as one of arrival.

DEMOCRATIZATION

"Simplicity is the ultimate sophistication."

———

LEONARDO DA VINCI

Since its origins, digital culture has aimed to make it easier to access knowledge, eliminating the power of elites and democratizing all the ways in which it can be accessed. This process has been carried out under the banner of **simplification** – allowing the masses to freely benefit from products, services and experiences – and **gamification**, or the inclusion of a playful dimension that makes every activity pleasant and light. This approach is in contrast to the dominant one, placing 'essence' and 'appearance' on equal footing, allowing the masses access to a world that was previously closed to them. In the fashion universe, such cultural reversal has laid the foundations for the birth of prêt-à-porter (also called **ready-to-wear**). This, in effect, represents a clear form of democratization compared to the paradigm of high-end fashion, which by definition was reserved for the elite.

DIGITAL DEMOCRACY

We mentioned earlier that a handful of pioneers in California gave birth to the web in the 1970s. And we focused on their idea of disintermediating access to information so that the masses could circumvent the elite's intermediation and to allow knowledge to flow freely. Democratization is, to some extent, the other side of this phenomenon and is its consequence. This is not to say that the web itself is an ambassador of democratic rule in the world, or that cyberdemocracy is an inevitable outcome.

By 'democratization' we mean that the web was created to be accessible to all. **The web had to be accessible to everyone and navigation had to be simple, so much so as to take on the features of the playful dimension typical of video games that constituted the professional backgrounds of many of its founders.**

And if we think about it, this is still the case. The millions of sites, portals and apps that we use every day are designed so that we do not need to read instructions first; you orient yourself with fun icons, move within attractive graphical interfaces, and if you make a mistake, you can easily go back and start over, evaluating your success on the basis of a score (e.g. Facebook likes or Instagram loves). This is how the complicated world of technology, which for decades had remained the preserve of a small circle of skilled people having the patience to study long instruction manuals, quickly became 'democratic,' accessible to the masses. Probably the most striking case that really represents this philosophy is the historic presentation of the first iPhone model. It was January 9 2007, on the stage of San Francisco's Moscone Center, when Steve Jobs proudly displayed a small, light, simple device, (even back then it had only one button) with the ambition to change the rules of the game. And he succeeded.

As Alessandro Baricco says in *The Game*, the iPhone perfectly symbolizes the reversal of the mental image that had dominated the 20th century. Until the last century, culture was based on the assumption that the essence of things, their substance, resided in depth. It was therefore necessary to go beyond the superficial understanding of things in order to understand and appreciate their value. The iPhone represents well the reversal of the pyramid to which we were accustomed, by hiding the complexity under the surface while letting the essence emerge. And this practice marked the decades that followed.

Technology is like a joke: if you have to explain it, it means it did not work. All products of the digital culture were created with assumptions such as: disintermediation, democratization, simplification of the user experience, trial-and-error learning, and recognition of success through 'scores' that are visible to all. Think of the aforementioned Facebook and Instagram, or even YouTube, LinkedIn and Wikipedia, the latter able to democratize and disintermediate even encyclopedic knowledge.

Contemporary culture, in fact, is based on this approach: essence and appearance must coincide or potential users will lose interest. No one has the desire or the time to read instructions before using a new device and no one expects to face a complex learning curve before being able to send an email with a newly purchased PC or smartphone. We do not have the luxury of devoting time and energy to in-depth study, with all that that implies. In hypermodernity, we celebrate attitudes such as 'done is better than perfect,' 'trial and error,' 'fail fast, learn quick' that reference the idea that in most cases the search for in-depth knowledge should be set aside and that we should proceed by trial and error, learning from experience – exactly as it happens in a video game. For companies to satisfy this type of need, it means they must resort to the democratization of what they offer.

However, it is clear that traditional companies were not operating according to these principles. Managers were not trained according to this logic, designers were not prepared to follow them, operating models were not designed to meet this sudden desire for convenience, business sectors could not sustain the pace imposed by a clientele that demanded everything at the click of a button. That is why companies in many sectors have tried to reject the wave of digitalization, labelling it as marginal or confined to sectors other than their own, thus failing to deeply understand the phenomena.

Digital is like electricity: it is an invisible 'enabler' that allows the creation of products, services and experiences that in some cases integrate with existing ones, and in others, replace them altogether. If one takes this view, it is easier to interpret the transformation that is occurring in a proper and potentially advantageous way. And it will avoid the risk of confining digital to a category of 'innovative tools,' or confusing the means with the end, as so often still happens today. If used well, this enabler offers companies the opportunity to detect current trends, generating a more democratic exchange of value between companies and people.

THE DEMOCRATIZATION OF FASHION: THE BIRTH OF PRÊT-À-PORTER

Some fashion dynamics, such as the possibility to freely choose what to wear and to buy new garments regardless of whether the previous ones were actually worn out, have historically concerned only a small circle of privileged people. In the past, it was only royal families and aristocrats who could afford periodic visits from tailors, from whom they commissioned fine clothing based on current trends and personal tastes. There were precise hierarchical rules to avoid clothes being made with the same fabric for members of the nobility with different social status. And there were laws to prevent access of the lower classes to the finest fabrics (the sumptuary laws), so that only the ruling social classes could possess such distinctive symbols of superiority.

As Vanni Codeluppi recalls, the birth of high fashion can be commonly traced back to 1857. In Paris that year, the designer Charles Frederick Worth opened an atelier that offered ladies of nobility and aristocracy finished clothing designed according to his style and presented using live models. The clothes were still made to measure, but we can clearly see the beginning of a system that led the designer/couturier to become a true artist. **It was no longer the traditional elites who determined fashion trends but the tailors, who from that moment on were acclaimed as stars and simply called designers or fashion designers.**

The same period witnessed a parallel development of progress generated by the second industrial revolution. In particular, chemical dyes and new textile machines gave impetus to the nascent garment-making industry, allowing mass production at affordable prices. The bourgeoisie and the people could buy these garments in department stores, and also thus buy the dream of belonging to the world of high fashion. In fact, many of the models sold in these stores were nothing more than simplified replicas of the prestigious outfits reserved for the wealthier classes. These two tracks ran parallel for about a century, feeding off each other in a virtuous circle of exclusivity, dream and emulation. However, it was not yet a real process of democratization, as high fashion and industrial manufacturing remained two separate categories.

Things changed markedly in the 1960s. As the industrial boom swept through advanced economies and created levels of affluence never before achieved by such vast swathes of the population, a broad demand for quality products at affordable prices was born. The new middle class, imbued with new, almost evolutionary ideas, was decidedly opposed to the privileges of the upper classes. The idea of elitist, 'dusty' and exclusive luxury was strongly rejected.

This is why in the 50s and 60s of the last century, and also due to progress in the textile and manufacturing industry, the 'democratization of fashion' was fully realized, leading to the birth of prêt-à-porter. Starting from this period, more and more people have been able to dress fashionably by wearing designer clothes of fine workmanship.

This democratic revolution reached its peak in the 80s, a period when the figures of designers and supermodels were revered as gods and the fashion system produced stellar sales. The eagerness to live in the 'possible world' offered by high-end brands was such that those years also witnessed the birth of many **brand extensions** in various fields, from furniture to hospitality; not to mention the boom of licensing by brands in the accessory, cosmetics and perfume industries. Some maisons also chose to launch second lines, known as **diffusion lines**, with the specific intent of creating a range of cheaper products linked to an ad hoc sub-brand. Emporio Armani and D&G are among the most famous for this. The fate of these extensions has been mixed, and the reverberations on their mother-brands have also posed significant questions for managers. In many cases, the maisons have had to deal with issues related to dilution of the brand image, resulting in lost clientele and a negative impact on sales. In others, licenses and second lines have proved to be decidedly significant sources of revenue, both in terms of customer acquisition and, of course, sales.

It is interesting to observe how some companies have had to make the difficult decision to stop licensing operations or halt diffusion lines because these risked pulling the brand toward the lower end of the market, inevitably undermining brand equity. However, there are numerous successful cases, mainly attributable to situations in which the ownership and management of the brand have been able to calibrate the magnitude of the extension, carefully ensuring gradual entry into other domains, and that all areas of diversification were inherently consistent with the company's DNA.

Continuing in the direction of democratization or – as detractors might say – 'banalization' of high-end fashion, examples such as **sportswear**, **streetwear** and the advent of garments once destined for the workplace, such as jeans, can be cited. The trends and partnerships that have often occurred between the high-end and brands in these segments have certainly contributed to making them more current, enhancing them with technical overtones and a more authentic soul, but at the same time sanctioning their transformation.

It is important not to make the mistake of confusing the phenomenon described with the actual accessibility of the asset in question. Jean-Noël Kapferer, one of the most eminent branding experts and luxury scholars in the world, has observed how democratization should be associated with the 'desire' for high-end products rather than the actual act of purchasing them, which remains in fact the prerogative of the few, in light of their generally high cost.

In this vision, the outstanding reputation of global megabrands would act as a universal indicator of status and, at the same time, fuel the perception of accessibility. On the other hand, the high price of the products would contribute to preserving their character as 'luxury' products, without which they would effectively become victims of a dangerous process of banalization.

The contamination between these worlds, which in the past would have seemed incompatible, announced the definitive end of the higher social classes authority to determine the tastes of the lower ones. That dynamic that sociologists of consumption at the end of the 19th century such as Simmel and Veblen had theorized and defined as **trickle-down** (dripping from the top down) has now given way to the phenomena of **'trickle-across'** (King) and the **'viral diffusion'** of trends (Wiswede), which can originate in any social class of the population and spread widely, just like a viral contagion.

The transformation is thus complete: high-end fashion permanently sets aside its elitist traits and ambitions of cultural hegemony in the determination of aesthetic taste, to sublimate itself in an accelerated, democratized and connected hypermodernity.

Having reached the end of the chapter, it should be clear to the reader how the compass points that have guided the strategic decisions in recent decades by managers in the fashion system have been challenged, if not overturned, by the five forces described in these pages. It is obvious that the pandemic has further complicated the situation, exacerbating and accelerating many of the trends already underway.

This is why in the following pages we have considered it appropriate to propose **a handbook of new rules. We hope that they may act as guiding principles useful in steering the decisions of companies within the fashion system, in a world that has been defined as 'without rules.'**

The Ten

Rules

1

BE INCLUSIVE

*In a society that is profoundly different
from that of luxury's origin, by being both
more open and inclusive, the elitism typically
associated with high-end brands risks
being out of context.*

*For this very reason, Be Inclusive means
balancing the exclusivity of products with the
inclusivity of its own culture, in order not to
lose its authenticity; nourishing the dream
component at the same time as making
the brand more culturally accessible.*

High-end fashion has gone through various phases of development that have seen the modification of its grammar in terms of actors, types of products, commercial methods, etc. What can be defined as the **first phase of fashion** dates back to the end of the 19th century. It was during that period that time and artisanship as a guarantee of quality and prestige were gradually overshadowed by the creative flair and genius of the first couturiers, beginning with Charles Worth.

These personalities, who tailor-made garments for the leading figures of the time, considered themselves, and were considered to be, artists in all respects. High-end coincided with the strictest definition of luxury and did not require commercial superstructures such as brands: it was only the names of the designers that made their products exclusive.

The next moment of discontinuity coincided with the advent of the 20th century. In this period, the upper middle class created a demand for high-quality clothing that did not come from inaccessible haute couture. It was between the 1920s, with Sonia Delaunay, and 1966, with the opening of Rive Gauche and the first ready-to-wear collection designed by Yves Saint Laurent, that the concept of prêt-à-porter was conceived.

In this new scenario, characterized by a different demand than in the past, the **second phase of fashion** took shape. Here the stylists, now more aware than ever that the value of their work did not lie so much in the uniqueness of the product itself as in their signature, seized the opportunity to transfer this prestige to a product packaged in a serial way. This led to the creation of the first maisons. In spite of the standardization that this philosophy required, buying a ready-to-wear garment from these brands did not mean buying a simple product, but rather an identity: that of the designer, made up of a set of values combined with the culture of the moment.

For the advent of the **third phase**, it was necessary to wait until after the economic boom, a period characterized by the spread of more democratic aesthetic standards (such as jeans) and the birth of quality industrial brands. In this period, the business strategy of the maisons, which had already abandoned objective scarcity as a distinctive feature in the transition from haute couture to prêt-à-porter, underwent a further change with the creation of the **diffusion line**. Through this, expedient high-end players segmented not only their own offer but even their own brand, creating ad hoc lines to satisfy diverse needs of various market segments, moving ever closer to mass-market.

The first steps of this phase began at the end of the 1980s, but it was not until the 1990s and the first decade of the 20th century that the greatest developments were seen. Examples of this are Versace with Versus or Roberto Cavalli with Just Cavalli. But the real pioneer of this strategy was Giorgio Armani, with the creation of Armani Jeans, Emporio Armani and Armani Exchange. The diffusion lines satisfied distribution necessities. And their existence made sense, especially in the pre-digital period, when the fashion business was primarily wholesale.

The transition to a retail perspective changed the game yet again. From that moment on, in many cases, diffusion lines proved to be ineffective in the long-term perspective: they increased yearly revenue, but resulted in cannibalization and, above all, ended up diluting the value and perception of the brand. For an average consumer, defined as a 'luxury hiker' (Dubois and Laurent), coming into contact with the diffusion line meant taking the price of these products as a reference point and no longer being willing to consider another item from the flagship line at a higher price. This led, years later, to many brands revising their portfolios to limit confusion and preserve their appeal.

The brand, in fact, is the biggest defender of price differentiation in the fashion industry. However, the contrary is not true: one cannot indiscriminately raise the price of a product with the sole objective of creating a specific brand image. To understand this dynamic, one can use the wine sector as a comparison. Any wine, even if it is excellent, cannot pretend to be a luxury wine. Its price cannot be justified solely by its function or characteristics. Its value is determined by its uniqueness, created with intangible elements such as heritage, history, country of origin and place of production. Brands that lack these components remain confined to the field of comparability. Even very good wines cannot be compared to various Ruinart or Château Pape Clément, because they lack a venerable quality.

Coming back to high-end brands, no one questions their prices or justifies them, because they are close to works of art. To build this image takes time, a vision or both. In this segment, the charm and mystery of their origin is the milestone for most brands. It is no coincidence that many maisons have their own names, founders' names or family names: they are the code that precedes all the other brand codes. High-end fashion brands that remain loyal to their heritage offer people a special reason to establish a relationship with them. Since the purchase of these garments is not necessary, profound motivations and values are the driving factors.

Dream and tradition are what segment brands within the market. To build a high-end brand, one must create a mythology and a cult of followers, much like those of a religion. Customers of high fashion are the most attentive and sophisticated, because they buy symbols and codes. That is why storytelling is the most important lever for a brand's equity. Even companies that are not a part of the segment, but aspire to be considered as part, have understood this: if fast-fashion owes its success to distribution and affordable prices for the masses, and the high-end is unattainable in terms of quality and prestige, premium brands focus on meaningful communication efforts to continuously sustain the image and superior margins of mass-market products.

Elitism, as demonstrated by haute couture, was the basis of luxury and its high prices. Veblen was one of the first of several consumer sociologists to theorize that its evolution in the past was the result of the continual struggle among the elites who tried to impose their own tastes, which they considered to be better than those of others. Since its inception, luxury has thrived due to its exclusivity. The high-fashion industry was built around the concept that we always want that which we cannot have. And, in line with the business tactic of strategic scarcity, the brand worlds created around these companies exploited established codes of **cultural exclusivity**: advertising that showed only a certain privileged demographic, a presentation of the product that discouraged interaction, and the deliberately complaisant and aloof manner of sales assistants.

Yet high-end fashion brands have had to face a cultural change: exclusivity has ceased being of value, at least for Gen Z. A report by the research firm Kantar, supported by numerous studies and documentation, shows that younger generations of consumers do not seem to appreciate conventional codes of exclusivity with strong conviction. Elitism, as it has always been conceived, contrasts with the profound values in which this group is reflected. Gen Z has proven to be more open and inclusive than its predecessors. The most successful brands with young people have embraced this sense of inclusivity and turned a 'right' value into a 'cool' attribute. It is easy to understand how this shift in perception could destabilize luxury players. This is not a trend, but a fundamental cultural shift in what drives consumer desire. And not even the maisons can escape these changes.

Retracing the three phases described before, it is possible to see a change in the way of identifying and perceiving something as 'exclusive.' Initially, exclusivity held both economic and class significance, while in the second phase, social segmentation gave way to brand recognition, hence a theme of awareness. But the real paradigm shift occurred later in the third phase, when the economic factor began to lose relevance (due also to the diffusion lines). Faced with the challenge of rebuilding equity often diluted with the need to feed the 'dream of growth' through guaranteeing high distribution, high-end players must now understand the necessity to rethink the meaning attributed to exclusivity and to integrate its opposite, inclusiveness, into their way of thinking and acting.

This change did not mean that these brands slid from the top of the pyramid due to typical mass-market dynamics as happened with the diffusion lines, but it did force them to **adopt a new strategy based on the balance between exclusivity of the icons, accessibility of the entry-level products and inclusiveness of the brand culture**. High-end brands are now resorting to extending their offer to make themselves more accessible. This practice is positive and works for the brand if it allows greater awareness and guarantees penetration for a restricted and limited number of secondary products. In this case, there is a maximization of the Customer Lifetime Value (CLV), as after time, buyers might push themselves to buy a flagship product of the brand that they could not previously afford.

The side effect of these more accessible products with their lower prices is that they may aspire to serve the same social function as those in the high range. In this case, however, the brand offers consumers the opportunity to trade down, affecting at the same time both the CLV and its equity.

In mature countries with market saturation, this is the strategy that has driven much of the segment's growth. The **accessorization of**

luxury phenomenon is an example: not everyone can buy a tailored suit from a prestigious maison, but millions of people can wear their sunglasses or buy their perfume. And its success is undisputed: take, for example, Chanel and its beauty line worth 60% of total revenue. The same goes for a brand like Givenchy, whose best-selling product in 2017 was a lipstick. These two approaches refer to two different marketing strategies: **brand extension** and **brand stretching**. The first relates to the expansion of the brand with product categories similar to its core business or already within it, whereas the second explores sectors far from the brand's original area of expertise. Yet it is not enough. To avoid side effects and preserve aspiration while creating an inclusive brand culture, the majority of high-end brands resort to another segmentation strategy of progressively raising the prices of their icons.

In order to better explain this concept, it is appropriate to introduce another theme, that of the archetype that characterizes the segment we are dealing with. In *Marketing 4.0*, it was defined as the **Trumpet model** (explained in the figure on page 65). The distinctive character of this model lies in its high level of affinity: people tend to trust the quality of certain brands, so they are willing to recommend them to others even if they do not buy or use them personally. In these cases, the number of advocates is higher than the number of actual buyers; advocacy therefore exceeds the act of purchase. In a Trumpet category, customers are deeply engaged. However, the evaluation process that follows is relatively simple, because most brands have already developed a specific reputation for quality, built over the long term by word of mouth. Those who feel attracted to certain brands, as we've anticipated, tend to group together. Their existence often influences potential buyers by encouraging them to learn more about the product's quality. Due to the high prices, there are admirers who aspire to buy these brands but cannot afford them. However, they happily recommend them to others anyway, because they embrace and share the values of the brand and the possible world it represents. And even if later they can afford them, it is not certain they'll be able to obtain them: most of the brands pertaining to this archetype are, in fact, niche. **Since scarcity increases a brand's attractiveness in the eyes of potential buyers, those who manage them must not make the product too readily available.**

It has been said that at every sales performance meeting, Karl Lagerfeld systematically decided to discontinue the maisons' first three products. And that the possibility of choosing a given colour for one's Kelly was discontinued when it became too popular among high-society women. Scarcity, once the (only) source of business for the high-end, is wisely used now as a marketing lever, specifically to artificially reconstruct exclusivity with a different meaning than that of the past. The element of 'sacrifice' in terms of resources, both economic and time, is a factor that should not be underestimated in this segment. Although the number of people able to buy luxury products remains limited, social media has expanded the opportunity to connect with brands and appreciate them. By becoming more accessible in attitude, luxury outperformed all categories in brand value appreciation according to the BrandzTM Global Top 100, with an increase of 29%, following the previous year of 28%. Therefore, it is clear how necessary it is today to attract and include the greatest number of people in the Appeal phase.

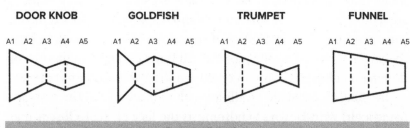

FIGURE 2.1: **SECTOR ARCHETYPES MAP, MARKETING 4.0**

To do this, high-end brands also need to engage younger generations. The industry has had to deal with stylistic issues not only in creative terms, but also in ethical, social and identity terms. For example, sensitive issues such as gender equality, body stereotyping and cultural diversity are now on the agenda for top managers. This has manifested itself in a number of ways: from making totally different casting choices than in the past for their fashion shows, to campaigns for humanitarian causes, through to collaborations with cultural leaders once considered antithetical to luxury. The perception of social inclusivity of high-end brands has benefited from the phenomenon of luxury accessorization (described before) and the trend of convergence with the world of streetwear, which is strongly linked to the theme of contamination mentioned at the beginning of the book. Seeing their brand worn by 'pop' cultural icons who are followed by millions of young people has allowed maisons to open up to the world and reach new audiences with a different proposition than of the past and finally be relevant to them. And this is happening without 'disturbing' those who continue to search for the most exclusive items from those brands. Nowadays, it is essential for any brand to adapt to cultural benchmarks, and high-end players are not exempt. At the same time, the importance of subcultures has increased. In order to win the favour of most people now, it is not enough to adhere to the dominant culture; it is also necessary to show respect for minorities.

In 2020, Gucci made headlines with two actions: in the first case, using a girl with Down's Syndrome as the face of the L'Obscur mascara campaign; in the second, going against the dominant ideology of the concept of beauty and choosing to use the model Armine Harutyunyan, creating a real media debate. In both situations, the brand's choices contributed to the representation of the value of diversity: there is room for eccentricity and a type of self-expression, free from prejudices and stereotypes of gender, ethnicity and beauty within the multifaceted vision reflected in Gucci's dress codes. Industry players will increasingly prioritize these issues and it is clearly understood that simply promoting them is not enough. They will also have to organize themselves internally to reflect this vision.

It is no coincidence that in 2019 the Camera Nazionale della Moda Italiana (CNMI) created the *Diversity & Inclusion Manifesto* in which the 10 founding principles are the exact opposite of exclusivity. For CNMI, it is not just a matter of changing the aesthetic standards on which fashion has always been based, but of working within companies to build a more open and ethical culture, so they can present themselves to the market with the same virtues. According to research carried out by the institute, **incorporating inclusiveness functions to support business and is an accelerator.** This explains why the market is moving decisively in this direction. Many brands, such as Chanel, have hired dedicated managers to demonstrate their commitment. Therefore,we can say that **the high -end has entered its fourth phase: inclusiveness.**

The consulting firm Bain & Company confirms that the crucial factors when buying luxury goods will be the degree to which shoppers feel aligned with the brand from a cultural point of view and its appropriateness to the values in which they believe. Therefore, the brand must communicate effectively in relation to them. It is clear that this is a very delicate and complex issue. Today, most high-end brands are global megabrands and consequently have to take specific details into consideration when developing these initiatives on a global scale. It is necessary to pay attention to everything: religion, minorities, animal welfare, customs and traditions. Further complicating the scenario is the deeply entrenched Western legacy for many of these brands, which for decades have spoken directly and principally to 'white and wealthy European and Americans.' Today this paradigm must change completely, in a world where social media and the web expose companies to ever more analysis and criticism, with the potential for heavy repercussions due to investigations and scandals.

To win this battle and conquer Millennials and Gen Z, **the maisons must amplify and nurture their culture, cocreating cultural objects.** Good examples are the abandonment of traditional advertising in favour of video productions made with emerging artists and rock bands, or collaborations with artists, such as the calibre of Maurizio Cattelan, to paper a city with art walls and create exhibitions dedicated to the analysis of multiple forms and the different meanings that the act of appropriation assumes in our time.

This conceptual model is fundamental in what we might call the 'age of expectations,' an era in which the phenomena (described in the book's introduction) have set increasingly high standards in the consumer expectations around the world. The empowerment of consumers, driven by ample information and online communities, requires brands to have a clear, differentiating and integral positioning. **Inauthentic brands will not survive in a world where word of mouth has returned to being the most powerful advertising channel and where consumers trust the judgment of total strangers (peers) more than what companies say and advertise.**

Even the high-end fashion brands must accept working in an era of horizontally integrated communications, where vertical control is less effective and the only requirement is to 'simply' remain consistent and faithful to their vision. That is why there is **more and more talk about inclusive brands with exclusive products.** This does not mean 'accessible luxury,' but rather a brand that includes more people culturally than in the past, and preserving exclusivity in meanings far removed from its elitist origins. An example of this was Giorgio Armani's choice to broadcast a fashion show on TV for the first time in history. "A message that reaches every home in an intimate way," said the designer. "I don't know if this choice of mine will be followed by others and if all of fashion will enter an era of complete democracy, but I chose television to reach a vast and real audience."

What has been said so far can be even more effectively developed on the web. Although many maisons still have a difficult relationship with digital media, it is clear that the online world and social media are preferred vehicles for building an inclusive brand culture. In terms of communication, the internet lends itself perfectly to the development of meaningful worlds and collective imagery in which communities of believers can immerse themselves.

This is why fashion megabrands have evolved into true media companies. A prime example is Burberry, already a pioneer of streaming fashion shows in 2010, then the first high-end brand to live stream on Twitch, presenting their S/S 2012 collection. Rod Manley, Chief Marketing Officer of the maison, said, "Twitch offered a new and exciting space where the Burberry community was involved; an interactive experience in which guests could connect and interact with both the brand and each other."

Consequently, online communication represents a great opportunity for the maisons. But there are still hidden risks. The first lies in the difficult balance between quantity and quality, between presence and absence. **If scarcity is a value for these brands, ubiquitous communications can generate negative consequences, such as the excessive distribution of product images**. It can happen that an item of clothing or an accessory loses its charm and desirability just because people see it worn too often by endorsers and influencers on the internet. And it also happens that a product that has not even arrived yet at a boutique has already become obsolete.

The second risk relates to the potential loss of control over brand messaging. High-end brands were accustomed to one-way communication, typically created through the use of glossy magazines and events, but today they need to adjust to the interaction of dialogue. To complicate the equation, there are also new figures in the picture: the **influencers**. The use of these ambassadors should aim to increase the notoriety, inclusiveness and desirability of the brand, without affecting the exclusivity and ultimately the rarity of the product. **To evolve the dream and fuel the myth of the brand, the high-end must communicate well beyond its core target.** Do not forget that these brands create value through the eyes of others.

2

BE A SYMPHONY

In an environment fragmented into a multitude
of touchpoints that have shortened the distance
between maisons and luxury customers,
Be a Symphony means orchestrating an optimal
selection of touchpoints, taking into account
the high-end's need for aspiration and scarcity,
even before consumers' desire for ubiquity.

In recent years, various models have been theorized to analyse and represent the management of channels used in client relationships. The most recent is that of **omnichannel**, which posits that people show an increasingly 'agnostic' attitude toward the channels through which they communicate, inform themselves, purchase and manage their post-purchase relationships. The new consumers want to live an experience of **onlife commerce** in which, as already described, the purchase is only the final piece of a broader relational process that enhances all the contact points between them and the brand. The result is a seamless experience based on their needs.

Therefore, all the digital and physical channels available to a brand today need to merge into a single ecosystem. This model represents the evolution of another precedent, namely **multichannel**. A multichannel strategy involves using a variety of channels to enable interactions and transactions between the brand and individuals, focusing only on the point of view of the company. This results in a lack of interconnection between channels that often do not communicate consistently with each other, and a lack of synergies. However, in the precise segment we are analysing here, we believe it is appropriate to evolve the concept of omnichannel in a new direction.

The essence of high-end is the balance between presence and absence, accessibility and exclusivity. This is why selective distribution plays such an important role in building the distinctive character of these brands. This reasoning does not just refer to the sale, but also extends to all the channels through which client relationships are managed. For this reason, high-end fashion brands cannot afford to be present always and anywhere, at the complete mercy of clients. Total submission to the customer's will does not marry well with the fundamental and founding prerogatives of this segment.

Just as the conductor of an orchestra does not always need all the instruments to perform a symphony, so too must brands focus on the channels that are most in harmony, to enact the experience that best suits their brand. Beyond the number and their various weightings, the key element remains the integration of every part for the work to be a success. This approach, which goes beyond the complex attempt to govern an ever-increasing number of channels, is referred to as **optichannel**. As the name suggests, it refers to choosing the optimal channels with respect to specific business needs and encourages simplifying the experience offered to customers. Instead of proposing every available channel and then integrating them, the optichannel experience benefits from clear guidance, optimizing effectiveness and preserving the aspirational and desirable qualities that these brands seek. In this way, as the metaphor suggests, only those channels suitable to the expected outcome will be favoured.

By putting ourselves on the side of the shopper, we can understand better the dynamics existing in the high-end fashion segment. According to data collected by the consulting firm McKinsey, luxury buyers use their smartphone 98% of the time in their purchase process (compared to a cross-industry average use of 65%) and 77% of the time they use more than one device (compared to a 35% average for other sectors). As the customer journey progresses, there are multiple touchpoints. For consumers with very high levels of digital literacy, like Chinese ones, this can reach an average of 15 touchpoints, confirming both the high involvement and the high fragmentation of the relationship.

Along the way, the overall experience is referred to as Research Online, Purchase Offline (**ROPO**). In fact, 80% of the purchases in this segment are motivated online, but only 22% are finalized through e-commerce. Once individual brands are taken into account, this percentage falls even further: for a high-end fashion brand that performs well online, sales through this channel do not account for more than 10% to 15% of their revenue. Therefore, we can see how the shopping experience in the high-end fashion segment is predominantly characterized by a **webrooming** approach (the opposite of **showrooming**, where a potential customer visits one or more physical showrooms but then tends to make the final purchase online). Ultimately, when luxury goods are purchased, the tendency is to complete the buying process in a physical store, despite the proliferation of digital options. But the sociocultural and economic transformations linked to the COVID-19 pandemic could make this logic questionable, and we could see a growth in showrooming. A buyer desiring to see the product could go to the store and get advice from the shopping assistants. However, since they might be unwilling to try on a garment that may have been previously worn by other customers, they conclude the transaction later online. In the future, the store display window could become an even more interesting way to showcase the product and create awareness, as well as offer advice and solve other tasks with technology.

Having debunked the idea that high-end fashion is based on a totally analogue journey, the importance of digital, beyond the possibility of making a sale, has been reinforced by the latest data released by Google: in the first half of 2020, online searches for premium and luxury segments grew by 30% and 22%, respectively. **In light of these trends and purchasing behaviours, even more than in other sectors, high-end players will have to structure a single income statement that takes into account overall performance rather than just evaluating single channels.** Doing so will also avoid cannibalization between different company functions: it is not important that each channel leads to a transaction – considered in a limiting way as the only metric capable of determining effectiveness – but rather that each contributes to the generation of one.

The webrooming approach is also driven by those brands that do not want to be at the mercy of total reliance on digital technology. In fact, there are brands, positioned at the top of the pyramid, that do not even want to expand their entire portfolio to e-commerce. They promote and publish their product on their own platforms but only allow in-store transactions. Often there is also a desire to couple the product with a sales practice that ritualizes the purchase, emphasizing the particular characteristics that justify its high price. Some point to them as 'digital unfriendly,' but this is a strategic choice. An example of this is Hermès, where entire sections of its website are dedicated to Birkin and Kelly bags that can only be purchased in select boutiques and through waiting lists.

In addition to this approach, high-end brands are increasingly resorting to sales by invitation only or the broadcasting of capsule collections that can only be booked via web-to-store. The data from some studies confirm this trend: with the growth of the aspirational qualities of the brand, the number of omnichannel solutions offered decreases. Even so, digital channels are still useful in the development of the purchase experience and also as a tool to check the availability of a specific item or accessory within the network of physical stores.

In terms of omnichannel, it now becomes clear how the existing gap between fast-fashion leaders such as Zara and that of high-end players is not necessarily a competitive disadvantage. In fact, for the latter, it is more important to focus on a relationship that may be less extensive, but is perfectly tailored to their own needs and those of their customers. Thus, we get to what the consulting firm PwC has named **luxury dilemma**, where high-end brands have the possibility of following two diverse paths: remain confined to their ivory towers or, conversely, open up completely and bow to consumer expectations of interconnectedness that they are accustomed to having in other sectors. PwC has also identified four fundamental pillars in managing both channels and touchpoints: research, purchase, delivery and customer care. In the comparison between luxury brands and mass market, as can be imagined, the latter outperformed in all areas. However, high-end players make up for this with their analogue particularities and accompanying human touches, such as gift-wrapping services or the custom tailoring of garments in-store.

But one area in which high-end brands have been unjustifiably late is in their delivery methods. For shoppers accustomed to fast and inexpensive services such as Amazon Prime, not receiving special treatment or frequently having to bear the delivery costs are sources of dissatisfaction and frustration for the type of purchase they are making. A best practice in terms of delivery is Gucci's 'Store-to-Door in 90 minutes,' in collaboration with the e-tailer Farfetch: customers in 10 cities in different regions of the world can purchase the brand's products from the brand's app or the partner's website and receive the items at their home within an hour and a half, delivered from the nearest boutique. The high level of integration between the players means that it is possible to check the availability of products in real time at the nearest Gucci boutique.

For high-end brands, investing in omnichannel solutions is therefore a tactical operation, in light of the preference for an optichannel strategy. This is unlike brands that are located at the bottom of the pyramid, for which such solutions are strategic, if not essential. That is why, in recent years, players like Boggi have invested in various different solutions, including click-and-collect (in-store pick-up of online purchases), click-and-reserve (reserving products online to pick up in-store), seek-and-send (to take advantage of the stocks within store networks for online order shipments) and click-from-store (to enable purchases in-store of products not in stock).

The focus of the strategy we are describing is control, in terms of both image and customer experience. In fact, we are witnessing the process of distribution licenses being repurchased by their maisons, starting with the Kering group that announced a plan in 2020 to focus mainly on single-brand direct management. **Every touchpoint of a high-end brand has to accomplish two important tasks: sustain storytelling and enhance the relationship with the customer through impeccable service.** Players at the top of the industry pyramid must demand even more of their stores now. In a scenario of reduced traffic, in part as a result of the pandemic, stores represent a rare and therefore precious opportunity to engage customers, transporting them into the symbolic universe of the brand. This activity is almost impossible in multi-brand stores, except by using the shop-in-shop formula, which has obvious limits.

Having said this, it raises a question for high-end brands when addressing the issue of the web. The presence in this space, by its very form, destroys boundaries that can usually be erected in the real world. On the web, everything is just a click away and the platform of a maison can be dangerously close to that of one of fast fashion. It is precisely because they did not have a brand to defend that the pioneers of luxury e-commerce were not the maisons but rather service companies created with this specific intent. However, it should be noted that the various e-tailers do not necessarily pose a threat to high-end brands, as they can act as an important commercial and communication vehicle. For example, one of the founding principles of YNAP is its **content-to-commerce**, which specifically engages users with content recounting the history and prestige of products in its catalogue. That being said, it is clear that the development of a **direct-to-consumer** approach creates an urgent necessity for the players of this segment.

Returning to the 'onland' environment, let us discuss **off-price stores**. Many brands decide to have a large presence in outlets where they can sell their garments at deep discounts while offering a middling shopping experience and then they counterbalance this with enticing high-level flagship stores. Ralph Lauren is an example of this: most of the sales volume is in off-price, especially within the label Polo Ralph Lauren, while the aspirational quality of the brand is guaranteed by the 'temples' that tell the story of the founder and celebrate the signature line, Purple Label. **For these players, the flagship is a celebration of the brand; the other stores serve a purely commercial function.**

While a fundamentalist vision of high-end brand management might view off-price as a threat, in its excessive expansion of potential demand and the dilution of the brand imagery, data collected in the latest edition of the Bain-Altagamma market report show that this channel is thriving, and that prior to the outbreak of the COVID-19 pandemic, it was growing steadily. Worldwide, off-price comprised 12% of the luxury personal goods market in 2018 for a turnover of 31 billion euros, with a positive trend of +7% compared to the previous year. Pre-pandemic data predicted growth to reach 36.5 billion. Furthermore, the latest data in the *Luxury Market Monitor 2020* estimates that outlets will lose 15% of turnover compared to 22% for mono-brand stores. It is clear how pandemic status will lead to an under-reporting of the figures, but it is plausible to think that their role will continue to be important for the foreseeable future. Pre-COVID, it was estimated that off-price stores would increase market share in personal luxury goods by one point by 2025, to hover between 43 and 47 billion euros in a segment worth 329–365 billion. Paradoxically, the advantageous prices of this channel could be an anchor for a market, like unnecessary goods, which will suffer uncertain repercussions.

The economic crisis generated by the virus has already made an impact: Tmall, e-tailer of the Alibaba group, opened an outlet on April 20, in the sector dedicated to luxury. Luxury Soho, the name of the new digital zone, aims to dispose of unsold stock, acting as a counterpart to Luxury Pavilion, the section dedicated to the high-end. The platform will gather highly discounted quality products so as to attract buyers, especially young ones, who love fashion but are price sensitive. As explained by Weixiong Hu, Vice President of the Alibaba Group and General Manager of Tmall's fashion business unit: "In the future, brands will be able to open two different types of stores on Tmall: the official flagship store focused on new seasonal products, located in the Luxury Pavilion, and the official outlet store, focused on discounted products, located in the Luxury Soho area."

In addition to lower prices, off-price has seen its rise thanks to the transformation, over time, of the outlets into real villages: places where you can combine high-level shopping with restaurants, where you can enjoy a gourmet break and even art exhibitions, concerts and events. These destinations have garnered the favour of consumers and led their operators to multiply their numbers. **Especially for tourists, some outlets have the same appeal as the main fashion arteries of European and world capitals.** For some customers, especially from countries such as China, Russia and the United Arab Emirates, these places offer more convenience, making it possible to pack sizeable purchases of luxury goods into a single stop and day.

For the high-end fashion segment, the income generated by tourists is fundamental. It is estimated that the maison boutiques located in Via Monte Napoleone in Milan lost about 85% of their weekly revenues in the initial stage of the coronavirus emergency due to the lack of sales usually generated by tourists. The fragile balance on which the success or economic failure of these players is based leads them to seriously question whether the exorbitant commercial rents of those stores, so important for the sustenance of the brand, can be borne.

The necessity of integrating the physical and digital channels arises not only from the needs of the customer but also from a reflection of commercial nature. A tactical response that was gaining ground among high-end players in the pre-COVID-19 period was the use of the **temporary shop** and **pop-up store**. These shops only operate for a fixed period of time, usually a few weeks or at most a few months, in heavily trafficked areas of the city centre, shopping malls, stations or airports and act contrary to traditional shops by pushing new products toward customers and not vice versa. Jean-Jacques Guiony, LVMH's financial director, said that the pop-up trend is highly regarded by the French conglomerate, as "it allows us to speak to our customers in a different way." In 2019, there were about a hundred of these stores under brand banners such as Dior, Prada, Valentino, Hermès and Moschino. According to *Forbes*, the strategy of temporary and pop-up stores is also an important weapon in terms of efficiency and effectiveness for luxury brands that want to establish themselves in emerging countries. For luxury brands, the pop-up fulfils the traditional function of testing, or exploiting a temporary opportunity, but also, and perhaps more importantly, of presenting capsule collections or special projects, where traditional mono-brand stores would not have the appropriate context for the exceptional nature of these events.

3

BE A VIBRATION

In a world dominated by dematerialization, luxury must claim to be tangible and therefore sensorial. Be a Vibration means enhancing the role of physical contact points, primarily mono-brand and flagship stores, making them the main vehicle of the brand essence.

"Luxury must be felt." With these words Nick Foley, President of Southern Europe, Asia Pacific and Japan of the brand consulting and design firm Landor, synthesizes the true essence of this market. Luxury is the sector of 'vibrations' because more than any other it manages to stimulate the senses and psychology of its buyers. The physical relationship with the brand and its products is essential to produce these vibrations.

Nowhere is this as true or as important as in the market we are analysing, namely fashion: high-end fashion is culture, a material culture, which draws its origins from craftsmanship, the quality of the fabrics and the materials, and is inextricably linked to the act of being worn. **That is why high-end fashion, despite the process of digitalization, will never see its physical role diminish.**

It is based on a multisensory experience and a feeling of privilege. Customers who approach the brands in this segment expect to receive special and unique attention and unparalleled service. These two concepts can never take place anywhere except in physical stores. For Vincent Bastier, former CEO of Louis Vuitton, "The true experience of luxury only happens in an interpersonal relationship." **Flagships** are therefore essential for high-end fashion brands. Purchasing a high-end garment or accessory must be something special, not just because of the product but also, and most of all, for the extraordinary experience connected to it.

This truth can be plainly found in the basis of human biology. Our species is visceral by nature: 40% of our neurons process external stimuli, transforming them into signals of emotional pleasure. A room's scent, the background music, the sensation of a garment on one's skin as it is being tried on and the pleasure of sipping a drink while deciding: **purchasing within a physical context creates a ritual and elevates the product accordingly. This is the reason behind the choice of many maisons to keep boutiques as the 'favoured place' in which to conclude customer purchases**, inviting not only the examination of the product but most of all the gratification of an experience. The goal is to fully activate the nervous system, creating feelings of satisfaction, excitement and loyalty.

Like any ritual, high-end shopping takes time. The process of selecting, examining, trying on, comparing and choosing is usually long and complex. So much so that the garment is as extraordinary as the fact that a portion of one's day has been carved out and dedicated entirely to it. That is why shoppers are willing to go to stores. While brands in the high-end range are fortunate to have these individuals' time, they need to worry not only about entertaining them, but most of all about creating memorable moments that become fixed in their minds.

This approach has rewarded all the brands that have presided over the main metropolitan arteries of the globe with their boutiques. But in recent years, something in these dynamics seems to have fractured. According to reports by Altagamma *Worldwide*, **foot traffic** in mono-brand fashion stores fell by 25% from 2012 to 2018, while the number of new openings contracted by 65%, also physiologically following a period of frantically pursuing new retail spaces. Another reason may be the new generation's lack of interest in traditional stores, which, in order to remain relevant in an increasingly fragmented and omnichannel context, find themselves having to periodically renew their value proposition.

We are convinced that mono-brand stores will always remain a key asset for high-end fashion brands. At the moment, these are the channel that records the largest volume of sales for these companies: according to data collected by Bain & Company in 2017, **mono-brands** account for as much as 30% of the total, compared to the digital channels (including both e-commerce owners and e-tailers), which are worth less than a third (8%). However, the forecast from the same research confirms the difficulties mentioned previously. For year 2025 projections, the consulting firm assumes a redistribution of the weightings, with the mono-brand decreasing to 25% and a growth of the online market until it ties in share.

However, these numbers may be misleading. We must remember two factors. The first is the material and tactile nature of the brands we discussed at the beginning of the rule. The second is the opti-channel approach dominating the segment, discussed in the rule Be a Symphony, in which a store might not make the sale but be able to trigger it in another channel. Therefore, we believe that even in the future a continued growth of e-commerce will not undermine the fundamental role that the mono-brand store plays in the global strategy of luxury brands.

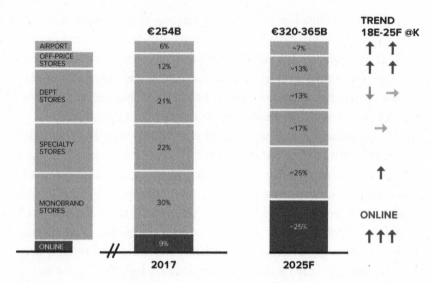

FIGURE 2.2: **PERSONAL LUXURY GOODS MARKET BY CHANNEL (€B)**

The same cannot be said for the fate that may await **department stores**. Bain & Company also reports that this channel will be the most affected by changes in shopping habits within the sector. It is estimated that there will be a decrease in sales from 23% in 2016 to 13% in 2025. The underlying motivation behind this drastic decline is a reflection of what has been stated so far: by their nature, **department stores do not always allow high-end brands to tell their story and demonstrate their uniqueness.** However, one of the reasons this channel may not totally disappear is that their window displays are able to create brand awareness. This lever is definitely not enough for high-end players, but it can help to generate sales from customers who had not previously shown a preference for them.

Now let us turn our focus back to flagship stores. As stated by Jean Noël Kapferer and already introduced in Be Inclusive, luxury is considered to be like a religion. To engage in worship, brands need 'churches' without which there would be neither religious initiations nor rituals. These are spaces in which to recreate a dimension that is almost sacred. **In these stores, which can be compared to actual temples, the products must be displayed like icons, to be venerated and sold through specific individual ceremonies.**

The comparison with religion does not seem to be risky if we consider the purchase of a garment from the high-end range as a need for self-realization, located at the top of Maslow's pyramid, which mirrors among other things, the category pyramid. The attractiveness of these places is so great that they generate a true form of pilgrimage: a city like Paris can be visited for its monuments as well as for the multitude of luxury shops. As spaces that celebrate the brand, they encompass its identity: past, present and future.

In the fashion sector, Prada must be mentioned for its avant-garde approach with the construction of its Epicentres, the highest expression of flagship stores. Even before 2000, the Italian maison had already grasped the importance of creating spaces with a higher purpose than only commercial. It was clear that the Epicentres were intended to bring events and sophisticated forms of culture together in a consumer context. These 'stores' were, above all, a means of communication, designed to consolidate opportunities to meet consumers. Among the first polysensorial and multisensorial projects in the fashion retail sector, they provided a place for the creation of numerous events designed so that people could truly participate in the brand's world.

When someone crosses one of these thresholds, they become totally immersed in its world. The dedication with which these brands control their image and try to preserve it allows customers to find and live the same experience, in every boutique, despite their global distribution. Therefore, we could propose another metaphor and speak of a **brand embassy** in every nation. For a citizen, every embassy of their country around the world is a meeting point, able to transport them immediately home. So for a foreigner, that same embassy is a way to get in touch with a distant culture, perhaps even half a world away. Although the customer may be reassured regarding the experience they will encounter, to some extent this strategy can be perceived as standardized and therefore not bring value to the visit.

That is why some brands decided to create their own specifically unique spaces. Gucci is one of these: in recent years, it has created several projects around the world, dressing each location with a unique mix of the brand's vision and the culture of the specific place.

Gucci Garden is an example of this. Opened in Florence in the historic Palazzo della Mercanzia and conceived by Alessandro Michele, Creative Director of the maison, the space houses a boutique with unique items and an exhibition area curated by the critic Maria Luisa Frisa. The Gucci Garden Galleria pays homage to the brand, celebrating it through various themed rooms with historic advertising campaigns, descriptions of artisanship and displays of vintage objects. It begins on the first floor with a room dedicated to the phenomenon called 'Guccification,' continues with another dedicated to the signature imagery and symbols of the maison, and closes with the history of its jet-set clientele and the evolution of the heraldic element of the crest. The visit ends on the second floor with the De Rerum Natura rooms that are reminiscent of natural history museums, and Ephemera, where it is possible to retrace the history of Gucci through objects, video and memorabilia. Not to be missed is the auditorium where special films are screened. There is also a gastronomic element: Gucci Garden hosts the Gucci Osteria, the restaurant bearing the signature of the three-Michelin-star chef Massimo Bottura. Gucci Garden embodies the desire for evolution that high-end fashion players will need to have as they adapt to the demands of an increasingly demanding clientele.

In this vein, a variety of luxury brands are experimenting with alternative formats to make experiences aligned not only with their values and principles, but also with the ideal lifestyle they want to promote. An example is Ralph Lauren, with its decision to open a series of elegant and refined restaurants in cities such as New York and Paris. These locations are "in perfect harmony with the aesthetics of the maison – as stated on the homepage of the brand's website – [...] a natural extension of the world of Ralph Lauren as expressed through the culinary arts." Burberry also created a destination imbued with the brand's imagery, Thomas's Café. Inside the Regent Street boutique in London, customers can immerse themselves in a unique atmosphere while enjoying delicacies of British cuisine. In February of last year, Louis Vuitton also ventured into this arena for the first time, opening a café and a restaurant, Le Café V and Sugalabo V, respectively, on top of his new Maison Osaka Midosuji in Japan.

All these initiatives are part of a consolidated trend: the introduction of the food service sector to luxury stores. It is a continuation of the interconnectedness between haute couture and haute cuisine. **High-end brands need to offer customers more than one reason to visit their stores and these restaurants entice new customers as well as build loyalty with the most important ones.** Within these places it is also possible to host exclusive experiences. Another option in the redesigning of the segment's mono-brand stores is to transform them into home environments, obviously sophisticated ones. This is certainly not a new trick for fashion brands: structuring your place as a living room takes the customer's perception of the brand from commercial to relational ambitions. The most daring examples are able to go as far as recreating the experience of a private personal dressing room, as Kleiderzimmer tried out. This store offers a unique experience: it can be booked exclusively so that one can try on proposed garments in complete freedom.

Another aspect illustrated by Gucci Garden is the ability high-end brands possess to transform 'four walls' into real museums where their history can be exhibited. For some players, the commingling with the art world is so strong that it results in the patronage or creation of cultural foundations. This is the case of ZegnArt for Ermenegildo Zegna, of Fondation Cartier, of the Espace Culturel Louis Vuitton or of the famous Fondazione Prada. The latter is the first institution entirely dedicated to art and culture owned by a maison. The project, which began in 1993, has been defined by the international press as "the most interesting cultural campus in the world." Fondazione Prada has always questioned the intentions and relevance of the cultural commitment of the moment and of the future, with a series of projects in continuous evolution. Its activities take place in two permanent locations, the main one in Milan and the other in Venice. The intent of Miuccia Prada and her husband Patrizio Bertelli was to enable artists to realize their ideas that otherwise could not be, and to offer everyone the opportunity to expand and deepen different modes of learning. For them, culture was something useful and necessary, beyond being just engaging and attractive, because of its capacity to enrich daily life and provide tools to understand change. The foundation reflects the soul of the maison: a visionary entrepreneurial energy, eclecticism, desire to experiment and fast-paced execution. In short: the concrete representation of Italian genius. Miuccia's aim to create 'echos and intersections' was captured in full.

In conclusion, in light of all the possibilities mentioned, and as stated in *Retail 4.0*, we can say that **to create a true destination, it is necessary to design a space for creative encounters between consumers and brands**; an attractive haven in which people can immerse themselves and where the values of the brand are not only showcased but can also be experienced first-hand. The levers described, in reality operate on needs deeply rooted in our minds and in that of intimacy. Sociability, for example, is inherent in human nature, an essential condition, and we think it will not disappear even when confronted with situations such as COVID-19. Compared to the past, brands will be required 'only' to ensure greater safety in these places. Paradoxically, returning to a previous statement, along with what was stated by the sociologist Mauro Ferraresi, for people it will no longer be time, but space, that will be considered 'a luxury.'

4

BE TIMELESS

In a market accelerated by fast fashion and
in which luxury companies are addressing
a global market, traditional distribution and
commercial models are falling by the wayside
and even seasons are ceasing to be a constraint.
Be Timeless therefore means taking advantage of
go-to-market actions such as see now, buy now
and capsule collections, but above all, espousing
a seasonless approach: a paradigm that invites
maisons to think about building the brand in
the long term, through a narrative capable of
connecting all its parts, rather than pushing
collections that are independent of each other.

From the very beginning, **time has always been an essential element for luxury.** The same was true for high-end fashion. It took time to make an haute couture dress; it took time in the boutique to find a garment admired during a fashion show; it took time to conclude the sales ritual of an exclusive product. Time increased the sacred dimension and value of the brands in this segment. But in a world accelerated by new technologies and intermediated by new actors, can it still be considered a key factor of distinctiveness and success? What is the relationship between high fashion and time today?

This identifying element of the industry has historically been marked by the relationship between maisons and buyers. Designers worked on a creative process that culminated in the runway show and could be questioned by their genius until the very last moment. The buyers chose garments for the stores months in advance and thus gave the maisons the opportunity to produce only on order. With this *modus operandi*, time was a true operational asset and guaranteed the high-end players maximum efficiency. The maisons soon realized, however, that the runway could be turned into a media event. By presenting their creations for the following season to the world, they could use the time between the discovery of a garment and its actual availability in the boutique as a strategic lever to increase its desirability.

The advent of digital provided the opportunity to extend the communication of these events to anyone who desired, thanks to streaming and social media. It is precisely at this moment that some players have chosen to question time as a value, in order to exploit the commercial opportunity of presenting a garment that is already available for purchase. They were aware that consumers, continuously stimulated by fast fashion and contemporary consumer society, showed an increased need for immediacy and gratification, and they decided to satisfy it. In order to meet this need, they transformed the fashion show into a direct sales event for the end customer. This phenomenon is referred to as **see now, buy now.** By eliminating the variable of the time needed to reach their clients, this practice has become popular, particularly with players who occupy an intermediate position in the pyramid, and who aspire to the highest section of the same. For them, time is a high cost in their budgets, and it is strategic to shorten the time between the launch of a product and its monetization.

For high-end players, however, critical issues soon became apparent. The see now, buy now model complicates production, logistics, and buying and retail planning. The distribution method is not unbiased because, particularly in the case of physical stores, it requires an ability to predict public success, and therefore the sales of individual items. Finally, from an industrial point of view, it means setting up production practically in the dark. The resulting disadvantages are mainly two: giving up one's own efficiency and exposing oneself to a conflict with the traditional sales intermediaries.

In 2015, the Council of Fashion Designers of America proposed a solution: preserve the traditional moment of sharing with buyers by making it private and move the fashion show, open to the public, as close as possible to the moment of distribution of the collection. **But for the Italian and French maisons, this strategy meant institutionalizing the logic of see now, buy now dangerously close to the operational model of fast fashion**, antithetical to its own from a symbolic point of view, and much more suited to the industrial/commercial one for flexibility and financial strength. Well aware that sacrificing the dimension of time could dilute the equity of the brand, which they considered essential to safeguard, they rejected the proposal, maintaining their traditional calendar.

Domenico Dolce and Stefano Gabbana were among the leaders who took this position. Before the calamity caused by COVID-19, the two designers had stated that creative work and the essence of high fashion should not be overshadowed by the instant satisfaction of the desire to purchase. "With see now, buy now, you force the designer to finish designing a garment five months in advance. We are talking about commerce, not creativity," said Dolce. The position of the two designers was clear, **but the pandemic has demonstrated the need to question even their most deeply held convictions**, leading the brand to organize a fashion show with this model in order to guarantee a faster cash flow. In accordance with the risks mentioned and following an approach more suited to the luxury segment, many maisons have decided to adopt the see now, buy now approach, with reasoning more oriented toward marketing and public relations than pure business.

A recent example of this is from Valentino. Right after the S/S 2020 fashion show, the Italian brand offered the new Valentino Garavani

Rockstud Spike Fluo bag online. For the first time, the maison chose not to wait for the traditional distribution time and to leverage the buying wave generated by the fashion show scheduled during Paris Fashion Week. The bag was immediately available on the official website and on the brand's Instagram account and sold using dedicated displays in only five boutiques in the world. Limiting the exercise to a single accessory puts Valentino among the brands that have decided to exploit the see now, buy now for special activities or for the extraordinary release of **capsule collections**.

It is this very concept that is receiving increasing attention. The term 'capsule collection' refers to a limited edition of selected elements of clothing, accessories or bags. Because of these characteristics, the release is always accompanied by strong interest and big media buzz. **The new generation of consumers is always seeking novelty but at the same time shows signs of fatigue in regard to the initiatives of fast fashion players.** For this reason, designers are collaborating with celebrities or other labels to launch more and more collections in limited editions, while maintaining a focus on quality. This type of collection finds its ideal partner in a particular launch methodology: the drop. The **drop** is a marketing technique that started in the streetwear sector and focuses on scarcity and exclusivity. The products that hit the market in this way are released in small quantities, only to selected stores and remain available for a few days, a few hours or even a few seconds.

The drop marketing model appeared first in the 80s, devised by shoe brands such as Nike and Adidas to create hype within the community of sneaker fans. In recent years, this tool has gone from being a niche occurrence to that of a mainstream practice. This is due to streetwear brands like Supreme that built their brand entirely with this dynamic. They released products that, once they were sold out, were never made again. **For these players, the sales lever is neither the quality of the products nor the cost of them, but instead the exclusivity: each piece is linked to the 'one-chance-to-buy' logic.** The widespread use of the drop reached its peak when people began talking about the real culture connected to it, endless waits in lengthy lines, frenzied purchases and parallel markets with inflated resale prices.

According to *The New York Times*, 2017 was "the year of the drop": it was at this point that high-end players cemented their relationship with streetwear and took possession of this marketing strategy. In that year, Louis Vuitton and Supreme created a series of T-shirts, backpacks, sweatshirts and even a series of trunks that immediately became some of the most desired items in the history of collaborations. The Louis Vuitton x Supreme collection was issued in eight exclusive pop-up stores around the world, with the locations and times being completely unknown until just two hours before the release. This generated lines of thousands of people in just minutes following the announcement. The objectives underlying this collaboration were, of course, opposed. The French maison wanted to increase its credibility and appeal to a target that, until now, it had believed to be far from the brand's identity. This was specifically the street world and affluent younger consumers. In fact, by combining the skater world with that of luxury, Louis Vuitton put its products under a new light and allowed this new generation to see themselves in it. But for Supreme, the objective was to be more appealing in the fashion marketplace.

However, the collaboration did not work as equally for both brands: for Louis Vuitton, the expectations were met, while Supreme had to cope with the indignation of its target audience, who saw this event as too marked a deviation from its original premise as a supporter of underground culture. Beyond this single example, the drop seems to work for more than just youths, because it is based on a dynamic that works across the board for all generations. It is based on the excitement that results from scarcity. "A drop does not conform to the traditional schedules of fashion, it's unpredictable, and therefore the products seem scarce," said Adam Alter, Associate Professor of Marketing at NYU Stern School of Business. "**Scarcity** makes them desirable because they are only available to people who are lined up for the release of the product."

Robert Cialdini, American psychologist, Professor of Marketing at Arizona State University and author of the book *Influence: The Psychology of Persuasion*, confirms that scarcity is one of the strongest forms of persuasion: "If you have something that others cannot get or work to get – in the case of fashion, also only because they are not aware of it – that signals a certain status." This uniqueness, which in itself generates emotion in people, is added to that of superior quality, and therefore social elevation, traditionally linked to luxury goods. But Alter also raises an obstacle for the longevity of the drop: by definition, it is a limited strategy because you cannot rely on endless surprise, novelty and rarity. The risk is that the increasing number of launches carried out in this manner will generate consumer fatigue and therefore a lesser response to the stimulus. **In a perfect world where everything follows the rhythms of the drop, the appeal of the drop ceases to exist.**

Another subject of discussion around the theme of time is the interval that exists between the discovery of a new garment that attracts a customer's attention and their actual purchase. It is often the cause of friction and dissatisfaction in all sectors. Even high-end players are focusing on reducing this source of discord and allowing shoppers to move from the generation of interest phase (Appeal), to that of the purchase phase (Act), as seamlessly as possible. While it is true that the luxury industry has felt the burden of this issue less so than others, players such as Amazon, Uber, Netflix and Deliveroo have exponentially increased people's expectations in terms of speed and ease of experience, changing attitudes forever.

An increased need for instant gratification has been created. This pressure is considerable today because consumers have also changed the way in which they are guided. In the pre-digital era, they received messages sent to them directly by brands and brokered only by magazines. But in the digital age, sources of information have been fragmented between influencers, social media, celebrities and so much more. Each of these actors continuously bombards users, creating an effect of estrangement and confusion due to the lack of a uniform communication between the product/message and brand. Therefore, the consumer, paradoxically, has a more difficult time than in the past in finding the answers to their needs, as they are forced to hypothesize the brand of a given product that they are attracted to, its characteristics, where it can be purchased, etc.

From a brand perspective, this fragmentation, and the new levels of separation it causes, create obstacles to converting 'inspired consumers' into buyers.

All this is exacerbated by the experience that can be had with mobile devices. Shoppers live with a smartphone in their hand, but it often happens that the experience designed for this media is not suited to their expectations or even aligned with that found on desktop devices. Some advances have been realized with the advent of **social-commerce**. It has intervened to simplify the previously long and difficult process in just a single tap. Simple shop windows have been transformed into true sales spaces parallel to e-commerce, with the help of direct links to online stores.

Even the high-end sector has discovered the logic of the continuous stimulation of desire and its immediate satisfaction – although it must be noted that the maison that performed best during the COVID-19 crisis is Hermès, a maison that still employs months-long waiting lists for some of its products, using this as a strategy to its advantage. A player by the name of 21 Buttons decided to build their business on these dynamics. Their social media app is designed to increase the potential of 'shoppability' in the industry. The platform allows influencers to share their outfits with their followers, listing all the clothes they are wearing and including the respective links to the e-commerce sites of the brands they are endorsing.

In this challenge, a number of technologies are also emerging alongside the fashion players. Screenshop is an eloquent example of this: the application launched by Kim Kardashian is considered the 'Shazam of fashion,' because it allows users to take or upload a photo, find out which clothes a star or influencer is wearing, and then receive the links to buy them. Some brands, especially e-tailers, are also developing proprietary search tools: analysts expect that visual search will help drive their sales growth by at least 30%.

The quintessential place for inspiration, at least for those in the sector, has always been the **fashion trade shows**. But today, even this traditional model is being put to the test by purchasing models that are increasingly open and directed toward the end consumer. The progressive loss in importance for trade shows is the result of the principal maisons progressively shifting from wholesale to retail business. As their dependence on distribution through a vast group of third-party retailers has diminished, so has the need to invest in such events. However, they do continue to play a prominent role for both niche brands and emerging designers, as well as for buyers of boutiques who use product research and curation of their offerings as their distinctive approach. Especially for these players, but in general, to play a role in today's high-end, **fashion trade shows must evolve to respond to these new direct-to-consumer dynamics, shorter fashion cycles and digitization**. To embrace disintermediation, they need to rethink their proposition and redefine their target audience. For them to differentiate themselves, or even just survive, these events will need to add attractions or launch new services and experiences to enhance relationships with traditional B2B audiences.

It is this direction that influenced the decision, made urgent by the consequences related to COVID-19, by the Camera Nazionale della Moda Italiana in July of last year, to launch the first Milan Digital Fashion Week. Thanks to the collaboration with Accenture and Microsoft, a digital platform was developed to experience the event. Brands, designers and industry professionals were able to use the hub to interact with buyers, media, influencers and consumers around the world. Chats, video conferences, bots, holograms and completely virtual spaces made one of the most important events in international fashion interactive and even more exciting. The platform is organized in three levels: a content hub for live streaming of fashion shows, virtual runways and other industry-related events and round tables; a virtual showroom system, with digital catalogues and virtual environments, which also provide support for the management of order processing; finally, a data-driven platform, accessible to professionals, to gain business insights from people's interaction with brands, events and content. This model could be replicated in the future by other major events in light of the transformations described above.

The last and perhaps most important change that has occurred in the industry regarding the concept of time is the abandonment of the seasons. With the trend dubbed **seasonless**, we mean the phenomenon that has led the maisons to progressively ignore the traditional fashion calendar, marked by the spring/summer and autumn/winter collections, and to release collections, individual pieces or capsule collections whenever they deem necessary. Its genesis can be found in a global market and a demand that, depending on the hemisphere, requires opposing collections at the same time.

To overcome this problem and satisfy luxury customers around the world who want to **buy now**, **wear now**, high-end players have begun to think from a seasonless perspective. This change has modified a centuries-old pillar of the sector: the importance of seasonal inspiration. Compared to the past, designers are no longer required to constantly rotate the styles, themes and symbols to be promoted for the next six months. In this sense, **seasonless comes even closer to the theme of timelessness, which is a characteristic feature of this segment**.

The model was even taken to new heights by the creation of a new company, AYR. The acronym stands for All Year Around and bears the signature of Peter Dundas, former designer of Roberto Cavalli. The approach has also been embraced by diverse brands. It is also worth mentioning the point of view of Giorgio Armani, who while not directly supporting the seasonless approach, hopes that luxury will find "it's time" and a "less fast and more human dimension." The Council of Fashion Designers of America and the British Fashion Council have also issued a joint statement emphasizing the importance of rethinking the fashion system, also in light of what has happened with the coronavirus.

One of the aspects that has dictated the success of seasonless is the need to find, define and cultivate a particular style, over time, that resounds vigorously in every collection. This is the case with success stories such as that of Balenciaga, which prioritized brand consistency over the frantic search for novelty in the release of its latest pieces. For analysts, its success lies precisely in drawing creative direction for the brand from a single font of inspiration, and then designing the different collections by building on it; a strategy that seems to bring luxury back to the principles that governed haute couture: when the unique pieces of a maison were united by the hand and unmistakable taste of its designer. By distancing oneself from the customary schedules of the fashion system and choosing an irregular pace, free from imposed deadlines that crush creativity, it is possible to follow a personal narrative that is more in keeping with expressive needs.

In its return to the past, this approach is actually very modern, because it invites the maisons to think about building the brand in the long term, through a narrative capable of connecting all its parts, rather than pushing collections that are independent from one another. In doing so, creative directors are more likely to think strategically, offering clientele an 'entire journey' and not a 'single destination.'

5

BE INSPIRED

In a scenario seemingly characterized
by two opposite poles, data and creativity,
even luxury must find its balance.
Be Inspired means recognizing how data
can be of great help for the maisons in
the development of customer intimacy,
especially in the personalization of service,
and how creativity must dictate its primacy
in defining the direction of brands
and products.

Creative industries, including that of fashion, have to respond to the same dilemma that has dominated meeting rooms of marketers ever since digital changed the rules of the game. The predictable battle between two seemingly opposite poles: data and creativity. It has always been difficult to find the common link between 'ideas and numbers,' often because they are assigned to two separate units, but in most cases because they are considered to be unable to converse and interact with each other. For creative directors and designers, as well as copywriters in advertising agencies, creativity is an instinctive process aimed at building emotional ties with consumers. For them, qualitative analysis makes the work sterile and 'reduces the magic.' Sometimes even the most purist CEOs are of the same opinion: "We don't have a marketing department. We don't do market studies and we don't ask people what they want" – said Axel Dumas, CEO of Hermès in 2014 – "because marketing is not necessary; staying true to your style is. We are Hermès, and we create the desires of our customers."

But this stance is a prejudice: **the idea that data and creativity are irreconcilable is out-dated**. There is research to indicate this, including a study conducted by McKinsey. According to the consulting firm, those who properly integrate these two elements increase their revenues at double the average rate of S&P 500 companies. If luxury is also one of the creative industries mentioned in the introduction, it is necessary to understand how high-end players can accomplish this integration.

First of all, it must be noted that data has great value on its own, regardless of whichever industry is being considered. As suggested in *Retail 4.0* for the digital age, **data is the oil of the digital era. Turning it into fuel is a complex process but also the only way to exploit its potential**. For some years, the idea of **big data** has been pushed, but the real question is the ability of the players to convert that to **smart data**, information that can be useful in gaining a competitive advantage. To end the metaphor, an oilfield would be useless in itself to power our car if we did not have a refinery to turn the crude oil into gasoline.

To consider this issue more deeply, it is necessary to clarify the difference between data and information. The first is an objective representation of reality, not one that is interpreted; the second is a vision of reality derived after processing and interpreting the data. Thus data becomes relevant for a company only when it has been identified, validated, aggregated, crossed-referenced, contextualized, analysed and then translated into explanatory or practical information.

In the field of fashion, reactive and predictive data analysis allows brands to respond quickly to an emerging demand and to develop products in line with a new trend. By doing so, companies can reduce production times and optimize distribution times. In a tumultuous and constantly evolving world, being able to adapt quickly and accurately to the market is a critical success factor. **The sector has suffered the effects of a seismic event in which supply, always having worked from the viewpoint 'push,' has been reconfigured with a 'pull' approach based on real market demand.**

This operating model started with fast fashion and has been reinforced by the success of the Inditex group. Zara is the most striking high-performance example. The brand is distinguished by an outside-in approach, an on-demand production based on data, a go-to-market made fast and lean by nearshoring – or the decision to delocalize the production but still remain close geographically – and an ability to ensure both wide diversification of styles and immediacy with the release of new garments.

This brings us to a rather extreme application (if we think of the characteristics of the fashion world), used in project 8 by YOOX. It is the e-tailer's propriety brand "powered by data, designed by humans": a collection of essential items for women and men, created with the use of AI. YOOX takes advantage of AI to analyse data from a wide range of sources: social media, sales data, customer feedback and more. The design team thus has a dynamic moodboard at its disposal, providing direction on varied trends: colours, sleeve lengths, neckline shapes, textures and much more. This allows the designer to create collections that customers really want, approaching the product development from data and not from intuition. According to a PwC report on the subject, an AI-based approach for projecting demand could reduce forecasting errors by up to 50%, while being able to reduce inventory overall by 25-50%. Yet most of the other players in the sector have not yet begun to grasp the opportunities offered by data analysis. The BCG *Dressed for Digital* report states that less than 10% of fashion brands personalize their messages in email and digital advertising and, at the same time, only a little more than a third of them have a fully personalized recommendation engine within their e-commerce site.

To rise above the performance of the rest of the industry, **high-end players must distinguish themselves by wisely using data to build so-called customer intimacy**. This concept is based on the empathy and closeness that a brand is able to demonstrate with respect to its customers, so as to understand and satisfy the customer's needs. In order to offer the level of service that luxury customers expect, the maisons need to capitalize on their data and increase intimacy by taking the relationship to higher levels. The basis of this practice relies on audience segmentation and a deep knowledge of it. These super-demanding customers with high expectations represent the real value of every high fashion brand. A maison is nothing without its flock of faithful, and one of the cardinal principles of luxury is the individual knowledge and loyalty that each one has of the other. That is why players in this sector should not undervalue loss of control regarding customer relationship management (CRM).

Luxury is not just knowledge but also acknowledgment: by inputting all the information that can be gleaned from the brand-persona relationship within CRM, it is possible to create real-life actions relevant to each individual. Since high-end is characterized through experiences, these brands must not only offer unique products, but also exceptional levels of service. The goal is to make every customer feel like a special 'member' of that brand. To do this, it is necessary to digitally reconstruct the profiling operation that a store manager once carried out in an analogue manner with their 'little black book': an actual diary in which characteristics, purchases, tastes and preferences were noted. It is only in this way that it is possible to create a personalized service because it is meticulous and informed.

Although not exactly in the high-end segment, M.M. LaFleur is a prime example from which to draw inspiration. The founder claims to have created the brand exactly with this aim: "to offer a service that can transform a wide range of products into a thorough, specific and personalized selection for each customer." In fact, a shopper can use the platform to book a visit to the boutique-show-room, share preferences, needs and physical details and, in addition, send selfies, reference images or preferred styles. With this information and drawing on the historical profile of the customer, a stylist will create a personalized lookbook and arrange for the selections to be available in-store for the appointment. The experience continues during and after the purchase: advice and suggestions to make the most from the purchased items, and proposals for future ones, will be added to the diary.

This example shows how it is possible today to put data and technology at the infrastructure level of the operating model, permitting personalized and relevant service, simply. **It may seem paradoxical, but today it is software and algorithms that support humankind in the attempt to be more genuine and authentic.** Historically, these are traits that distinguish the luxury sector. To provide an ad hoc service to an intimate few, it was necessary to build a relationship over time. Now with digital, maisons can easily scale it. At one time Louis Vuitton wrote handwritten letters with specific suggestions recommending travel bags; today, technology extends the boundaries of customer intimacy from a privileged few to many, without losing its charm and relevance. With the automation of 'who,' 'what' and 'when' and taking advantage of the information from the collected data, brands can find new opportunities to provide their services in a unique way for each customer and occasion.

As we have established above, **service** must be a *conditio sine qua non* of luxury. However, in the eyes of consumers, it rarely determines its essence. According to their statements, service is never mentioned among the first five elements spontaneously associated with the segment. Making this worse, some pure digital players believed that by basing their proposition on this aspect, they had elevated themselves to be an experiential benchmark. To fill the existing gap, high-end brands must work on two fronts: innovating on the back end to reach the minimum standards required by digital-era consumers, while at the same time enhancing the front end to (re)gain their true differentiating factor and competitive advantage.

All of this, in accordance with what was noted in Be a Vibration, can occur in a physical store, but most of all through the attendant staff.

The place, and the people within, allow the human relationship to be linked to the purchase. Assistance, pampering and advice generate a value that is rare in a world where relationships are increasingly intermediated by technology. The latter forces humans to question their true added value. **The value of empathy and the ability to grasp the needs of customers will be the killer factors for the luxury experience. And they will only be viable through shopping assistants.** The experts of Global Luxury Expert Network (GLEN) insist that an approach founded on aggressive sales in the luxury industry must be eliminated and replaced with a zealous culture of providing value to customers through long-term relationships. For this reason, high-end players will have to select people who love to help and look after others when it comes to choosing those who will be the face of the brand. These people will then have to be loyal to the maison, feeling its vision as if it were their own, becoming its first ambassadors. **Without solid employee loyalty, high customer loyalty is a much harder goal to achieve.**

Information released by Boggi shows that in-store staff are not just the supervisors of the final sale, but an asset capable of influencing the entire customer experience, determining the success or otherwise of a boutique. By shifting the attention paid to the client from the checkout to the shopping phase, the Italian brand racked up a 20% increase in transactions, but even more surprisingly, has seen a growing readiness of customers to provide personal data so as to receive information and promotions. A small change to sales rituals brought tangible and net results for the business.

Some players have observed the aversion luxury buyers have in using chatbots and have consequently upgraded with direct lines to their store managers in the aim of instilling a human approach to remotely managed services. One example is Burberry. The British fashion house is about to launch a chat dedicated to a small elite group of customers. The service, under the name of R Message, will allow them to interact, in a preferential and personalized manner, directly with boutique staff for various services. Customers will be selected by invitation. "With this tool, we will offer customers the same luxury service that occurs in-store," said Mark Morris, Vice President of Digital Commerce for the brand, in an interview.

The latter case shows how now more than ever, after the recent events related to COVID-19, **companies will have to be able to nurture and convey typically human social and emotional skills even through digital channels**. Of course, an effort to adapt will be required on both fronts: companies in terms of training budgets, and employees in terms of adopting new fully digitized approaches.

In understanding the importance of personalized service, the question arises: can luxury also work at the product level to increase customer intimacy? Before answering, it is necessary to clarify the difference between two concepts often used interchangeably: personalization and customization. As explained in *Retail 4.0*, **personalization** consists of the proactive use of information collected about the customer, to anticipate their expectations and offer tailor-made solutions; **customization** is instead a process that enables the user to make a product 'their own,' choosing a certain combination of possibilities from a finite number of alternatives. This leads us to analyse the activities of various maisons. Burberry, for example, allows customers to add their initials to scarves, similar to that of Louis Vuitton, who makes its leather products customizable through the Mon Monogram program. The idea of engraving, embroidering or painting a product with initials is the ultimate ploy to make it unique and personal in the eyes of consumers. A superior level of customization allows clients to choose some product elements, such as patches on jeans or textures and clips on sneakers. And beyond that, some brands have dedicated entire areas to DIY within their e-commerce platforms or stores, as Gucci in Wooster Street, New York, has done through an interactive digital tool to see sneakers and modify them at will in real time thanks to augmented reality.

Another technology that can help the maisons in these activities is 3D printing. Thirty per cent of the top managers interviewed by McKinsey are convinced that it will have an impact on the luxury brand business by entering the in-store experience.

In conclusion, it is evident that customization options are diverse, but still confined to small decorative details rather than structural modifications of products. This is because **luxury is only interested in allowing light customization of the original design, to preserve the mastery of its artistic and stylistic direction and its artisanal quality.**

What would happen, in fact, if luxury brands were to adopt a structured approach to the **co-design** of products? This is the starting point for the research project carried out by Emanuela Prandelli, Associate Professor of the Department of Management & Technology at Bocconi University, together with Christoph Fuchs, Martin Schreier and Darren W. Dahl and published in the *Journal of Marketing*. The article shows that while fashion brands with a more mainstream positioning can generally benefit substantially from collaboration strategies with users in product development, the same does not hold for luxury brands. Instead, consumers in the high-end segment seem to perceive products designed by other users, or even by themselves, as lower quality and, more importantly, do not convey the same high status. This is due to the importance that these two drivers hold in purchasing decisions within this sector. Based on a series of interviews, the study revealed that, in general, the origin of the design determines the customer's preferences at the time of purchase.

For mass-market brands in the fashion sector, 'user-generated design' leads to positive results, as in shoppers' eyes a product designed by one's peers acquires greater value than one produced by an unknown designer inside the company. In light of this, fast-fashion players could push this practice to the extreme, using a common design form and entrusting the entire creative process to the masses.

Instead, the diametrically opposite effect occurs in the high-end world. Here the design of the maison is preferred: when the design is by other users there are negative connotations. The reason is simple: with origins in 'the masses,' the design is not associated with the same quality and artisanship. **A luxury product receives its status from the combination of 'design' in its broadest sense, and the source of creativity that gives it life; when that is changed, the emotional aspects connected to it, such as charm, magic and prestige, are lost.**

If the co-design is in partnership with an artist or celebrity, consumer aversion diminishes. The study reveals that when consumers are more emotionally involved with the purchase, because it is linked to an iconic product of the brand, a modification is less appreciated. It is tolerated more in relation to entry-level products that are less 'sacred,' such as T-shirts, sneakers and accessories. By focusing on this second possibility, high-end brands can build a good relationship with their audience. Hopefully it will have a positive impact from a financial viewpoint too, with customers becoming more interested in the maison's flagship products.

Now we come to the point of defining how high-end players should implement the integration between data and creativity. On the one hand, the former is necessary and fundamental in knowing the client and building a one-to-one relationship with them, intimate and therefore personalized. On the other hand, the latter cannot be sacrificed by creating products based on the tastes and expectations of the market, as creativity is the hallmark of high-end brands. That is why, even if the fashion houses have the necessary data to produce their products using customer preferences, they should not leave the creative ownership in their customers' hands. Even in the early days, high-end fashion designers provided their aesthetic interpretation of current socio-cultural trends; customers are left with the choice of whether or not to recognize themselves in these stylistic expressions, as different from one designer to another as there may be interpretations of the same reality. The key is in understanding the implicit stressors and inclinations of the consumers and surprising them with an exceptional product.

Unlike the fast fashion segment that can follow a data-informed approach in understanding market support and is data-driven in the offers it directs to the masses, the high-end must instead adopt a data-inspired strategy. Not by shelving the data, but by putting it at the service of the creative director. Numbers do not count for much at the top of the pyramid without talent capable of transforming them into insights and glimpsing their potential. High-end fashion thrives by picking up weak signals, coming more from culture and society than from sales. The creative genius that sustains the maisons lies in transforming these signals into unique pieces, sometimes contradictory, but capable of starting a trend. To conclude, being **customer-centric** in the luxury sector does not have the same meaning as in other sectors.

6

BE RELATIONAL

In a sector in which loyalty cannot be identified with customer retention, without suffering brand erosion, Be Relational means structuring membership activities through high value-added services. By treating their clients in a unique and special way and making them part of an exclusive and very small group, maisons can move from a promotion 'to the customer' to branding 'through the customer.'

The market for customer loyalty management is set to reach a value of 30 billion dollars in the coming years. Loyalty programs have proliferated: it is no coincidence that in 2019 there were 3.8 billion memberships in the United States alone, for an overall average of almost 29 enrolments per household. However, according to some studies, customers of brands that offer loyalty programs are not recognizably more loyal than the customers of brands that do not. This is also due to the fact that most of them do not know their actual rights and benefits precisely. In addition, Accenture points out that nearly a quarter of consumers have neither increased nor reduced their readiness to spend after subscribing to a loyalty program. This is because the vast majority of these activities are based on merely functional or economic incentives. One tactic has come to be known as **earn and burn**, because it is based on the accumulation of points through repeated purchases that can be used for premiums or discounts. However, by utilizing this lever, many brands are wasting large sums of capital on incentives for customers they would have little chance of losing anyway. They are subsidizing purchases that would have been made anyway. In addition, they are simultaneously losing the opportunity to establish and build a deeper relationship with them.

Therefore, it is imperative to change this approach. Two essential aspects of human nature must be taken into account: emotional ties and sociality. A sociological study conducted by *HBR* revealed that **an emotionally engaged consumer generates an incremental value 52% higher than that of a highly satisfied but unengaged customer**. The name given to this occurrence is **attitudinal loyalty**. It is an evolutionary stage of loyalty following both the cognitive stage, which relies on functional and practical elements, and the emotional one, based instead on satisfaction that does not include total commitment. Therefore, we can say that the majority of current loyalty programs do not generate true loyalty.

So what would happen, then, if brands rethink the relationship they have with their customers, evolving loyalty that is only transactional today and therefore transitory? What mechanisms would be capable of flipping the relationship to ensure that the most loyal customers pay the brands rather than the brands paying them for their loyalty?

An exceptional **membership program** provides a quick answer to this. Amazon Prime is an example worth more than any theoretical definition. The service was created as a paid option, so customers could receive selected products with guaranteed delivery within two working days. The program is still widely known and chosen for this feature, but its effectiveness in terms of membership has been created and consolidated over the years with the creation of its very own ecosystem of services. More and more users are happy to pay an annual fee to benefit from the available previews, music and video streaming platforms, digital books and cloud storage space.

In the United States, as many as 82% of households with incomes over $110,000 per year are members of Prime. Amazon's ability to retain its customers is demonstrated by the data: research by Consumer Intelligence Research Partners shows that 73% of those who chose the free 30-day trial end up subscribing, and 91% of subscribers renew after the first year, followed by 96% of subscribers renewing the relationship for a third.

Amazon Prime creates a real 'addiction.' It is not by chance that what has been called 'Amazon-first mentality' has manifested itself. The experience is disruptive: at the onset of need or desire to purchase, one in two users search first on Amazon rather than anywhere else. In addition, one in five users said they had reduced their shopping at other retailers, instead deciding to rely heavily on this platform. All of this obviously has an impact on sales: the average annual spend for an American Prime member is $1,400, compared to $600 for a nonmember. That is a gap of 130%. The example shows us that **loyalty does not mean being able to put a loyalty club card in a client's wallet, but instead ensuring a privileged place in their heart and mind.**

Joining a membership program seals a mutual commitment: the membership, regardless of the fee amount, creates a sense of exclusivity and transforms the customer's experience in a structural manner. Likewise, charging a membership fee creates an obligation for the reseller to provide added value beyond the expectations it creates. This philosophy is also suitable for premium markets, as demonstrated by the Centurion program that defined the success of American Express.

The service from the famous financial company, connected with the iconic black card, is based on a catalogue of rewards intended for a limited elite. The fact that this card is issued by invitation only and with very strict conditions has made it synonymous with exclusivity and cloaked it with an impressive cultural cachet. All the services, including enhanced security, various airline or luxury hotel chain privileges, and an around-the-clock concierge offering entertainment planning, gifting and business services are designed to accompany these individuals at all times, providing a level of incomparable experience.

At this point, it is fair to ask if these dynamics can be applied to a market with delicate and unique aesthetics such as high-end fashion. This subject is complex. The definition of **loyalty** alone opens up countless scenarios. In fact, more than 200 have been written, each of them emphasizing multiple and different aspects related to the theme, highlighting its many facets. But let us start from an axiom: **in luxury, loyalty is not just a matter of retention**. As sustained in Be Inclusive, high-end brands must aim to preserve their extraordinariness in the eyes of customers.

Owning several products of the same brand diminishes the appeal that their uniqueness usually exerts. **The more you buy luxury, the more the dream fades.** If, for consumer products, repurchasing increases behavioural and emotional fidelity, the same cannot be said for high-end products. Structurally, this segment has to deal with reduced purchase frequency. Rare shopping opportunities coincide with limited opportunities to establish meaningful relationships. For this reason, activities to ensure customer loyalty must create new and more frequent moments of dialogue, support the appeal of the brand and, consequently, continue to make it desirable.

Further complicating the equation is the prejudice of many maisons who believe loyalty programs are not aligned with their image or brand proposition. Believing, in fact, that traditional versions make the products appear 'cheaper' and therefore too accessible, the offer diluting their equity. However, according to a report by Deloitte Fashion and Luxury, 44% of customers in the segment would like to be rewarded with gifts in exchange for their loyalty.

So it is obvious that it is possible to exploit this opportunity by structuring more effective programs, capable of going well beyond the simple mechanics of discounts.

Luisaviaroma is one of the brands that has invested more in this area, with its Privilege and Sneakers Club programs. The first one works on the frequency of purchase and is a 'traditional' earn and burn program, redesigned to complement the brand's level of quality and style. It is structured on four levels, where access is determined by points thresholds. Points can also be accumulated through interactions outside the purchase process, with activities such as sharing content on social channels and competitions. The higher the level reached, the greater the value of the exclusive experiences reserved as a reward. Today the Privilege program has one million members worldwide. The second program is a true membership club, since it is necessary to pay a fee equal to 2,000 points to be admitted. Members then receive early access to all the drops for a full year. Most of the time, the shoes offered by the retailer do not even reach the store or the digital shelf because they are sold out with the club members. In the month it was launched, LVR Sneakers Club reached 1,000 members. The combination of these two assets generated an ROI of 293% in the first three months of their launch and in two years put 16 million euros into the brand's coffers.

One of the strengths of this program is undoubtably its tiered structure. In general, this is an excellent device to recognize different clusters of customers through their spending habits and be able to offer them relevant solutions accordingly. But not only that, the levels create a strong sense of privilege among members, especially when reaching the next level up, as they grant exclusive benefits making members feel special and giving them a sense of achievement. And it is precisely the absolute exclusivity, and the ensuing access (or not) to the benefits, that should be the cornerstone in defining membership programs for the high-end segment. The fact that only a very small circle of 'chosen' people can benefit from certain features makes them much more desirable.

Armed with this knowledge, some players have gone as far as developing solutions that are even 'invisible' to the eyes of 'normal' customers. This is the case of Louis Vuitton, with its House of

Vuitton in London and Singapore: actual physically private spaces with restricted access. The high-end sector lends itself perfectly to a strategy described as **invite-only marketing**. It is based on increasing the desirability of a product or service by making it accessible to only a very limited number of people, chosen by the brand, by virtue of certain characteristics.

This stratagem is not a prerogative of the high-end: many brands, especially in the start-up phase, use it to generate willingness to join and positive word of mouth. Such was the case with Facebook when it was launched as a platform for American students. The big difference is that invite-only marketing is used by products and services that aim at the mass-market in the initial growth phase and then it is abandoned once a sufficient critical base of penetration is reached. High-end players, on the other hand, can make it a structural element of their membership programs. For these brands, **this can be accomplished by having dedicated store hours for individual shopping experiences in reserved events that are unknown to most, or in specific products unavailable to members who are not selected**. The invite-only concept can even go as far as restricting access to a medium that is by definition open to all: the web. A maison could choose to restrict its website, or a section within it, to specific customer profiles, such as its most loyal customers. Alibaba made this decision in positioning its Luxury Pavilion, which we mentioned previously in Be a Symphony. The entry point for this luxury e-department store is only visible to a very small percentage of Tmall's 500 million users.

The invitation strategy works well with the need of high-end brands to know and recognize their core customers. According to estimates by Bain, for some e-tailers such as Net-a-Porter, Matchesfashion and Moda Operandi, anywhere between 1% and 3% of customers make purchases totalling up to 40% of revenues. That is why Net-a-Porter coined the acronym EIP, Extremely Important Person, to distinguish these big-spender clients. With an expectation of a high level of service, the brands guarantee these individuals attention beyond the norm, whether it is advice on WhatsApp and WeChat or even organizing last-minute appointments for them to try on clothes right at home. Added to this are invitations to reservation-only events such as fashions shows or private dinners. Business of Fashion reports that an EIP customer has a fashion-related spend of about $64,000 a year. It is not surprising that Net-a-Porter made the most expensive sale of the year in 2017 through WhatsApp, with a Cartier watch worth over $130,000.

In conclusion, we can argue that, in addition to the reasoning adopted, these relationships between customers and the maisons must presume 'permission,' which commits both parties and eliminates any ambiguity about the relationship. Luxury customers do not want to feel pursued or bombarded by unwanted offers, but they are more inclined to share their personal information if they know that in doing so they'll allow brands to design an out of the ordinary experience for them.

The ultimate goal of membership clubs, and the direct consequence of a meaningful loyalty relationship between brand and person, is **Advocacy** (the last phase described in Kotler's '5A model'). The term is certainly not new in marketing. Word of mouth has always been fundamental and is considered by some as the oldest form of advertising. But in the era of connectivity and social media, this reality takes on a much greater scale.

The most important form of loyalty, in the era of peer reviews and widespread purchases, is the willingness to recommend a brand to others. A customer does not necessarily continue to buy products of a certain brand, or is even always able to, but if they are satisfied, they will be willing to recommend them, both to acquaintances and to strangers with whom they share specific interests. Loyalty goes well beyond the purchase if individuals feel engaged and actively involved in a brand's proposition. Indeed, if the brand has successfully set up its initiatives, the customer will become the actual spokesperson of the message, becoming media in their own right.

Today, in fact, **branding 'to the customer'** is no longer enough, but it is possible with this logic to activate **branding 'through the customer.' Digital luxury is increasingly a customer-to-customer economy**. Consumers of high-end are very active on social media, constantly seeking inspiration from their peers and non-peers, and fleetingly step into the spotlight when they post their outfits. A 2017 analysis by McKinsey on Instagram, and confirmed by recent data collected across the platform, makes it clear that in the volume of content related to the maisons, it is the consumer citations that dominate, not the proprietary posts. With a very similar number of posts published, a brand like Chanel, for example, has almost twice as many mentions as Zara. Even the high-end brands, which have always tried to maintain and centralize the management of their image and conversations about them, will have to live with ambiguity and accept that some aspects of their online presence are created by customers and fans, rather than unilaterally controlled.

FIGURE 2.3: **COMPARISON BETWEEN PUBLISHED POSTS AND MENTIONS OF THE BRANDS CHANEL AND ZARA, INSTAGRAM, DECEMBER 2020**

A cross-industry study by Bain & Company found that **just a 5% bump in customer loyalty could increase a company's profitability by 75%.** Furthermore, the average amount spent by a repeat customer is usually two thirds higher than that of a new customer. And Gartner Group reports that 65% of a company's business comes from existing customers.

In conclusion, as brands face increasing pressure and competition from all sides, loyalty is a true competitive advantage. Since it is estimated to cost at least five times as much to attract a new customer as it does to retain an existing one, given both the considerable cost and value of each, investing in ancillary services can enable high-end brands to benefit from both loyal fans and long-term cost savings. Brand loyalty is one of the structural components of brand equity and working with these principles allows the maisons to defend their price differential. The demand for loyal customers is inelastic and this is even more important in a sector that tends to increase prices over time rather than decreasing them.

7

BE PURPOSEFUL

In a scenario that requires brands to operate in an ethical and transparent manner, and in one of the most polluting industries, Be Purposeful means trying to define your goal in the world. Luxury is often singled out for its decadence and waste: the maisons must demonstrate that they are sustainable, have a place in society, and can have a positive impact on people's lives and in the world.

Given that sustainability is one of the forces that have shaken the foundations of the fashion industry in recent years, let us try now to think about the strategies and methods that high-end players can implement. If fast-fashion brands have found it impossible nowadays to avoid the implications of this issue, it is necessary to understand whether a segment as structurally different as the high-end range should be subject to a similar demand. The answer seems to be affirmative if we consider that one in four buyers admitted to having removed luxury brands from their department store portfolio due to environmental, social justice or animal welfare reasons. This is what emerges from data released by McKinsey & Company. Americans seem to be the most mindful toward the issue: almost a third of them have enacted these decisions.

Therefore, this is an issue that affects professionals in the market, even prior to final customers. **It is the entire system of stakeholders (institutional representatives, investors, governments, public opinion) that demands this attention to sustainability.** And there is no doubt today that most consumers are sensitive to these issues while shopping. According to data collected in a global survey by BCG-Altagamma, 56% of luxury customers search for information regarding the social responsibility of the brand they are interested in buying. Even more surprising is the growth, by 10% from 2013 to 2018, in the number of individuals (61% at this date) who consider a brand's commitment to sustainability as an element capable of influencing their purchases.

Today, high-end brand managers face a critical issue: in what ways they can cultivate the relationship between luxury and sustainability. Let us start from a premise: it is difficult to demonstrate to consumers the link between these two worlds given that some of the characteristics perceived to be intrinsic to the high-end, such as being unnecessary, superfluous, unequal and having high visibility in terms of media exposure, often lead this segment to be viewed as an 'exaggeration.' On the other hand, the theme of scarcity, implicit in luxury, refutes this idea at least in theory. By definition, **the high-end production philosophy respects typical sustainability elements**. Among them, we can easily recognize artisanship, localism (the famous 'Made in') and the conservation of primary resources.

The products designed by the most consistent maisons are inextricably linked to specific territorial roots, precious and limited natural sources, specialized technical know-how, as well as a rare and finite human expertise. These companies have an interest in preserving and safeguarding these elements of uniqueness and value over the long term and, consequently, embracing sustainability. However, the evolution of companies and their parallel growth in size have led, over time, to changes in the production and operating systems, often making them profoundly different from their origins and far from those values that distinguished them.

Yet, as stated in the book *The Sustainable Values of Luxury*, 'real luxury' is found only in the defense and enhancement of environmental, economic and social dimensions. So, for high-end players, sustainability cannot be perceived as a choice. It must be recognized as a necessity. Luxury does not just represent high quality products; it is also called upon to convey relevant social issues. In short, luxury must aspire to be recognized as **social luxury**, bringing value into the lives of its customers, but also to the entire ecosystem that produces that prestige. The offer of a high-end fashion piece, made by a community of artisans with refined raw materials, must be a choice aimed at more than simply gratifying a customer's wishes but also encompassing a desire to preserve the cultural and natural heritage that allowed the creation of the products themselves.

The high-end will have to concretize the shared value theory of Porter and Kramer: namely, the existence of a link between competitive advantage and corporate social responsibility. The hope is not that there will be a miraculous decline in growth, but that luxury's original intrinsic principles of sustainability can make their way into current and future market settings. Managers will need to juggle between the restoration of these principles and of reinterpreting them in a contemporary manner in the understanding that today, these changes can be of enormous operational and economic complexity.

So, sustainability also plays a fundamental role in the high-end range of fashion. But by itself, is it able to feed the dream linked to this type of purchase? If the brand has already built its equity, it is fairly intuitive that communicating sustainable attributes can feed the dream, making it both ethical and responsible. However, if the brand has not yet established its heritage, and sustainability is used as the first and primary selling point, it is hard to justify a position at the top of the pyramid.

Perhaps the only one who has managed to build a brand beginning with the asset of sustainability is Stella McCartney. In fact, the designer founded her own maison, explicitly with the desire to create luxury products that are both beautiful and respectful of the world in which we live. But her success would have been more complicated to achieve had the designer not been able to assert her talent and creative genius through previous experiences with Chloé, one of the leaders of luxury prêt-à-porter. Outside this particular case, we can reach a conclusion: **a high-end brand may be sustainable, but an exclusively sustainable brand rarely falls within the segment.** The challenge of sustainable luxury, first of all, is to be perceived as luxury. It is only after this occurs that the perception of being sustainable can then be stimulated.

This is linked to a more general dogma that exists in the fashion sector: it is always possible (and simpler) to dilute one's positioning by descending through the pyramid's segments (as already noted with diffusion lines in Be Inclusive), but it is almost impossible to climb back up to the summit after placing oneself in the lower levels. Therefore, it is time for those luxury brands that are structurally able to position themselves as sustainable to give more prominence to this asset, fortified by the fact that in today's society, sustainability is the most relevant trend. This is why events, such as the one involving Burberry in 2018, should be avoided today. The British fashion house suffered a harsh backlash of public opinion after deciding to burn 37.6 million dollars of unsold clothing, accessories and cosmetic products rather than selling them in secondary markets.

We are witnessing an increasing groundswell of demand for transparency and accountability from companies and not even the high-end can escape. According to global data collected by Business of Fashion and McKinsey & Company, despite geographic differences, 90% of Gen Z members say that the sector's brands must address issues of social and environmental responsibility. It is emblematic that #*WhoMadeMyClothes* has spread specifically among these new young consumers, reaching 727,000 mentions on Instagram alone from 2013 to the time this book was written.

The issue of sustainability in fashion seems to have reached a point of no return: **what was once the prerogative of activists alone is now part of most people's consciousness**. This change is partly due to the reduction in information asymmetries between companies and consumers, thanks to the spread of the internet and new technologies. This has created the opportunity for the most radical to control the maisons' sourcing and production processes, and the ability, for any individual who is interested, to find this information online. Access to this, in an era of global social media, means the possibility of public exposure and simultaneously triggering demonstrations at an international level. Deloitte speaks of the 'era of transparency': an era in which unethical commercial practices become difficult to hide and risk leading to actual boycotts against brands that fail to be responsible. The most critical dimensions and issues for which fashion actors will be under the microscope are the supply chain, conditions for workers, data protection, authenticity and creative integrity.

The most striking example of this last point is @DietPrada. This Instagram account has become famous for its posts aimed at unmasking instances of plagiarism, by naming and shaming the brands that have stolen designs from other designers. Its success can be counted with 1.8 million followers at the time this book was written.

The most recurring theme that has been on the agenda for several years is, without a doubt, environmental sustainability. Back in the 1980s, environmentalist Jay Westerveld coined the term **greenwashing** to identify a communication and public relations strategy (which unfortunately continues to be used today), aimed at aiding and enhancing the environmental reputation of a company without the support of real action and credible evidence. These practices, easily identified and exposed by attentive consumers, have had a profound impact on trust in the ecological and ethical claims of brands.

Companies that have understood the crucial importance of the issue are moving in the complete opposite direction. They are embarking on the path of so-called **radical transparency**. This term, coined in the *State of Fashion 2019* report, indicates the desire to make any information regarding a company's work easily accessible and clear. **For many fashion players this has resulted, for example, in the introduction of blockchain technology to ensure the traceability of materials.** Kering, aware of this need, created an app in 2017 dedicated to sustainability called My EP&L, in collaboration with the Chinese messaging platform WeChat. Using the Environmental Profit & Loss methodology, the luxury group allows both customers, and also designers and production managers, to calculate scores relating to the environmental impact of a product.

Another relevant example is one offered by Farfetch. The e-tailer of high-end-range fashion chose to collaborate with the independent agency Good on You with the aim of selecting sustainable garments with a positive impact. Thanks to the classifications of the agency, which examines environmental, social and animal wellbeing, consumers can purchase products labelled as Positively Conscious. An increasingly widespread predisposition is dedicated to the purchase of products, not so much for their intrinsic characteristics, but for the effect that choosing them generates on the community.

The pursuit of complete transparency has even inspired the birth of a new brand. Honest By is a women's clothing brand launched in 2012 by Bruno Pieters, formerly the creative director of Hugo Boss. Disillusioned by the excesses of the industry and inspired by his experiences in India during a sabbatical year, Pieters created his brand with the idea of total transparency of all information: starting from the production process and the materials used right up to the precise income distribution for his products. The designer believes that practices like this not only honour fashion, but also the history behind it, giving consumers the opportunity to make informed, aware and responsible choices about their purchases. Honest By was recognized worthy of the LVMH Prize, awarded by the holding company to reward young visionary talent.

The latest Fashion Transparency Index created by Fashion Revolution, an impartial foundation active in the field of sustainability, states that the trend toward transparency is growing. In 2020, 40% of brands published a list of their top-tier manufacturers, compared to 35% the previous year, while the details regarding suppliers of raw materials has grown by 40% since 2019.

Nowadays, it is necessary to consider that transparency is not a goal, but rather a starting point. **Brands must demonstrate not only how they manage their production process but also how they are trying to improve it.** There are numerous examples of this, including the pioneering Stella McCartney, even in the high-end segment. In 2018, Chanel launched a new strategy for the research and development of materials and leathers generated by agri-food industries. To succeed in this venture, the maison coupled its financial strength with the innovative momentum of the start-up, Evolved by Nature. One day, not too far in the future, an ecological silk may be the chosen material for making a Chanel scarf. Associations between luxury brands and start-ups will be big news in the near future: Orange Fiber is a start-up already in the process of collaborating with major fashion companies. The young Italian company patented and produces sustainable material made from citrus by-products and worked with Salvatore Ferragamo for a capsule collection.

A more recent initiative is that of Gucci. In June of 2020, Alessandro Michele announced Gucci Off the Grid, the first collection from the Florentine brand based on sustainability. The creative director stated that it wants to be a symbol of modern society's need to rediscover a serene, symbiotic and respectful relationship with nature. It is an important step for Gucci, with this collection choosing to use materials that are recycled, organic, from sustainable sources, and created with renewable materials. The key fabric is Econyl, 100% reclaimed nylon from pre- and post-consumer waste. Off the Grid marks an important movement toward a more ethical view of fashion than that of the past: a good starting point for this philosophy of circular rather than linear production, which will be extended in the future to the brand's entire production.

A further step forward has been taken by brands that not only respect the environment, but also work to restore or even enrich it. This concept is called **regeneration** and is implemented through tangible means. Instead of just maintaining the status quo, companies must try to leave the planet and its population in a better condition for continued existence. Forward-thinking brands work with nature, and for society, not against them.

In adopting a regenerative approach, it is clear that the ultimate aim of the company's work is to create a positive impact in the world. We said at the beginning that high-end players, even more than the protagonists of other industries, can exist and succeed only by virtue of the communities and the environment in which they operate. They will need to engage in **brand beneficence**, which, as defined in an article published in the *Journal of Marketing* and discussed by Kotler in the book *Brand Activism: From Purpose to Action*, consists of activities that do good for society and the world.

In the evolution of a brand, beneficence is the last stage to generate competitive advantage. The business return is supported by a law underlying social psychology, the principle of reciprocity: if an actor gives something to society, others unconsciously have a tendency to make a gesture of gratitude in return. For a brand, this translates into a greater predisposition to purchase or to offer spontaneous advice. Brand beneficence aligns with the concept that defines the era in which we are living, **purpose economy**, as dubbed by Aaron Hurst. Purpose is meant in the general sense, and it is as much about why a company exists as why a consumer ends up preferring its products. Choosing brands for what they represent, and not just for what they sell, is an intrinsic need that we all have as human beings in our constant search for meaning.

In a historical period animated by numerous political, social and cultural causes, brands are required to take an 'active' and no longer 'passive' position to face them. Today, people expect brands to take real action. The *Trust Barometer 2020* published by Edelman reports that globally, 64% of consumers are guided in their purchase choices by the belief that companies should catalyse change and solve social problems. For these people, "I vote with my wallet" is true. Aspiring to be recognized as a purpose-driven brand implies integrating 'value' associations (social, political, ethical, cultural) into one's identity. This is certainly an opportunity, in line with the zeitgeist – typically Western – but it exposes the company to risks such as conflicts with cultures or groups, even in major markets, which are based on incompatible values, and entails attention to maximum transparency, consistency, and a predisposition to criticism or even the loss of potential customers.

For some customers, **the association of a brand with a relevant cause makes it easier to justify a self-indulgent purchase**. Data from Brandz shows that the actions taken by luxury brands in this direction are helping bridge the gap in people's perceptions, making the brands seem less arrogant and more responsible.

Other examples that created great public interest and appreciation were Armani and LVMH's initiatives in response to the first wave of the COVID-19 epidemic. The Italian fashion designer's maison ordered all its Italian production plants to be converted to the production of disposable medical gowns intended for the protection of doctors and nurses, while the French holding company started producing disinfectant gel to be distributed free of charge.

However positive all the actions mentioned so far may be, they remain unrelated and appear as sporadic incidents. And in the eyes of the most critical, even opportunistic. Unfortunately, these accusations are often well founded and may continue to be so in the future. We hope that more and more companies, led by visionary leaders, will be better able to balance short-term goals with the lasting impact they will have on society, and that this vision will be what allows them to continue to operate and prosper.

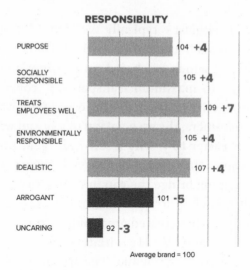

RESPONSIBILITY

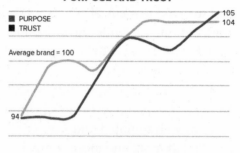

PURPOSE AND TRUST

GUCCI

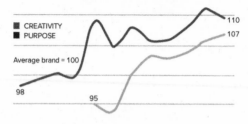

CREATIVITY AND PURPOSE

CHANEL

FIGURE 2.4: **THE CHANGE IN PERCEPTION TOWARDS LUXURY BRANDS (GRAPHICS: BRANDZ)**

The real difference between single actions, which still pertain to CSR, and a broader strategy based on shared values, lies precisely in clearly defining the purpose and aligning all activities accordingly. Only in this way will it be possible to appear authentic and not be seen as doing benevolent work solely for the publicity.

Regardless of the industry, there are few brands that have really managed to define a core meaning and purpose, building their entire organization upon it, and then their relationships with the outside world, and not subsequently contradicted themselves with their actions. Two examples in fashion are Patagonia and TOMS. The first was started and developed from the belief that nature is an asset to be preserved and has consequently always pursued a 'Made to last' philosophy. Adhering to its purpose has led the brand to make specific decisions such as self-imposed 'tax' of 1% in favour of the planet, or to create dramatic initiatives. Their latest, being aimed at political leaders who have not been attentive enough to environmental protection, was a bold statement printed directly on their clothing labels. The second example, TOMS, is globally recognized for its attention to the most needy, which is embodied in the donation of a pair of shoes for every pair purchased.

If looking forward and understanding how to positively change people's lives is obviously complex, in luxury the difficulty increases as the maisons are driven to focus on their own history and heritage. As stated in Be Inclusive, this almost self-indulgent attitude must be addressed by the answer to a question: what is their role in the world? Finding one's purpose is a mission, not an obligation. Activism must be a sincere reaction in the face of the threat to the design the maison aspires to achieve. A difficult goal, certainly one more challenging than the easy error defined by **woke washing**: that is, to boast about brand activism through communication, embracing social causes or giving an ethical value to products and services solely for the purpose of visibility, reputation and economic objectives, without all that must truly permeate throughout the organization.

8

BE A SERVICE

In an era in which the relationships between companies and clients have been disintermediated, and a shift from ownership to access has taken place. Be a Service means reviewing the usual high-end business models, integrating new ones such as rental and second-hand, and developing an enhanced service component.

Very few product categories have the aspect of intimacy typical of clothing and accessories. Yet fashion, including that of high-end, has been influenced by the idea of **post-ownership**. This concept means **a market economy that is no longer based on the possession of things, but instead on access to them**. There are many categories that have already embraced this logic and have been reconfigured to it, namely transport. The most exemplary case in this sense is certainly Uber. The American, now ex-start-up, has changed the experience of mobility, allowing anyone to become a 'taxi driver' or to enjoy a ride at any time, anywhere.

The impact on society has led to a new word: **uberization**. This term refers to a market transition in which access to resources is guaranteed at more favourable economic conditions, thanks to a system that allows easy matching of supply and demand. This change has also altered the mindset of car owners, especially in large cities, prompting them to question their real need for ownership. In turn, this has paved the way for a real revolution in the sector, culminating in the sharing economy. Millions of people around the world now prefer not owning a car, instead renting different cars for a few minutes to reach their desired destinations, paying only for their actual usage. These dynamics follow the **product-as-a-service** business model. Rather than focusing on the timely sale of an asset, manufacturers find it advantageous to make the product accessible as a service that can help the user achieve a purpose or objective, extracting from the tangible object its true value. Continuing this reasoning within the automotive market, it is clear why groups such as BMW and Daimler decided to develop proprietary car-sharing services.

These dynamics, quickly tested and then adopted primarily by Millennials, soon spread to other sectors in response to the demand of this generation. Even the high-end has been affected. They can solve two otherwise irreconcilable needs: **on the one hand, the desire for sustainability and to make choices that have a positive impact on the community, as discussed in Be Purposeful; and on the other hand, by satisfying the personal desire to always be seen in different outfits**. One in three women in a country such as the UK considers a garment 'old' after only wearing it once or twice. And one in seven considers it to unacceptable to be photographed twice in the same outfit. It is clear that if a customer in this segment indulged this impulse with continuous purchases, they would end up buying a disproportionate number of items destined to remain in the closet, a practice that is not exactly sustainable. So high-end consumers are considering new behaviours, such as renting, buying used and even reselling.

The basis of this behaviour is not only the search for a 'bargain' in the sense of economic savings: these people will pay full price for an exclusive Hermès moccasin and wear it with a vintage Armani and then gladly tote a rented Prabal Gurung. The choice derives instead from the desire to keep up with 'ever-faster-fashion,' which makes products obsolete (even luxury ones) through social media and communication, to make responsible purchases, and to demonstrate individualistic stylings and therefore one's uniqueness. The trend is rapidly increasing. In fact, the data indicate that in the coming years, the value of the used market could exceed even that of fast fashion. It is for these reasons that many new companies, as well as the larger maisons and their groups, have started to develop services that previously did not seem related to this industry. These services are able to generate greater value for customers, without any changes to the products themselves.

Let us consider the **rental**. In reference to the premium segment players, the first to embrace this logic were, once again, those in the automotive sector. Several years ago, Audi launched a program through which people could share a car with others: users paid a fixed fee for the service, plus a variable portion based on actual vehicle use.

Returning to high-end fashion, the most emblematic case among the many start-ups that have moved in this direction is undoubtedly Rent the Runway. The American company has raised $176 million in financing and, as the name suggests, offers members the opportunity to rent clothes and luxury accessories for a monthly fee. Specifically, it is a **subscription** model with plans offering a different number of rental items per month, from a minimum of four up to an unlimited number. Alternatively, customers can also rent individual items for just a few days at a time.

Allied Market Research states that the revenues from fashion-renting will reach a value close to $2 billion by 2023. If high-end 'as-a-service' reaches this critical mass, fashion houses may soon consider the option of launching their own subscription services. **The ultimate goal would be to directly manage their customers' experiences, collecting information to improve the personalization of the service itself and, as a result, increasing loyalty to the brand.** This strategy could be developed by the Kering, LVMH and Richemont groups, using high-profile models capable of generating a significant competitive advantage over Rent the Runway and other players.

Moving on to the analysis of the **used market**, a figure extrapolated from BCG-Altagamma, before the COVID-19 pandemic, clarifies how the phenomenon would have followed an upward trend. In parallel with a projection of +3% for the market for luxury personal goods for 2021, revenue for second-hand goods was estimated to have grown by 12%. The same research showed that in 2018, 60% of consumers already had an interest in second-hand luxury items. The drivers guiding this predisposition were not only a better quality-price ratio, but most of all the possibility to buy sold-out, limited edition, vintage or otherwise unavailable items. The final evidence emerging from the study focuses on the importance of the digital channel for this type of purchase: as many as 80% of those buying second-hand luxury did so with at least one purchase made online and for 37% it was the only channel used.

This is due to the rise of many specialized platforms such as TheRealReal, Vinted and the leader, Vestiaire Collective. The latter is the first social media shopping site specializing in second-hand quality and luxury fashion. It was launched in 2009 in France with the aim of offering a marketplace for used high-end clothing and accessories, where people could buy and sell with full confidence and transparency. Every week, more than 30,000 new products are selected by a team of designers and uploaded to the platform, with the permanent catalogue having more than 600,000 pieces. The site stands out from its competitors because of its strict quality control: all the articles are screened by the expert eyes of a specialized team, offering only impeccable products to the approximate 8 million members of the community.

In the case of TheRealReal, the expansion of its business in 2020 is noteworthy, as a result of opportunities generated by the situation related to the COVID-19 pandemic. In fact, the platform has doubled its product range from that of the previous year, thanks to new B2B program partnerships. TheRealReal allows maisons to sell unsold stock on its e-commerce site.

The advantage for high-end players is that they can dispose of this inventory without having to do so within proprietary channels; an increasingly frequent need in a hyper-fast market, and one complicated by the uncertainty that has rocked the world so recently.

Beyond these latest events, one of the most important partnerships they have signed is with Burberry. Luxury has begun to think in a more circular way, also seeing the opportunity to dispose of stock, together with, or in place of, off-price. Thanks to the American platform, the British fashion house has begun to encourage owners of its garments to resell them on this site and thus create further shopping opportunities within their boutiques. While Burberry will not sell its products directly on the site, it will reward consumers who do so with an incentive for their next shopping experience in one of its 18 stores in the United States.

Until just a few years ago, fashion looked at second-hand with indifference, but also with apprehension. It was carefully avoided in the fear of negative repercussions on the sales of new products and that it would lead to an overall devaluation in the perception of the brand. But the points we have just made, as well as the successes of the aforementioned platforms, have persuaded high-end players to consider entering the business of used.

Today's ambition is to try and even control the phenomenon, making a profit from it. The competitive advantage for maisons lies in the possibility of centralizing the entire experience, having total control in terms of accessibility and distribution. For customers, the benefit would be to interact exclusively and directly with the brand. This would minimize one of the barriers highlighted by research, namely the concern about the authenticity and quality level of the product.

In general, luxury players are gearing up to meet the potential risks associated with products passing from hand to hand. In this sense, blockchain technology is a potentially useful tool to track the path of goods. LVMH has already partnered with Microsoft and ConsenSys, a blockchain company, to create a tracking and tracing platform for luxury. **Services structured like this could comple-ment the approach reserved for those enrolled in membership clubs**, both in the sense of peer-to-peer sales and actual resale, by having the security of dealing with people belonging to a small circle of selected users.

Even e-tailers are open to these dynamics. The pioneering player is Farfetch. In line with the initiative mentioned in Be Purposeful and included in the broader sustainable mission of the brand, called 'Positively Farfetch,' the company, led by José Neves, took its first steps in second-hand in the spring of 2019, with the launch of a pilot program for customers to resell high-end-range handbags for credit on the site. The enterprise, called Second Life and currently only available in Europe and the UK, may soon be expanded to new types of products and new markets. Furthermore, within the Farfetch site, there is a section entirely dedicated to used clothing: Farfetch's pre-owned range aims to give new life to style icons from the most famous maisons on the planet. And in October 2019, an experimental charity project, available only to British customers, also began in partnership with Thrift+, a start-up specializing in the donation of used items. Users can donate their used clothing and, once it is sold, receive a third of the proceeds in credit for use toward future purchases on the site. The remaining amount is split between Thrift+ and a charitable organization chosen by the user when they signup. At last, motivated by the desire to reinforce the benefits of a second-hand purchase, Farfetch has launched a tool that allows customers to understand the environmental impact of the purchases they want to make.

As already shown with rentals, even second-hand creates an opportunity that is not insignificant for the evolution of business in the high-end segment. **If the essence of a luxury strategy is control, these players will benefit enormously by directly managing the second life of their garments.** That is why Richemont decided to purchase outright some of the rental and resale companies that managed the brands for the group.

Developing their own 'as-a-service' model will bring numerous benefits to high-end brands. The first will be in having a new source of data and information intentionally provided by customers regarding their propensities, preferences and tastes. All this will mean that everyone's experience can be more personalized and unique. The second, intrinsically linked to the first, will be the possibility of establishing a real relationship, a relationship that goes well beyond the single purchase. By bonding with their own clients in a deeper way, as stated in Be Relational, maisons will be able to increase customer loyalty and work on creating new business opportunities.

This second benefit brings a third, related to cash flow. Instead of receiving a single proceed, **brands will be able to multiply their revenues over time, thereby exploiting the entire life cycle of the product, whether it is rented or sold again as used.** In their own review, Deloitte confirmed the advantage of developing this type of business model: the service component is 75% more profitable than any other company operation. Service can be leveraged in many sectors, but in reaping the benefits luxury is probably more favoured due to some of its structural characteristics already discussed. Consider the outstanding quality of the products and their consequential longevity: having timeless goods allows a high-end player to successfully feed, over time, a model based on a continuous service. This has been evident with hard luxury, watches as a prime example, and now this model is ready to make its mark on the fortunes of apparel.

It is even possible to mention a fourth and final advantage: demonstrating being in step with the spirit of the times, adopting increasingly sustainable if not even circular models. **Being more aligned with the needs of consumers, and also being more profitable for companies, it is expected that rental and resale will become increasingly important in the strategies of many maisons and groups.** These processes are redefining the boundaries between inclusiveness and exclusivity, concepts described within the rule of Be Inclusive. Today it is possible to be part of a 'community of style' no longer through the possession of a garment, but instead through temporary access to an icon of the brand; and in the future, this will become easier and easier. As the once well-defined boundaries between product and service dissolve into a new and better way to shop, the spirit of the times are changing, even in luxury.

9

BE COLLABORATIVE

In an era in which the ability to innovate and reinvent oneself has become a critical success factor for even the high-end, Be Collaborative means abandoning a closed innovation approach and embracing an open logic. Alongside licensing and co-branding, activities not new to the segment, the concept of coopetition and a specific focus on relationships with e-tailers are gaining ground.

Today, no market can escape the external forces that determine its current volatility, unpredictability, complexity and ambiguity (VUCA). When it comes to developing the new skills necessary to face this scenario, every company must answer the following question: should they develop them internally, buy them on the market or obtain them through a partnership? Given the overall character of the industry, this latter option seems to be the most efficient and effective. Historically, high-end fashion has always been based on a model of supply chain collaboraton. The contribution of yarn, fabric and leather producers to high-end innovation has been, and still is, incalculable, and it has determined the success of some players such as Italy, especially in geographical terms.

Being willing to collaborate with the outside world is the basic principle of **open innovation**, which can be viewed as a further extension and evolution of a phenomenon already known to the industry. This expression represents a paradigm and model of innovation in which companies cannot rely only on internal ideas and resources to promote and increase their value but need to take advantage of technological tools and expertise available from external sources. Sources of added value for players of any size can be universities and research institutes but also start-up incubators, business partnerships, customers, freelance professionals and consultants.

The open innovation approach is in contrast to the traditional **closed innovation** process, where research is carried out within the confines of a company, which no longer seems adequate in a dynamic and unpredictable market. The flow of innovation that was once vertical – from companies to the market – has now become horizontal.

Even high-end brands can use strategic partnerships integrated with in-house expertise, in order to create new products and exciting experiences for customers. This assumption is the basis of the concept **exponential organization,** discussed in the book of the same name written by several of the founders of Singularity University. Exponentiality means, among other things, transcending the boundaries of what you offer by making use of third-party assets, allowing you to make progress with relatively low costs and in much shorter time periods. Of course, the leading maisons need not radically transform themselves in following this principle, but can instead draw inspiration from it with a view to evaluating new modes of evolution. They will be able to enhance what they offer by ensuring accurate time-to-market, without needing to exit their own core business of research, development and implementation.

This concept fits perfectly with the fashion industry's need to keep pace with technological innovation and digital transformation. An example is Farfetch offering to collaborate with companies on the construction of their e-commerce sites, beginning with a white-label solution called Black & White. Another notable agreement is the one between YNAP and Armani. Through its Next Era business model, the luxury e-tailer will allow the maison's customers to manage purchases in a flexible way, benefiting from the full potential of the various channels: it will be possible to access the products available in the entire network of the brand's stores, both online and offline, with increasingly fluid means. Orders will be processed not just though YNAP's distribution network, but also from the distribution centres and boutiques of Armani.

Other players have decided to collaborate with another universe, that of start-ups. Relationships with this group can encompass diverse aspects from promotion and incubation to acquisition. Analysts expect more and more large-market players to allocate venture capital to invest in innovative start-ups.

LVMH, together with Luxury Ventures, is already doing this with an initial capital of 50 million euros. The group also established the Innovation Award in 2017, a prize created to recognize and tangibly encourage the development of start-ups and promote best practices with the maisons. It is a way to reflect the values LVMH holds dear, such as creativity, excellence and entrepreneurial spirit. By learning from the operating models of start-ups and native digital companies, those in fashion will begin to accept new ways of working and new types of talent.

Another initiative by LVMH demonstrates an example of open innovation also involving its employees. The DARE (Disrupt, Act, Risk to be an Entrepreneur) program, again launched in 2017, calls for the group's best talents to compete in a contest, with the aim of stimulating corporate entrepreneurship to find innovative and winning ideas to enter untapped markets or to launch new products and services.

After exploring the two principle options that companies possess to apply open innovation, either by collaborating with external partners or engaging internal stakeholders, we can now consider another type of collaboration: one with competitors. The term **coopetition** is used to define a strategy that combines characteristics of both competition and cooperation and happens between companies that choose to collaborate only for certain activities. **It is an unexpected partnership occurring between two usually rival companies who interrupt their competition on one or more fronts in order to achieve a common goal.** Ultimately, the goal is to obtain results that are difficult to achieve using only their own strengths, thereby increasing negotiating capacity and bargaining power.

This path has its advantages but also requires caution. The fact that the collaboration unites two competitors implies that a certain amount of competitiveness permeates the entire relationship. Consequently, a company that enters into a coopetition arrangement must stay alert to possible situations that can generate tension, or worse, negative consequences. These include an imbalance of power in the relationship, opportunistic behaviour, loss of intellectual property and weakening of competitive advantages. Nonetheless, coopetition is considered to be an excellent lever to increase performance and achieve certain objectives.

Perhaps the most interesting example in the luxury market is the partnership between Kering and Richemont in producing Cartier's eyewear. The same Richemont also proposed that competitors invest in the new company formed by the merger of YOOX and NAP to create critical mass and prevent Amazon from entering the luxury market. This attempt, however, was rejected by LVMH, as it decided to develop its own proprietary platform.

In the retail world, an innovative, albeit complex, form of coopetition could be that of **co-retail**. We can imagine stores literally shared by two brands linked by a certain affinity, relational or situational, in which they feed one another's propositions; also benefiting from savings in rental costs and the possibility of 'cross-seeding' customer data.

The relevance of coopetition is even more evident in times of crisis, such as that of the COVID-19 pandemic. Emergency situations that mark moments of strong discontinuity can be the opportunity to apply this stratagem and survive the instability of the market, making operations more efficient, or even rewriting the rules of the game. **Collaboration with third parties is useful in setting up systems in which the individual parties work together, more or less permanently, to provide services with greater added-value or to achieve a higher 'common good.'** Periods of rupture with respect to normality, such as the one we witnessed in 2020, should be considered as opportunities for construction rather than a need for reconstruction. It is precisely in these moments that new and disruptive business models emerge or a sector's quality standards are raised.

In the world of high-end, coopetition is even more important to achieve results related to crucial issues, including traceability, counterfeiting and sustainability. Without finding common standards, it will never be possible to accomplish the CSV described in Sustainability and continued in Be Purposeful and to bring positive change to the industry. Kering's decision to develop its My Ep&L platform in an open-source version – also mentioned in Be Purposeful – must be viewed from this perspective. Michael Beutler, Sustainability Operations Director of the group, defined the development as an 'open innovation concept,' precisely because it was designed to provide guidelines in terms of sustainability, even to competitors. By giving each player and external stakeholders the ability to use the tool, Kering is working for the good of the entire luxury industry.

Collaboration with other companies and suppliers has been the basis for the development of luxury brands and their expansion, not only in new merchandise categories but also in uncharted markets and customer segments. The mechanism that has made this possible is **licensing**. This form of commercial agreement requires one company (known as a licensor) to grant another (called a licensee) the rights to use its trademark, a patent, draw on know-how or use any other element that constitutes intellectual property, with the goal of creating a new product or service and bringing it to market upon payment of a fee.

Historically, fashion houses have used licensing within the eyewear and make-up segments. It is precisely because of this operating model that Luxottica and Safilo – along with L'Oréal and Estée Lauder in the beauty sector – have seen the number of luxury brands in their portfolios grow exponentially and have become key players in the licensing world.

There are three motivations for fashion brands to rely on licensing for these types of products. The first is that eyewear, like perfumery, watchmaking and jewellery, requires technical expertise that these players do not possess but which can be provided by their partners. The second lies in distribution advantages: these companies, in addition to their substantial know-how, have global sales networks, which would be costly, complex and time consuming for a new entrant to develop, and they have strong bargaining power that allows them to easily integrate with the retail distribution sector. The third is linked, albeit not with the highest margins, to an increase in revenue, as most consumers see the products mentioned above as a gateway to the world of luxury. Designer eyewear usually has a considerably lower price point than that of a flagship product from the maison, such as a suit. It is no coincidence then that licensed products feature conspicuously in the revenues of many companies.

However, some critical aspects regarding the adoption of licensing on the part of luxury brands should also be highlighted. The expansion of its target base and the exponential spread of the brand can dilute the equity of the brand – as already discussed in the previous chapters – and cause a loss of operational control over the brand. The players who have overextended their licensing activities in recent years have fallen into these circumstances. To avoid this, others are taking steps to bring items now managed by partners back under their control. This was done, first and foremost, by the Kering group that, with the creation of Kering Eyewear, put a stop to the licensing of eyewear collections such as Balenciaga, Bottega Veneta, Cartier, Gucci and Yves Saint Laurent, outsourcing only production and internalizing the more strategic phases of the process, including design, marketing and sales. Among the brands mentioned, the most striking rationalization of licenses was the one performed by Saint Laurent: according to a Reuters estimate, the brand had reached 160 before reducing them to just two in 2012.

Managing these aspects in-house allows companies to closely monitor every stage of the value chain and decide when and where to take action in terms of efficiency or value enhancement. Simplifying, we can identify three main advantages: control, profitability and integration of skills. This would be the optimal situation for every maison, but they are forced to face high complexity in management, substantial investments, costs, time and risks, along with losing focus on the business. Relying on a licensee therefore is an opportunity from a practical and economic point of view.

It is for this reason that the choice top management must make is not about pursuing or ostracizing licensing, but about choosing which stages of the value chain it is strategic to control or outsource. Burberry did this with its beauty line, managed in-house since its creation and licensed to Coty in 2017.

A more recent but equally powerful practice is **co-branding**. It can be defined as a strategic alliance between two companies aimed at offering the consumer a new product or service, characterized by intrinsic and extrinsic qualities attributable to both. Co-branding really happens when the two parties work at the same level, each contributing to the creation of something new that bears their dual signatures. For this reason, it is essential that the two brands have a common vision and share the same principles and values.

There are two macro-types of agreements: functional and symbolic co-branding. The first involves the collaboration between companies from different sectors but who have a mutual need for each other; the second relies on the partnership of two players active in the same market who aspire to positive contamination between their brand images. **In functional co-branding, technical expertise is used to enhance the functional attributes of the new product; in symbolic co-branding these same attributes are used to generate new value associations.**

In most cases in the high-end world, co-branding has been adopted to create a 'third way,' claims Karl Lagerfeld. The two polar opposites of the market, luxury and mass-market, unite to create a new mid-range that, according to the designer, "mixes high and low." This has occurred because in an ultra-competitive context, high-end brands are constantly looking for new ways to grow, but at the same time, reduce the costs associated with launching new products, thereby minimizing their risks. Collaborating with mass-market companies allows them to increase sales by being able to draw on a wider pool of customers, usually out of their reach, while selling a product momentarily more affordable. In the future, perhaps this group of customers will return to the maison and buy one of its flagship products. At the same time, mass-market players benefit from the prestige attributed to the partner, also gaining in aspirationality. If the opportunities for high-end brands are evident, the risk, especially in the short term, is once again a negative impact on their image and perhaps even the loss of a clear and defined identity in the long run. This possibility increases when luxury meets fast-fashion.

There is an emblematic group of agreements between some of the largest maisons and designers, and that of H&M, one of the major fast-fashion players. Back in 2004 the Swedish giant launched its first collaboration with Karl Lagerfeld, limited to the Christmas season. After the sensational sales results, with an average of 1,500 to 2,000 pieces sold every hour in the New York Fifth Avenue store, and the entire collection being sold out globally in less than a day, H&M decided to continue this strategy. Every year, the brand collaborates with at least one prestigious high-end label, creating long lines of consumers outside its stores, who are motivated by the hope of getting hold of their first piece of 'signature' clothing by Stella McCartney, Roberto Cavalli, Kenzo and so on.

According to Alber Elbaz, former creative director of Lanvin, this type of collaboration elevates H&M rather than lowering the positioning of the maison. Emmanuel Diemoz, former CEO of Balmain, offered a matching opinion at the time of the collaboration, describing co-branding as a "further driver of high-end exclusivity." While the mass market believes they are accessing a luxury product, the true customers of a maison know that they are the only ones who can really afford it: the real proof of the brand's aspirationality. **We could even go so far as to suggest that co-branding between**

luxury and fast-fashion brands is an evolution of what diffusion lines were in the 1990s. They share the same goal of expanding the market, with a lower risk of diluting the brand's equity due to the temporary nature of the initiative, with the acceptance of lower revenues being the only compromise.

Another segment of the mass market that luxury often allies with to forge collaborations is that of **streetwear** and **sportswear**. In particular, the most used product to unite these two worlds is sneakers. The first case of co-branding in this sense dates back to the 90s with the signature sneaker of Japanese designer Junya Watanabe, Zoom Haven, and Nike. The first maison to decontextualize the concept of sportswear from athletic lines was Chanel, through a co-branding exercise with Reebok in the early 2000s. Since then, the world of 'sneakers' has changed forever. In fact, a true cult for designer sneakers was created, so much so that almost no high-end brand has been able to refrain from launching its own: from Yves Saint Laurent to Balenciaga, from Alexander McQueen to Versace and Valentino.

It is interesting to note how in just a few years sneakers have gone from being an item not considered to be within the domain of luxury to becoming a legitimate part of it. These special collaborations often give rise to capsule collections that are drop launched, as described in Be Timeless. It is no coincidence, according to data collected by BCG-Altagamma, that three of the five most popular global co-branding collaborations involve sneakers: Adidas with Yeezy, Chanel with Pharrell and Off-White with Nike. The only more successful collaboration than these three was the aforementioned one between Louis Vuitton and Supreme. Closing out the top five was Fendi and Fila with **handbags**.

In light of these examples, it is clear that special editions released in collaboration with other brands have great potential for attracting luxury consumers. BCG's own research reveals that half of these customers say they have bought at least one collabo in 2018, with even higher penetration among Generation Z and Chinese buyers. If the fashion industry was already characterized by competition between pyramid segments with increasingly blurred boundaries, these disruptive instances have added an element of further complexity, bringing high fashion to sport. The result of these moves is a convergence between the various markets as they merge into a single one.

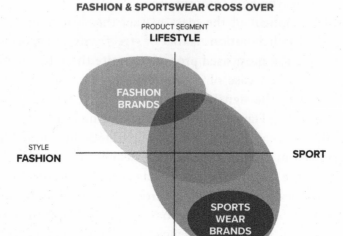

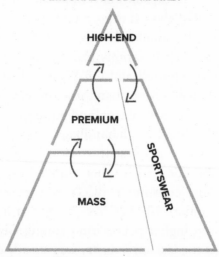

FIGURE 2.5: **CONVERGENCE OF MARKETS WITHIN (FASHION SOURCE: BAIN ALTAGAMMA)**

In light of the new market configuration, luxury brands must compete for relevance within new segments and deal with different players than those they have dealt with in the past. However, maisons have the advantage of being recognized as lifestyle brands. Being true icons and benefiting from positive associations and distinct values, they are qualified to extend their semantic universe into sectors other than their original one.

This represents a rare opportunity in terms of brand stretching, a concept already introduced in Be Inclusive. The good fortune of being recognized as cultural reference points enables these companies to enter fields such as travel and hospitality. A pioneer in this was Giorgio Armani who, after brand extension work with diffusion lines, redesigned the boundaries of his own maison with the inauguration of discos (Armani Club), restaurants (Nobu), hotel chains (Armani Hotel), furniture shops (Armani Casa), bookstores, etc.

The need to create a true ecosystem that starts from the original proposition is due to what can be called the **dematerialization of luxury**. People are less and less interested in the object itself, in favour of the experience it enables: this is why luxury buyers are happy to rediscover the same care and attention connected to a designer dress in a hotel stay or at a table in a restaurant. And to satisfy this desire, the top maisons have often entered into **joint ventures**, with big names in real estate, or renowned service companies, to spread their offer. The ease with which high-end players can create multiple new expressions, however, must take into account a structural limit. In reality, the maisons should never stray too far from the bounds of credibility defined by the values expressed in their brand DNA (Aaker). As McKinsey & Company highlights, the risk otherwise is to become mere 'labels' with no added value to offer. **Lifestyle must be the end result of the brand's work and not its predetermined goal.**

A final mode of collaboration to examine in this chapter is the **concession**. In this case, a 'grantor' gives the rights to a 'concessionaire' to resell its products in a certain 'territory,' usually exclusively, and respecting the commercial policies which have been decided upon by the grantor. In this context, an important issue for high-end players to manage today is how to relate to e-tailers. The desire for expansion must take into account the need for quantitative limitation and the qualitative preservation in the distribution of its products. In general, consumers are increasingly attracted to multi-brand e-tailers by virtue of their large assortment of products and sometimes cheaper prices. These platforms, which have already grown by 31% between 2017 and 2019 in terms of products sold (KPMG Luxury Summit), will continue to establish themselves with increasing importance in the market, taking on the role that department stores have historically played.

Fashion brands can no longer ask themselves 'if,' but must choose 'how' to collaborate with these players. The challenge is to find ways of collaboration that are advantageous for both and that allow the maisons to control their online presence: from distribution to price through to image management. This imperative is what grounds Kering's choice to operate online only through concessions, as stated by its Chief Client & Digital Officer, Grégory Boutté. Burberry has also moved in this direction in its collaboration with Farfetch. It chose to integrate with the e-tailer using its application programming interface (API) to make the entire inventory accessible through the platform while still maintaining control.

In light of what has been described, it is clear that there is no single or best method of collaboration. In reality, high-end players can draw numerous benefits from an open innovation approach, choosing their strategic partners based on current needs and the specific challenges they face. Whether it is working alongside third parties, hiring the best employees, allying with the competition, merging assets with those of another brand or licensing or granting concessions of the brand, collaboration is a solid direction for the development of the sector. **Putting this principle into practice empowers otherwise limited capabilities and potential and has a direct impact on generating new business ideas and in creating value.**

The advantages associated with this practice range from greater agility in responding to market shifts to an increase in industrial efficiency and effectiveness. Deloitte claims that we are in a **collaboration economy**, and as proof of this, calculated that companies that consider it an important component of their business strategy are four times more likely to see profits grow than competitors who do not.

10

BE ANTIFRAGILE

In a constantly changing world, luxury companies face even more complex challenges than in the past. Be Antifragile means not only managing the balance between revenue growth and brand protection, but also between the current and future market, the logic of which is beginning to change. This requires them to be ambidextrous and constantly be able to reinvent themselves.

It is a common opinion that every company's ultimate goal is to increase their value and revenues. Growth – a condition intrinsically and inextricably linked to the capitalist world – is seen as an objective to be persistently pursued. This reasoning, excluding a more holistic vision of the impact of companies on the world and on society (as in the triple bottom line, for example), is certainly befitting of almost all industries. Even the high-end cannot escape it, but the thinking behind it requires an in-depth analysis.

It all starts with a question: can rarity and scarcity – founding values of luxury – be reconciled with the demands of shareholders for ever greater growth? As mentioned already, luxury is fed through dreams. **The more a brand grows, the more this growth threatens its appeal and puts its essence into question.** But if the luxury megabrands that are present in the market today had started with this assumption, it would not have been possible to create them. This is because growth itself was incompatible with the original luxury model, based on haute couture and artisanship. But since the dawn of time till now, **it has always been possible, using various ways and means, to shift rarity and scarcity from an objective level to a qualitative dimension.**

Today, in fact, these players operate on a global scale, and in place of the restricted offer there are now sporadic releases of limited editions and the waiting list; the objective rarity of raw materials has shifted to a focus on fine attention to detail and presentation; the inaccessibility of a single tailor shop has been replaced by selective distribution in a limited number of mono-brand and selected multi-brand stores. Growth and pressure regarding higher revenues exist, but the managers of these brands must always worry about preserving aspirationality through limitations in terms of accessibility. This clarification is fundamental, as in this sector, the desire to increase revenue often clashes with the erosion of brand equity, because it generally corresponds to an expansion of the customer base and thus to greater accessibility of products.

The issue of balancing short-term and long-term results is even more pressing than in the past, precisely because of the changed nature of companies. While the maisons were once led by their founders or their descendants, today it is increasingly common to find external managers at the top. It is clear how delicate the question is, because the far-sighted vision of the entrepreneur-artisan and that of his family has become an evaluation – at times cold and ruthless – of the objectives achievable by top management. The need to generate short-term results to satisfy targets has made it increasingly difficult for many brands to think in the long term. But for a sector like high-end to not preserve the brand – an asset that has been consolidated over time – it means destroying its very foundations. To avoid this, Patrick Thomas, former CEO of Hermès, maintains that luxury must not "aim to become a best seller, but rather a long seller."

In the past, this belief has led the maison to quickly stop the production of clothing or accessories that were selling too well, to preserve the exclusivity of the brand. Other less 'extreme' strategies have also been adopted. The first is a price increase. By moving the entry point higher and higher, it is possible to control the maximum proliferation of a product in a given market. The sector is accustomed to using this method: consider that prices of watches and jewellery have almost doubled in just 15 years or that the iconic Louis Vuitton Speedy 30 handbag has undergone a price increase of approximately +20% year-over-year from 2016 to today.

The second strategy to prevent excessive penetration is based on controlling availability. **In addition to selective distribution, brands can manage the release of a product by limiting access, for example, through sales by reservation.** This method is mostly used for entry-level products, with the aim of not saturating the market with the brand's own logo. Prada is a great example, managing to balance economic success with brand preservation. After having achieved significant results in terms of their geographic expansion, due to substantial growth in the network of distributors and resellers, the maison chose to reduce the latter by 80% in order to give priority to sales through direct channels.

We can note that **the central issue of luxury is not to sell as much as possible, but to remain luxury.** This last aspect is put to the test by a structural feature of the fashion industry, its **cyclicity.** By definition, fashion moves with the times and a garment, a style or even a brand itself will find its fame and appeal waxing and waning over recurring periods. One solution from the industry has been to structure itself over the years into large financial groups, with portfolios holding several maisons. In this way, through careful analysis and shrewd planning, the managers of these holding companies can define the cycles of each brand, shifting attention and investments, avoiding inefficiencies and cannibalization, and eliminating financial stress from individual entities.

While the theoretical framework proposed so far is useful in giving context to the dynamics of the industry, it encounters the volatile nature of the world in which we operate, made even more unpredictable and difficult to understand by the effect of COVID-19. Recognizing the importance of controlled growth and the ways to achieve it, it is necessary to present other approaches, processes and skills that companies must have in order to not only survive but thrive in the present and future.

In light of the macroeconomic, political and social characteristics of the scenario, now more than ever, every company should be configured as an **ambidextrous organization**, according to the definition coined by O'Reilly and Tushman. That is, a company efficient in the management of the current business and, at the same time, capable of pursuing alternative paths. It is a strategy that will allow it to be ready to confront any sudden changes in demand and not see its stability challenged by uncertainty, thanks to the conscious abandonment of risk aversion. An ambidextrous organization is one that has prepared to embrace a future without shocks.

To achieve this state, there are several actionable inside-out and outside-in models. For example, as explained in Be Collaborative, one can opt for the establishment of an innovation team or a centre of excellence, in which employees are called upon to get involved and act as change agents, even with colleagues, or of an intrapreneur program or 'business incubator' (inside-out). Many large companies have adapted their organizational structures and practices to self-organized teams and interactive networks to improve speed, flexibility and innovation.

Other cases (outside-in) choose to follow a more traditional collaboration with external consulting firms, which help the company identify the right path of evolution or transformation. Yet creating the conditions for this fusion of skills means embracing a high degree of cross-functionality and cross-mediality. In other words, the organization must be prepared so that the silos – the different departments in which it is traditionally structured – increasingly assume the form of communicating vessels and ensure that information circulates in a fluid way.

In this vision, companies will have to adopt – if the conditions allow it, and according to the skills and responsibilities of each – an agile model; one that favours **cross-pollination**, permitting anyone to make their contribution in an open and collaborative environment. In fact, innovation can no longer be the prerogative of just those who are tasked with pursuing it. Innovation, like the creativity so fundamental to this industry, cannot be limited to a job title.

Consequently, the position of CEO has become much more important in the digital age. Today they must be bastions of innovation and corporate vision: a role that places them on par with the mystical and always revered creative director.

To preserve the brand's DNA, without compromising the long-term stability, it is essential to create and maintain a symbiosis between creativity and managerial skills. The maisons must continuously seek the right balance between the artistic soul and the managerial spirit. For this reason, the partnership model, in which the designer and the manager share ideas and exert the same influence on the company's decision-making process, is now considered the most effective approach.

For the past decade the success of Louis Vuitton, for example, has depended heavily on the close working relationship between designer Marc Jacobs and executive Yves Carcelle, like that between Tom Ford and Domenico De Sole. Companies are made up of people, so to have agile companies capable of embracing change, its people must have these same characteristics. And in the making of an ambidextrous organization, the fundamental piece that needs to be established is its leadership.

Now more than ever, CEOs, and all management in general, are required to adopt a mentality based on **continuous improvement**.

This relentless goal of improvement is only possible if the concept of **learn to unlearn** is accepted and adopted. The objective in recent years, as pursued by many of the most important figures in business, is to 'never stop learning.' But there is one problem in this paradigm: not in learning, but in unlearning. As human beings, we are accustomed to working with the mental patterns we have created for ourselves. But over time, they can become outdated and obsolete. This can even happen at a company's helm, where the risk becomes using models that are no longer suited to new challenges.

But to adopt a new mindset, first you must rid yourself of the old. We tend to think of the knowledge and skills we have learned as a positive thing, and that they add to our capabilities. But unlearning what we already 'know' means letting go of this belief so that we can open the door to previously unconsidered new ideas and processes. So 'unlearning' does not mean 'forgetting.' **Unlearning is the ability to deliberately choose an alternative mental model, fully aware that the previous one no longer aligns with the needs that the context requires.**

In an article published in *HBR*, Mark Bonchek theorized that the unlearning process follows three stages: the first is the recognition that our old mental models are no longer relevant and effective – this is the most complex step to overcome, as we are unaware of our own mental patterns or afraid of abandoning them; the second stage is the need to find or create new models that best suit the objectives we want to achieve; the third is to make these new patterns habitual. This process is no different from classical learning, but it has the added difficulty of eradicating something already present before incorporating the new. Learning to unlearn therefore is essential for managers now and in the future, in these times of profound transformation. **They will have to become ambidextrous in their actions, conscious of the fact that it is not possible to solve a problem using the same way of thinking that created it.**

Not surprisingly, two of the terms most used by fashion executives to describe the industry today are 'uncertain' and 'challenging.' It is already clear to them that they need to be able to live with a perpetual dose of instability. As maintained by Pozzoli in

Create Uniqueness, if faced with curiosity, **change** can open up unforeseeable opportunities; what matters is the spirit of exploration and the ability to adapt. From interviews conducted with numerous top managers of the most important Italian and international companies, it became apparent that it is exactly the ability to embrace change, the attitude to live with uncertainty in a constructive rather than anxious way, and the passion for one's work that are today's key elements for survival.

In particular, some have emphasized how the combination between soft and hard skills will be crucial: a fusion of intuition, passion, entrepreneurship, creativity, data and technology. One word consistently emerged from all the interviews: **curiosity**. This concept is indispensable in rewriting the rules of leadership models.

The new leaders will have to act by pursuing a model that Paolo Gallo – author, coach and former Chief Human Resources Officer of the World Economic Forum and Chief Learning Officer of the World Bank – has defined as **5C**: Care (attention to people); Causes (a purpose that goes beyond short-term financial results); Collaboration (both inside and outside the company, including the social partners, institutions, competitors); Creativity (the stage requires a certain amount of 'improvisation,' the application of creativity in the broadest sense possible); Courage (acting, questioning their own certainties, even without having the ability to calculate all the risks and without having access to all the variables).

The fears and barriers that we impose upon ourselves after failure often put us back in the same place of repeating that failure, blocking us. The practice called 'pattern recognition,' which is based on learning from mistakes, can be a brake now on change and innovation. Just because it has failed once does not mean that it will happen again. That is why, by proceeding with learning to unlearn, we'll be able to set aside these fears with the intention of writing a new future.

There is a pitfall lying behind this suggestion: beginning with looking at a new situation in exactly the same manner as the previous one. This is what the phoenix does in the allegory. This mythological animal rises from its ashes, each time the same as it was before. But consistent with what the philosopher Nassim Nicholas Taleb argued,

there are times when resilience – in the business environment it is the ability to keep the system operational in the face of a shock – is not enough. Instead, it is necessary to focus on **antifragility**. This concept expresses the ability to thrive in chaos and transform errors into one's competitive advantages. It is no coincidence that Taleb offers the hydra as a metaphor for antifragility, a monster that, in the battle with Heracles, sprouted two heads every time one was cut off. This theme weaves together all the arguments made so far and is the basis of every attempt to build a prosperous future, both on a personal and corporate level. **By adopting an antifragile approach, it is no longer necessary to seek perfect tranquility and to remain indifferent and unshakeable in the face of uncertainty, because of a conviction of not being broken by it. Instead, one can enjoy living with volatility as it can potentially bring opportunities and improvements.**

In other interviews conducted, diverse top managers all spoke of having set up, in the midst of the crisis linked to COVID-19, task forces devoted to defining diverse scenarios for post-lockdown. The ambition of these companies was to seek a type of dynamic inertia, in the effort to accelerate a restart as soon as conditions allowed. This explains how these players have taken advantage of a difficult period, thereby reducing the risk of succumbing to it, and prepared themselves for other possible future crises. Many believe 40% of Fortune 500 companies will cease to exist within the next decade. This is demonstrated by the continuous and profound transformation within the rankings of the *Most Valuable Brands* year after year.

TOP 10 FORTUNE 500

‹ 2010 2009 2008 2007 2006 2005 2004 2003 ›   ‹ 2020 2019 2018 2017 2016 2015 2014 2013 ›

The Top 10		The Top 10	
1	Wal-Mart Stores, Inc.	1	Walmart
2	Exxon Mobil Corporation	2	Amazon
3	Chevron Corporation	3	Exxon Mobil
4	General Electric Company	4	Apple
5	Bank of America Corporation	5	CVS Health
6	ConocoPhillips	6	Berkshire Hathaway
7	AT&T Inc.	7	UnitedHealth Group
8	Ford Motor Company	8	McKesson
9	J.P. Morgan Chase & Co.	9	AT&T
10	Hewlett-Packard Company	10	AmerisourceBergen

VS

MOST VALUABLE BRANDS, BRANDZ

	Logo	Name	Value ($M)	Last		Brand
1	Google	Google	114,260	1	1	amazon
2	IBM	IBM	86,383	4	2	(Apple)
3	(Apple)	Apple	83,153	6	3	Microsoft
4	Microsoft	Microsoft	76,344	2	4	Google
5	Coca-Cola	Coca-Cola	67,983	4	5	VISA
6	M	McDonald's	66,005	5	6	Alibaba Group
7	Marlboro	Marlboro	57,047	10	7	Tencent 腾讯
8	CHINA MOBILE	CMCC	52,616	7	8	FACEBOOK
9	GE	General Electric	45,054	8	9	McDonald's
10	Vodafone	Vodafone	44,404	9	10	mastercard.

VS

FIGURE 2.6: **COMPARISON OF TOP 10 FORTUNE 500 AND BRANDZ'S MOST VALUABLE BRANDS RANKINGS, 2010 VS 2020**

The mantra of "reinvent or die" has never been so important. On the contrary, wanting to "innovate as before (because so far it has worked)," becomes the most risky idea that a company's managers can employ. Successful brands have had to reinvent themselves, remaining true to themselves while adapting in the right direction. Hermès originally designed equipment for horses and travel luggage; hence their logo with a carriage. When visiting their website, you will still notice a strong equestrian section, but travel luggage is now represented by smaller items that will accompany private jets. **Because times change, and brands must do the same.**

Contributors

LEO RONGONE

CEO @BOTTEGA VENETA

THE FASHION-CREATIVITY COMBINATION

Fashion has seen the emergence of those brands that were able to give creative answers to an extremely concrete question: how to reflect people's identity and values in everyday life.

Everything comes from a constant balance between these two elements; a real need satisfied by a creative response. Fashion responds to the desire to express your personality with the right dress or the most appropriate accessory, whether it's for work, to meet a friend, seduce your partner or attend an event. In this context, creativity is not an end in itself but is nourished and stimulated by demand. Clothing, in particular, represents the highest expression of the creative response and is characterized in our industry by distinct seasons marked with different types of materials and colours.

THE CALENDAR AND THE ACCELERATION OF FASHION

While it's true that over the years the combination of desire and creative response has remained unchanged, it's also true that the relationship between these two factors has completely changed. Nowadays, creativity finds itself responding primarily to the logic dictated by commercial calendars, rather than the seasonal calendars related to customer demand. The change stemmed from the economic power of the wholesale market, particularly the American one, which pushed for an ever more aggressive competitive scenario. At the end of the last century, a substantial portion of the world's demand for fashion came from the United States. On the one hand, they were increasingly important players and, on the other hand, the heart of global consumption. The constant demand for novelty clashed with the need to have long enough sales periods to dispose of the goods. Wholesalers demanded a shorter delivery time for new products, and this was inevitably at odds with the necessary time to produce the collections, research materials and manufacture the product without compromising the quality. The basis for the end-of-season discount is nothing more than a desperate response to a frenzied calendar that causes the same collection to suddenly depreciate, for the sole reason that it must quickly make room for the next commercial opportunity.

This was what gave rise to the pre-collections, which split a calendar usually divided into two six-month seasons (spring/summer and autumn/winter) into four collections of three months. Over time, different names have been given to them (cruise, resort, pre fall, pre spring, etc.), but the consequence is that these new offerings are created simply because of a desire for something new. As a result, the products, their inspirations, design time, material research and development have now multiplied, while the completion time for each phase has been cut in half.

This creates a lot of problems. For example, if during the production phase of a garment you realize that the material being used doesn't live up to your expectations, it's very difficult to search for a substitute in the remaining time. But insiders continue chasing this goal, often forsaking the right cost, quality or sustainability and stressing out the human resources who have to sew the garment at a speed that's not appropriate for a luxury product. The physiological creation times conflict with the commercial presentation times of the collection, and it's the latter that prevail. Thus, the division of two seasons into four collections has increased the pressure on creative activity and has generated an excessive cost and waste related to the amount of work, materials purchased, movement of people and goods, and production of products that will never be used.

THE VALUE OF TIME AND A NEW SUSTAINABLE MODEL FOR FASHION

I believe a sustainable model exists. One that allows a balance between creative supply and demand, safeguards the growth of brands, respects partners, improves working conditions for employees and supports emerging designers.

In such a model, national chambers of fashion, as is still the case today, coordinate calendars for fashion shows and collection presentations, so that emerging designers can have a presence alongside the big brands and develop, thanks to buyers and press moving in unison at the same times and to the same places. Prêt-à-porter is ideally divided into only two genderless seasons: spring/summer and autumn/winter. Each season has a six-month period prior to the show for design, research and development of the collection and is followed by a six-month period dedicated to the manufacturing, processing and delivery of the collection.

The model remains based on genderless PAP fashion shows that are held in physical or digital form, or more likely, a combination of the two, similar to what occurs today. All of the other PAP men's and women's shows are kept to a minimum in order to reduce travel to the fashion capitals for the buying activities. Of course, there are always other opportunities for shows and communications throughout the year that are not linked to these buying events. Each collection is divided into creative packages, ensuring a continuous supply of novelty in the store, even greater than today's.

The fashion show, in whatever form it takes, would continue to represent the culmination of the creative process, the peak expression of the artistic director. The show is based on the same inspiration as the collection and completes the process that gave birth to the dream. Postponing the creation of the fashion show until that same collection arrives in-store would mean the art director would be working simultaneously on the collection being developed and on the previous one just to create a presentation. So it restores the clear difference in value between the current season's collection at full price and the one on sale from the previous season, which in terms of colour palettes and materials, is the opposite season and the previous year's creative expression, not the tail end of the season itself.

The product is the result of the best possible creative process and of a careful and responsible search of materials. The collections reflect a real need that begins with people rather than commercial calendars. Longer development times allow better control of merchandising and planning, improving the level of sell-through and thereby minimizing the waste related to unsold products. Having just two periods for presenting collections won't diminish creativity; on the contrary, creativity will have multiple forms of expression in a society now accustomed to a frenetic consumption of novelty, be it product, service or social content.

Communication and product delivery will adopt the approach of always on, every week and every month, as brands continue to propose different ideas and expressions of creativity and this will be helped by having only two collections rather than four, because creative directors will be able to dictate the timing of creativity rather than submitting to the market.

Digitization will obviously continue its course, being an integral part of this model and evolving our business. However, I believe that the real challenge imposed by the pandemic that engulfed us this year is linked to the way we interact with one of the most important resources for our profession: time. The time needed to create a collection, to research quality materials, to manufacture, to publicize and distribute our products, the time to do all this while safeguarding the environment and securing the best conditions for our artisans. The most significant evolution of our sector will be represented by an innovative management of this precious resource, which, free from the constraints of the current commercial calendar's rhythms, will not just elevate creative expression but allow us to generate value for our customers and the community.

I would like to add one last point about sustainability. We're living in a state of constant awareness regarding this issue. And we can expect that in the near future wasting resources will no longer be tolerated. It will be a duty, rather than a virtue, to minimize the impact on the planet, an obligation to transform the created value into something useful for the community.

AFFINITY WITH
NEW CONSUMERS

Even consumers have changed over the years, becoming more and more informed – thanks to the accessibility of information online – demanding and seeking unique experiences that involve them online and offline. Thus, attention progressively shifts from the product to the consumer, a selective consumer who chooses a brand for the values it represents. In today's context, it's increasingly important to communicate the authentic values of the brand. Ultimately, it's these that generate interest in the target audience and lead to purchase and brand loyalty. The emotional dimension and rapport of values lets us fully live the dream that luxury brands create, intensifying it. Moreover, presenting the entire line compared to individual products is an essential step to convey a lifestyle and benefit from the desirability of a lifestyle brand.

GLOCAL MINDSET

During the recent months of isolation due to the pandemic, we wanted to offer moments of distraction and inspiration. Using Bottega Residency (a platform with content linked to art, literature, music, cinema and even the kitchen), we entertained our followers on our social channels on a weekly basis, showcasing the voices of eminent curators in these fields.

Consistency is a fundamental element in communicating the values of a global brand through relevant messages and respecting local cultures. For this reason, we've chosen Shanghai to be the physical address of Bottega Residency, and it will be our creative hub in Asia for the coming months. This represents an important moment in the history of the company, signalling the cultural transition from a headquarter-centred mindset to an increasingly glocal (global and local) philosophy. The Residency will not only host local and international artists who will periodically collaborate with us on content creation, but will also be the operational base for our Global Digital Director and home to an exchange program for the Worldwide Marketing team in Milan.

BRUNELLO CUCINELLI

EXECUTIVE PRESIDENT AND CREATIVE DIRECTOR @BRUNELLO CUCINELLI SPA

THE HARMONY BETWEEN
PROFIT AND GIVING

I grew up in the country, in a house with no electricity or water; people worked the land and lived with animals. I remember that my grandfather gave the first sack of wheat to the community; one tried to find a balance between profit and giving. This concept of balance was passed on to me during my first 15 years of life and has guided my choices ever since. When we came to live in the city, my father started working in a factory. He was humiliated, and so I decided that I would live a life of mutual respect and dignity.

When I was 24 years old, I came across a book by Theodore Levitt and I began to think about economics and globalization, developing the idea of producing something truly special. That was when I chose cashmere, because I wanted something of quality and that could be handed down. **Without renouncing profit, I have always remained respectful of all human beings and for Creation; this is why I have stayed the course, maintaining the values of harmony, human sustainability and an ethical idea of humanistic capitalism.**

FAR BEYOND SUSTAINABILITY:
HUMANISTIC CAPITALISM

I prefer to talk about 'human sustainability' because I find the concept of sustainability insufficient. At Solomeo, we have always sought a moderate profit, in harmony with human dignity, and for this reason we are committed to making high-quality artisanal products that do not cause damage to Creation, or at least as little as possible. In the country, my family and I lived in harmony with everything: when we chopped down a tree to warm ourselves, we made a mound of earth and moss to help it grow back. Too often we 'parents' have passed on to our children the idea that we must fear the future, when instead we need hope. I found it very interesting that the Japanese emperor Naruhito chose, as the name for his era, the terms 'hope' and 'harmony'.

My dream is for a shared custody of beauty, where everyone feels responsible for some part of the Creation that hosts us, even if it's small. Kant says, "Act by considering humanity, both for yourself and for others, never simply as a means but always also as a noble end."

The great Dutch Bernard de Mandeville of the 17th century said something I find fascinating: "There is no love but what implies a care to preserve the thing beloved." When we take care of both nature as well as our employees, we expect all our partners to do likewise.

OUR 'IDEALS OF LIFE AND WORK'

The great ideals that inspire us in our life and business are:

I.   We love and respect Mother Earth, cultivating it according to nature and receiving its fruits as most precious gifts.
II.   We do not use more than is necessary and natural. We treat the universe with kindness.
III. We always act as faithful and loving guardians of Creation.
IV.   We believe in the moral and economic dignity of the human being.
V.   We work by supporting fair profit and the harmony between profit and giving.
VI.   We seek harmony between a fair day's work and personal privacy.
VII. We remember our parents. They taught us to respect the law, and our history is written in their word.
VIII. We believe in a universalism of the world, and we act with respect toward all cultures.
IX.   We accept just changes to live the best we can in our times.
X.   We love the young and pass on to them the hope and dream of the bright future that awaits them.

ALL THINGS COME FROM THE EARTH

I always start with Xenophanes' maxim that "Everything comes from the Earth." Because of this, all our corporate building, construction or renovation work and in general any improvements to the land are carried out in harmony with the places and with their original spirit. Hence the attention to the landscape design, the architecture, to the maintenance and to its durability. **The Earth must be restored by respecting its resources and ancient natural laws.** Inspired by Francis of Assisi, we pay great attention to every element of nature, and we care for our crops of oil, wine, wheat and fruit according to nature, as well as in their use for the food in our company restaurant.

THE ART OF REGENERATION

We learned from our mothers that the act of repair signifies the value of things. John Ruskin said that we must accept the end of the objects we use, but we must strive to care for them by prolonging their existence; this is why an entire area of the company is dedicated to the art of repair and renewal of garments. I believe that in the future, production will be in an increasingly respectful and gentle way and that we will return to govern the world with science and soul because we cannot do one without the other.

AN AMIABLE
ARTISAN KNOWLEDGE

Our workplaces are carefully thought out and designed to be welcoming, and those who work there can raise their head and see the sky. We all observe the proper and same work hours; after 5.30pm and on weekends no one is connected. I still believe that we can understand each other better with a phone call and can also better understand the state of mind of the person with whom we're talking. Human relationships come first. In our organization, everyone has equal opportunities and deserves financial reward because dignity must be both moral and economic.

I.   We have devoted the utmost care to healthy relationships of esteem and trust between workers, whom we consider as thinking souls.

II. We believe there to be great value in culture as a factor for human improvement. For this reason, we try to amiably encourage it.

III. We are aware that sharing knowledge develops genius at work. For this reason, we established the School of Arts and Crafts in Solomeo.

IV.   If our company lasts for centuries, as we hope, this will also be due to the generational change that we have taken care with over time.

V.   It is our habit to meet periodically throughout the year and talk to each other, so that everyone can know how the business is evolving.

VI.   We never cease looking for the instinct of genius in people, and when we recognize it, we try with care to enhance it.

I think the company's job is to put the creativity and genius of every collaborator to good use, which is only possible by creating a virtuous circle of esteem and respect for skills. From the internet to robots, a humanistic use of technology is an immense help for the conscious and far-sighted protection of Creation. For centuries everywhere, artisanship has supported a humanistic economy and even today remains at the forefront, a precious asset between art and technology. This is the philosophy of the Solomeo School, which teaches a contemporary reinterpretation of ancient crafts and artisanal knowledge.

CHANGES, DIGITAL, THE FUTURE

As Voltaire warns us in a masterful way, "If you do not accept the changes of your time, perhaps you'll miss the best part." Let's accept the changing world without fear: humanity has overcome dark and terrible moments, wars, famines ... Today we must manage digital in an intelligent and balanced way so that technology helps us without taking time away from our humanity.

We are present as a brand in over 64 countries, we're listed on the stock exchange, and still we are always thinking of how to grow gracefully to keep the soul of the company intact. To be credible, you have to be true to yourself. That means large enterprises must think in terms of a thousand years. To my esteemed friends in Silicon Valley, including Jeff Bezos, I've asked, "What can we design for humanity?" Let's go back to designing for a thousand years: having this kind of perspective stimulates genius and creativity, constantly renewing the growth of the spirit.

ALFONSO DOLCE

CEO @DOLCE & GABBANA

BEYOND THE CLOSET: MAKING DOLCE & GABBANA PART OF EVERYDAY LIFE

We certainly cannot ignore how the pandemic we are experiencing has generated an impact on many levels. However, crisis periods have always been invaluable occasions to switch off, reflect and start again, looking at the world with new eyes. In the near future, a greater ethical and sustainable commitment, a more sincere relationship with the customer, one that is more linked to a complete experience than to the sale of a single product, all lie ahead of us. We are constantly looking for ways to have a closer relationship with the public. At Dolce & Gabbana, that translates into the major events we have been organizing throughout the country for years. They represent an opportunity for visibility, enhancement and support of the local cultural, folkloric, enogastronomic and artistic heritage, which we have always regarded with admiration and respect.

I believe the winner will be the one who manages to create a strong marriage between the available products and that of real lifestyle experiences. We offer the Italian lifestyle interpreted not just through the use of needle and thread but also through the commingling with other worlds – that of food and beverage, for example – of which we are particularly proud.

Some examples are our partnerships with Smeg for household appliances, Fiasconaro for confectionery products, Di Martino for pasta, Donnafugata for wine, and Martini, with whom we have also created an actual physical experience, thanks to the bars and bistros attached to our boutiques. We collaborate with all of these brands known for excellence in the production sector. **This way the consumer can also bring the DNA of Dolce & Gabbana into their daily lives, not just to their wardrobe.**

The democratization of luxury should not be considered a penalty; on the contrary, it represents a great opportunity: that of being able to entertain a wider and more receptive audience, while sharing the brand values.

THE BALANCE BETWEEN VIRTUAL ACCESSIBILITY AND THE UNIQUENESS OF LOCALISM

The evolution of consumption, along with the pandemic, have significantly influenced the quality of the coexistence between physical and digital dimensions: today we talk about omnichannel. We believe, in this unusual period, that the balance between online and offline is essential and will continue to be so in the future. As an example, the DG Virtual Boutique Experience was one of the ways we responded to this new order, at a time when the retail experience was necessarily diminished, if not cancelled altogether. A way of shopping, midway between digital and real, which takes the best from both worlds: the accessibility of virtual and the irreplaceable warmth of the human relationship, guaranteed remotely by the support of a real salesperson.

Now, more than ever, it's necessary to protect and enhance the relationship between brands and consumers, especially at a time when the customer loyalty experience now occurs between both the boutique experience and that of e-commerce: two worlds that will become more and more entwined. However, the emotional experience remains dominant in the physical store, as it is the natural place that allows a stronger coexistence between the DNA of the brand, the sense of belonging and the individual customer. It will always be the real meeting point, because it's there that the human relationship between company and customer, which represents an irreplaceable added value for us, really takes place.

In 2015, we inaugurated a one-of-a-kind boutique project to help enhance these 'sacred' spaces. Each store is a unique space whose architecture reflects the prevailing character of the city. The uniqueness also continues in the differentiation of the product assortment, offering the international customer the opportunity to enjoy unique shopping experiences and to pick up ever-new local messages.

BREAKING NEW GROUND

Fashion has always moved faster than other worlds. Anticipating trends and predicting social phenomena are intrinsic character-istics of fashion. At the same time, it has also been in a hurry to redefine its communication and distribution tools, adapting to the world and the way we live today, hyper-connected and hyper-stimulated. The disintegration of barriers that has occurred, thanks to technological development, has also allowed brands to create a genuine channel of preferential one-to-one conversation with the end customer, from which they can gather feedback and points of view in real time. While this phenomenon is undoubtedly positive, the downside is that it runs the risk of the content being freely inter-preted, which can end up distorting the intended original message.

In order for the fashion world to thrive, evolve and continue to create, it's essential that it does not follow rules that constrain it; in the long run, following the beaten path deadens creativity and con-sequently business. Investing in the new generation, with particu-lar attention to new social and cultural phenomena (which mirror what is happening in society), is vitally important to keep that flame burning. The Dolce & Gabbana brand has always been a pioneer in this: it was the first to have bloggers in the front row at fashion shows, the first to want Millenials and young royalty on the run-way, the first to invite dozens of international TikTokers to discover the value of 'handmade.' It was also the first to use drones on the runway, when this technology still seemed futuristic. **Everything is about tracking down opportunities and taking risks; that's just how we evolve, in work and in life.**

KILOMETRE ZERO
AND CIRCULAR ECONOMY:
A MODUS OPERANDI FOR FASHION

Sustainability is an issue for which we must assume responsibility. It's of fundamental importance as it represents a form of ethical respect toward mankind, society and the consumer, who is more demanding than ever nowadays, and for the environment in which we live, which needs more special care than ever.

Unfortunately, this often takes the form of some corporate jargon within communication and marketing plans – today any activity must be labelled 'sustainable' to be socially acceptable – whereas in reality it's not just a theoretical concept but also a practical approach that has an extraordinary influence on the intrinsic quality of the product. There is a lot of talk about 'kilometre zero' and the circular economy in relation to the agri-food chain. We like to think that this could also be a *modus operandi* for the fashion section, where the 'Made in Italy' label can now also refer to the raw materials and processing techniques, not just the finished product. It's a virtuous approach that is worth the effort, even if it's not easy to maintain, due to the difficulty of finding the right raw materials, guaranteeing their quality over time and supporting their use.

GILDO ZEGNA

CEO @ERMENEGILDO ZEGNA

THE NEED TO RECONNECT WITH THOSE WHO NEVER LEFT

The world we live in today is radically different compared to less than two years ago. The pandemic has only accelerated processes that were already in place. We are witnessing significant changes that will stay after COVID-19: all of them have a common denominator that they bring to digitization. We have changed as individuals and we have changed as a society. This is particularly evident in the luxury fashion industry where disruption to trade, as well as the limitation of international travel and in-person experiences, has pushed us to rethink and reinvent concepts and ideas that have been a bedrock of our industry for decades. We must reconnect with our local customers in new and different ways. Creating luxury experiences through in-store appointments, digital showrooms and personalized digital services is key to fostering the close bond we have with our valued clients across our various markets while tailoring programs to local customs and preferences more than ever before. We saw an incredible success even during lockdowns, with no physical fashion weeks and events, with our collection presentations through digital fashion film formats as a true expression of creativity and a true evolution of products arriving to a much wider audience globally.

BEING A POSITIVE FORCE FROM THE FOUNDATION

In the post-COVID world, companies can simply adapt to changes or choose to be a positive force in driving these changes. At Zegna a responsible development has always been at the heart of our company. My grandfather Ermenegildo Zegna had a vision to create the world's finest textiles ethically and sustainably. But his dream was not limited to creating a fine product; he also wanted to make his home town – and the world around it – a better place, ensuring the highest quality products without compromising the quality of life for future generations. When he built our first wool mill in Trivero in 1910, he set us on a path of excellence and quality, innovation and a pioneering approach. Social and environmental responsibility

190

have been our roots for more than 110 years and this legacy continues to manifest itself in #UseTheExisting, Zegna's commitment to making the dream of zero waste possible. Oasi Zegna, moreover, has always been the centre of our sustainable ethos. It represents the place where everything started, where the philanthropic vision of the founder became reality through sustainable projects that tangibly involved the environment and the community. Zegna is the only brand that owns a natural reserve, 30 times larger than Central Park, located in Valdilana, Piedmont, where over three generations of the Zegna family have continued to nurture the green soul of the founder. At the beginning of the last century, Ermenegildo Zegna started an incredible program of reforestation, planting over 500,000 trees, taking care of the environment and the community. As a family, even before speaking as a company, attention to environmental and social sustainability have always been a fundamental value for all of us. Since 2019 Zegna is among the first group of signatories of the Fashion Pact, the global coalition of companies in the fashion and textile industry committed to a common aim of key environmental goals in three areas: climate, biodiversity and oceans. I think the fashion industry is trying hard to reach high standards in terms of sustainability; the way forward requires many more efforts, but this is the right thing to do not only because our clients demand it but, most importantly, because it's for the good of the planet we live in. The fashion sector is dependent on a number of natural commodities such as cotton, wool and leather, and for luxury companies like Zegna, the high quality of these natural materials is of utmost importance. For this reason, protecting nature – and the larger goal of pursuing sustainability in how we run our company – is extremely important to us, as it allows continued access to these materials.

A GROUP AS A PLATFORM: SOLID INTEGRATION MAKES ZEGNA DIFFERENT

Since its founding, the Group has evolved from a producer of textiles and menswear into a leading purveyor of luxury goods to clients from around the globe. At its core, the Zegna Group is built upon key pillars: heritage, quality and sustainability. The flotation that we have recently announced, planned at the end of the year on the NYSE, will allow the Group to continue its successful strategy while maintaining the Zegna family's control. Zegna is highly vertically integrated, making it unique in the luxury industry and allowing sustainability to be a focus at all times. This vertical integration, alongside its one of a kind 'Made in Italy' luxury platform, ensures the highest level of excellence in all products and allows Zegna to also serve some of the world's top luxury brands as a supplier. The Group is uniquely well situated in China, having been the first luxury menswear brand to enter the Chinese market in 1991 and is today among the most renowned brands in the rapidly growing Chinese luxury market.

The Group has an established platform for growth in the luxury space: after the incredible success of its 2018 acquisition of the majority stake in the American luxury fashion brand Thom Browne, the Group is ready to use the proceeds from this transaction to continue its M&A strategy. Zegna's ability to scale brand names and integrate them effectively into its global platform have resulted in Thom Browne doubling its sales since the acquisition. Zegna's management has capitalized on the unique strengths of the Thom Browne brand, namely its consistency and recognition, its younger customer base, its high digital penetration and its iconic collections. The success of Thom Browne under Zegna's management is yet another example of the Group's ability to grow through successful acquisitions and leverage its textile and manufacturing platform effectively by creating opportunities for integration and efficiency.

More recently, the Group has found new growth opportunities through the expansion of its corporate portfolio. Zegna has acquired a number of top-tier Italian manufacturers to strengthen its one-of-a-kind 'Made in Italy' luxury textile, clothing and knitwear laboratory platform. This platform, which brings together a number of Italian luxury companies known for their excellence in textile and clothing manufacturing, allows greater collaboration to further the growth of the Italian luxury market. It also allows the Group to deliver the highest quality in made-to-measure goods, as well as luxury leather accessories. Over the years, we have brought together a pool of manufacturers who represent the best in their fields, such as Dondi for jersey, Bonotto for technical and innovative fabrics, Tessitura Ubertino known for tweed and jacquard, and Filati Biagioli that we bought in partnership with the Prada Group. All of them have been able to embed technology, research and artisanship in their products. Lanificio Zegna is a pioneering wool textile development facility.

Italy has a wealth of capabilities when it comes to design, innovation and craftsmanship. The greatest challenge is to keep this wealth alive while artisans fight for survival in a world where size and speed are paramount. That's why we are the centre of luxury Italian craftsmanship, and our aim is to continue to give this incredible tradition a future. Beyond supplying Zegna's own brands, the platform is also the provider of choice for some of the world's most highly regarded luxury names.

The Zegna Group remains one of the last, great independent fashion houses, and the third and fourth generations of the Zegna family continue to lead the Group's successful strategy to this day. Becoming a public company underscores the success of Zegna's strategy of continuously focusing on the Group's brand equity while also continuing to build upon its heritage, its ethos of sustainability, and the unique craftsmanship that has made its name synonymous with quality and luxury around the world. Four generations of the Zegna family have contributed to this success by carefully balancing science with nature and craftsmanship with technology. Last but not least comes style. Zegna, as a mono-brand, has always been synonymous with luxury menswear. That's our commitment and our force as it highlights our consistency and our success. And while we strive to keep the pace with the changing habits and needs of our customers, both our Made to Measure and Bespoke services offer our clients top quality suits made just for them.

A UNIQUE DEFINITION OF STYLE (TO WIN TODAY AND IN THE FUTURE)

Mirroring the progress of our times, Zegna has transformed its very idea of luxury to envisioning a casually wearable category of clothing. A move away from utter formality, but not from a thoughtful sartorial approach, is Zegna's new definition of men's style that we call Luxury Leisurewear. A new style approach, and therefore offering, is what strengthens our global leadership in the luxury men's market. Moreover, the great success of recent collaborations such as with Jerry Lorenzo, Fear Of God, allowed us to legitimately talk to a new and wider audience, while maintaining the core of our client base and demonstrating the brand's versatility.

I think that the future of high-end fashion and, in particular, of Italian family-owned fashion companies rests on staying true to their identity and unicity; and at the same time, to always innovate, also welcoming the next generation. This is what keeps Italy going. In the end, it is about roots and it is about family roots. It is about respect for what has been created in the past, and the ability to embrace the future. The fashion industry in general is actually undergoing a paradigm shift which will present challenges to some brands and opportunities to other companies. We as Zegna Group see opportunities.

JOSÉ NEVES

FOUNDER, CO-CHAIRMAN & CEO @FARFETCH

DIGITAL TRANSFORMATION
AND DEMOCRATIZATION

I started 22 years ago as a computer programmer. It was only later that I arrived in the fashion world. My background in technology enables me to understand precisely the transformations that are affecting the industry. The main areas are in regard to the internet and digitalization. The fact is that these transformations aren't just about transactions, but the entire journey: how you find the product, how you obtain information and so on. In addition, there's the advent of fast fashion to consider. Along with digitalization, fast fashion has forever disrupted how the industry works.

It's easy to see the overwhelming acceleration that is happening today. It's also possible to see a strong convergence between industries: fashion intersects with music and food, for example. Furthermore, fashion has been democratized; in the past, it was impossible to get in touch with the big fashion entrepreneurs, characters remote from 'normal' people. Today, everything is just one click away; bloggers and influencers have enormous power. WeChat has the ability to influence any industry, even that of fashion. And finally, cross-cultural contamination is a phenomenon made possible by this accelerated scenario.

A DIGITAL PLATFORM
FOR HIGH-END

In some ways, fashion is an industry that doesn't move quickly. It does from the creative and trend point of view, but in terms of business models, it tends to be cautious. However, changes have occurred so rapidly that companies are still trying to figure out how to balance online and offline, and how to manage direct to consumer. Personally, I've always been fascinated by how digital platforms have been reshaping the world. In 2007, Net-a-Porter was a great success, as was Luisaviaroma. So, it seemed clear to me what the consumer's goal was, and I also realized that the industry didn't have a platform. In music we had Spotify, in hospitality Expedia and Airbnb, in entertainment there was Netflix, but in luxury fashion there was nothing similar. There were retailers that were trying to become platforms, but no one like Farfetch.

We created something the industry had never seen before. Instead of buying inventory from brands, storing it, managing it and then selling it to consumers, we simply offered an entirely service-based platform to customers, so they could buy what they wanted from the major boutiques and fashion brands around the world. For me, it was a truly simple idea. The execution was a little more complicated, but from the start I believed it was an idea that could evolve naturally. I thought the industry needed this, and I worked hard to make it happen.

THE PHYGITAL FUTURE

The convergence between physical and digital retail is what excites me the most. Despite the disruption caused by digitalization, 90% of transactions are still completed offline. We'll probably reach a point when they drop to 80% or 70% but the truth is, **new models need to be designed so that the charm of physical interaction can be integrated with the convenience of digital**. The physical retail experience will always be part of the magic of fashion, even in a post-COVID world.

We expect that our augmented retail initiatives, developed in the last three years through an exclusive technology partnership with Chanel, will become even more important for luxury brick-and-mortar, as the industry's leading brands try to optimize sales per square metre in a post-COVID scenario of lower in-store traffic. We look forward to unveiling the next generation of our solutions that will help physical retailers as they try to create pleasant and personalized shopping experiences in the 'new normal.' In the foreseeable future, we also plan to launch our revolutionary Store of the Future experience in our flagship Browns boutique. It will be an exciting demonstration of the capabilities we have developed.

The intent is to create new hybrids between the two worlds, leveraging an extraordinary customer experience, with personalization through data and so forth. I think personalization will become crucial in retail. Online it already is; if you don't use it there today, you have no hope. However, offline the industry simply doesn't apply it in the best way. From a consumer's perspective, the experience is very impersonal. Very often, there are no data streams. People enter the store and leave the store, without any data being collected unless a transaction occurs. Even when a transaction takes place, there is a poor connection between the different touchpoints within the customer journey. This is very important, and it's the basis of our Store of the Future, and it obviously requires giving the consumer the opportunity to opt-in and be recognized or not.

Farfetch's work will lead to brands benefiting from the real application of innovation connected to data and various forms of personalization. It's a huge challenge, which is why we have around 1,500 technologists including product managers, engineers and data scientists. This is what Farfetch is right now: a player that connects you in real time with the world's most beautiful products. And we'll go beyond this.

(OPEN) INNOVATION

I'm sure there is a lot more to do in this industry and even more room for innovation. At Farfetch, we're absolutely convinced that open innovation is a key factor in terms of competitive advantage. **We definitely see the importance of incubating and accelerating ideas, and we work a lot on innovation with the start-up ecosystem. We believe in utilizing open innovation to face our challenges.** How far can we push our limits? We're working to scale and have expanded the platform into related sectors such as fine jewellery and watches, and children's fashion. Our goal is to become a 'curated platform,' a high-level marketplace.

SUSTAINABILITY

Speaking of open innovation, we collaborated with a start-up called Upteam to design a Farfetch 'recycling project.' The result exists in the resale platform called Second Life, and it's one of the ways we are demonstrating our commitment to a sustainability strategy. The site allows consumers to sell their designer handbags as second-hand in exchange for credits that can be spent on the site. We hope this will change the attitude of Farfetch consumers by encouraging them to recycle old accessories. In addition, we've developed a partnership that is the natural extension of our resale program. With Thrift+, an on-demand donation service for second-hand clothes, we've connected our customer base with an innovative service that improves the donation experience and has a positive impact; we give good-quality clothes another useful life by supporting various charities. Through the partnership, customers can order a branded Thrift+ and Farfetch donation bag online and select the charity of their choice.

Another partnership we've created is the one with Good on You, a rating system for ethical shopping within fashion, that lets you make informed decisions about the clothes you buy. Good on You researched and spoke with experts to arrive at a simple and intuitive rating model to determine how much impact a brand has on three key areas: people, planet and animals. The system scores each brand on these issues and generates a general rating that ranges from 'We Avoid' and 'Not Good Enough' up to 'It's A Start,' 'Good' and 'Great.' The 'Positively Conscious' tag on Farfetch products uses the Good on You rating system.

MARCO BIZZARRI

CEO @GUCCI

THE DIGITAL ERA

The digital revolution has been the biggest change in recent years, but it hasn't had the same impact on all companies. For those working in fast fashion, technology has offered significant opportunities, particularly in the back end, behind the scenes. However, for luxury, where there's still a big focus on human intuition and the ability to read and interpret sociocultural changes, the impact has been on the front end. For companies like ours, the opportunities have gone far beyond just e-commerce: digital has allowed us – especially through social media – to articulate our vision of beauty, openness and individuality to a much wider audience, in particular, to Millennials and Generation Z.

HIC ET NUNC

I think one of the most delicate tasks for managers has been, and still is, fully understanding the parameters of this revolution, and how to make their company's approach consistently uniform. Gucci has developed an innovative way of creating multi-channel involvement so that the experience is always seamless, whether the user is on a smartphone or entering one of our stores. We always talk about growing revenue but growth starts on a personal, individual level; it's a learning curve that never ends.

When I was given the opportunity to take the lead at Gucci, I was ready; only a few years earlier I wouldn't have been, there wouldn't have been a good alignment between the contribution that I could have made, due to experiences and skills that I've since gained, and the direction that the company and brand could have taken. To achieve outstanding results, there has to be a perfect match between the career stage of top management and that of the company's life cycle. And the arrival of Alessandro Michele's creative direction was both timely and fortunate, as his contemporary interpretation helped accelerate the growth of the brand in the last five years. The results show us that we have truly benefited from market globalization and the spread of digital tools. We were able to create a proprietary language that is unique and global.

THE IMPORTANCE OF
CORPORATE VALUES

Values create value. In our case we chose to offer, in seeming contrast to technology's disruptive advance, a focus on traditional values such as joy, respect, sharing and belonging. And underlying that is a base of sustainability, understood as a respect for people, coworkers, suppliers and the environment.

It was five years ago when we decided to set this new course for the company and the brand, based on these values and a new concept of creativity. I'd like to say that we anticipated the success we enjoy now, and that it's the result of a thorough strategic plan masterfully executed, but in all honesty, I admit that's not the case. We started with an idea, pursued it with determination, took risks, made mistakes and never gave up. When I took over the company in 2015, I had half the direct reports I have now, so I made many of the decisions myself, assuming the risks, because that was what was needed. Today, many of my reports would be perfectly able to fill in for me at any time. They are capable of making important strategic decisions for the company even without my active involvement.

DISRUPTION AND
CONSOLIDATION

Coming back to the subject of lifecycle, we have dedicated these last few years to disruption, experimentation and innovation. And we risked a lot. We can't think about dedicating the next five years to more disruption; now we need to consolidate, get things in order and create efficiency. Which is not easier, actually. There's a risk of sitting back, repeating what we know how to do and what has worked, and then entangling ourselves in the bureaucracy of processes. This is contrary to a world in which it's essential to remain dynamic, to be contaminated, to be receptive to the outside world and reinvent oneself continuously.

MARKETING AND CREATIVITY

The cyclical nature of fashion is a well-known factor, and we're not immune to it. So we try to remain relevant to our audience by working with a lot of data and putting that at the service of our creative director. We've nurtured a team of data scientists and marketing technicians who work behind the scenes to measure our performance accurately and who share insights from around the world with our creative team. From this perspective, **social media is a precious resource as long as there's talent to interpret the findings. There are faint signals in society and in the market. And very few have the gift of knowing how to grasp them, interpret them and send them back in a way that's relevant to the public.** There's also the risk of getting sucked into the vortex of social networks, becoming a slave to the instant feedback that users are accustomed to now, as that risks clipping the wings of ideas that, although they might not break through initially, could spread and become a trend. Social media is fantastic for spreading a language, but it also has the power to destroy your brand if it's badly managed.

E-COMMERCE FOR WEBROOMING

For us, e-commerce is essential, in that many people view our product catalogue online before going to the store. The webrooming aspect is real and growing rapidly. E-commerce is our first showcase. Also, from a communications perspective, it's often our digital campaigns that are the starting point rather than vice versa with print. We've done a lot of work on our site and there's more to do still. We've modified it several times to find its role and to enhance the content. I'm thinking back to what I said on social media before, that it could become a new sales channel rather than just being online communications. In China, where the consumers are profoundly different, and thanks to super-apps, we're already embarking on a path that will lead to a new role for these platforms. In Asia, they pretty much skipped the 'print generation' and are much more technologically advanced than us, so the speed of acceptance to adopt these solutions is completely different.

THE IMPORTANCE OF PHYSICAL STORES AND THEIR DIVERSE ROLES

In an interview I said, **"Millennials don't go to stores because they are boring." I want to say something quite specific: shops are very important, and I don't think they will disappear. They won't disappear if within them there are people who are capable of providing added value for the customer: if they are knowledgeable with advice, call you, treat you like an expert but also like a friend, making suggestions and never hard selling.**

Obviously, not all stores are the same. In Soho, New York, we were able to create a certain type of store with Gucci Wooster because we had the idea of a destination store in mind. Tourists don't pass by; they go there because they really want to. And why? Well, because there's the book, the 3D experience, but most of all because none of the kids who work there come from the retail world with direct sales experience. They are all artists, designers, fans of the brand who know how to bring brand storytelling to the people. What has to be clear is the situation regarding the store space, why it's there and why it exists.

If you build a store for tourists, like the one in Via Montenapoleone in Milan, for example, you need to shift the focus from experience to transaction. Because a tourist in Milan comes in with a clear idea, with a photo of the product from the e-commerce site, and they want that product in the shortest possible time. Even an airport store, for example, has to be purely transactional. It's all about knowing your customers, how to recognize them by the places they frequent and the motivations that drive them, so that it's possible to offer them the most relevant experience.

SUSTAINABILITY: BETWEEN FEASIBILITY AND 'CALL TO ARMS'

Second-hand, circular economy and sustainability are all very important issues for Gucci. And we've moved ahead of many other players. Today a start-up can be created carbon-neutral but for an organization like ours with an existing supply chain, it's impossible without a time frame of 50 years. We are an industry that pollutes. That's a fact. But it doesn't mean that we're not investing in innovation to address this. There just isn't any technology yet that allows for sustainability and quality from a scalable point of view. When there is, we'll use it.

In my opinion, the problem around sustainability is that we are trying to achieve it with insignificant and never really decisive enough actions. The United Nations is ready with a project – there is an in-depth article on *Bloomberg* – that, with $300 billion, would stop global warming for 20 years. In our global economic system, this amount is nothing. If every company agreed to 'stop' polluting instead of waiting for technology to reverse the trend, then something would be done for the planet. In November 2019, I launched a challenge to all CEOs to try and make this a reality.

INNOVATION, START-UP AND READINESS FOR CHANGE

We're working on the innovation side and investing a lot, both with former eBay and Facebook consultants, and through H-Farm, who every three months selects start-ups that we can sit down with to find out what opportunities they can offer us. **We make plans and invest. And it's interesting not just because it gives us a competitive advantage but also because it stimulates in-house thinking.** The reasoning is that if we need to continually reinvent and question ourselves, we need to breathe innovation all the time. I probably do it more to cultivate this mentality than for the economic return.

THE FUTURE OF
THE INDUSTRY

It's been obvious from the beginning, unfortunately, that the COVID-19 crisis would be an epic challenge; an event that happens once in a century. One issue that the virus has brought to the forefront is the protection and preservation of the supply chain. In light of this, working with an existing infrastructure, we launched the 'Sviluppo Filiere' (Supply Chain Development) program. It has given companies in the Gucci supply chain, of which there are many branches that are fundamental to the brand and made up of SMEs of exceptional skill, the ability to rapidly obtain credit at favourable terms. **Gucci's dream of beauty is an Italian dream that shows the world the power of imagination and the incredible skill of Italian manufacturing. Without those Italian artisans, there would be no Gucci. Supporting them was our duty.** It's a crucial issue for the industry: fashion is the second-largest manufacturing sector of Italian industry, involving over 60,000 companies and about 600,000 workers.

COVID-19 has signalled the end of a system. A system that, in my opinion, would be wrong to revive. The present and the future are different. It's a new era of corporate responsibility: mitigate the environmental impact, commit to transparency, equality and respect. Fashion is an incredibly important industry for Italy, which has never really been able, in my view, to truly create a 'system.' I would really like it if Italian fashion came out of this pandemic with a greater sense of belonging. And that institutions started listening a little more.

In regard to the commercial aspect, in order to gain market share, you need to focus on truly impactful projects. It must be said that even if it's good to have your head in the clouds, you have to have your feet firmly planted on the ground. So, keeping an eye on the small things (which may become big one day) is always a good idea.

I don't know if it will be luxury that does the buying or if luxury will be bought, but there will be contamination with the world of media, entertainment, food, etc. It will be a very challenging fusion of sectors.

REMO RUFFINI

CEO @MONCLER

CUSTOMER-CENTRICITY
AND DIRECT TO CONSUMER

The world is in constant evolution and fashion has also been the expression of this evolution, of this continuous change, that's becoming incessantly faster and faster over the years.

Let's start in 2003, when I acquired the company. My first opportune insight, that came from observing people and their behaviours, was that we had to make our product relevant for everyone. Instead of focusing on a small target, we had to find a way to talk to those over 55 as well as the boy who wears one of our garments when skateboarding or the 20-year-old girl who wears one to go to a party. Over the years, the way of communicating with consumers began to change, as numerous new methods for interacting with customers were created. Companies like ours that had begun in a world where the product and sales network mattered, suddenly realized that that model no longer existed, and that it was essential to focus on the consumer, to talk with them and understand them.

Then, as it happens in life, a revelation hit me. I remember that in 2017, as I was walking down a street in Tokyo, all of a sudden I realized how outdated our business model was. That's when the idea of Genius began. In 2018, we launched this project that entirely changed the company by moving from a traditional strategy that followed the seasonality of fashion, to a new model of more daily interaction. Previously the supply chain followed an order: orders were collected and then there was a wait of six to eight months for delivery. With Moncler Genius, we began to have focused projects and content every three weeks, and a constant relationship with our customers.

The real revolution is that we wanted to speak even more directly to the consumer. **We were looking for continuous contact and began to solicit more customer feedback, establishing a different tone of voice and content so that we could interact better with them.**

In this context, e-tailers have become more of a dialogue channel for us. We are very selective regarding sales channels so, from that point of view, e-tailers didn't attract us very much. But we saw that an editorial project on these platforms performed incredibly better than one in a traditional trade publication.

Underlying everything is a clear awareness that it's essential to build a strong brand and feed a dream. In a digital and global world, with so much content and stimuli, the brand is a very powerful asset and we must continue to invest in it, even if these actions don't always offer short-term results like product promotions might do. In the long run, the difference is appreciable. Making these changes a reality has been difficult. In some ways, it probably would have been easier to launch a start-up, because not only did we have to set up a new business, but we also had to change an existing corporate culture.

DIGITAL-FIRST MENTALITY

Let's take a step back. In 2003, Moncler was 100% wholesale and had $40 million in sales. Over time we reorganized the company, moved to Milan where it would be easier to establish a retail culture, and started opening mono-brand stores. Today we're evolving even more. And now we're in another phase: that of omnichannel, where retail, wholesale, e-tailer, social media and e- commerce are all part of the same customer journey and where the digital world is quite often the first point of contact with the brand. It seems simple, but it's another powerful revolution: you need to engage consumers first through digital and then they'll choose if and where to buy. Until recently, companies were mostly focused on store furnishings and locations. That's fine, but it can't be the priority. The cultural transformation means that now companies create a business model starting from e-commerce. Today it's essential to think, first of all, about the digital ecosystem when designing products, deciding on the collections, choosing what to put in the store, how to design the furnishings, how much to produce, etc.

FUTURE PROSPECTS UNDER THE BANNER OF TRIAL AND ERROR

The biggest mistake would be to think that the consumer will want just digital experiences. We have to contaminate physical with digital in a completely new mix that originates with digital and at the same time redesigns all the experiences of the other channels. Digital experiences can never replace the emotions that accompany a real experience. But I also believe that the real experience will radically change and be greatly influenced by digital and the tools it will provide to sales assistants.

The uniform business model for luxury is boring and has had its day. Without Asia, the sector's growth is small or next to nothing because that's where the new consumers are. In mature markets, there's a struggle to create innovation and energy. **To return to growth, there's a need for uniqueness, excitement, more experimentation, the embracing of trial and error in a systematic way and the creation of new business models.** For years we'll try different directions before returning to converge on a new model. If, from a communication point of view, we're arriving at a model of interaction with the new consumer, which in my opinion works, we now have to devote the next few years to understanding how to sell in a new way. The acceleration brought about by the pandemic requires equally fast reactions, flexibility, ability to redesign paradigms, and interpret a new, albeit still uncertain, concept.

CONTINUAL IMPROVEMENT

Changes are never easy. For example, if I think of our transition to the Genius model, nothing was immediately and completely perfect; we made some mistakes. We had no industry benchmarks to go by.

Along the way we simplified our tone of voice and language because it was too complex when we started out. We understand now that communicating throughout the world requires dealing with different cultural nuances and channels. You're faced with markets that react differently from each other, made up of men and women who sometimes have contrary shopping habits. We haven't yet 'fine-tuned all the notes,' but we're happy to be in a company where there's been a cultural transformation. We hear it from our employees, our collaborators, people in the stores. I believe that Genius is still a powerful and modern project today. Modern, also, because in its DNA there is a sense of evolution and openness to the world.

The social, economic and emotional impact of the pandemic will lead to a new start that once again begins with observing and listening to the consumer. It's difficult to say if everything will change or remain the same, because what we're experiencing now will be forgotten and quickly filed away.

I've always found my answers in the streets, observing people and their behaviours ... but maybe this time I might also find them while surfing between a website and social media, analysing online interactions, once again trying to decipher the message the consumer is sending us.

DAVIDE DE GIGLIO

CO-FOUNDER @NEW GUARDS GROUP

EXPERIMENTATION, CURIOSITY AND MISTAKES ARE AT THE CORE OF SUCCESS

I was studying architecture but I already had a passion for fashion and I knew that I would never become a good architect. I took the decisive step when helping my professor to design new stores and concepts for the fashion company Replay. "You have to do fashion," he told me, finally convincing me to take this path.

I started with 'Vintage 55,' which I began importing from the United States. That's where I learned a lot about the logic of fashion, not fashion with the capital 'F' of Italian designers, but the one I liked, vintage, used jeans. The decisive period was the return to Italy, with Vintage: nine very interesting years, but also full of mistakes. It is important for me to point this out. I risked bankruptcy after opening stores in Shanghai, Hong Kong and Paris and found myself in a liquidity crisis. First I sold to a fund that Sundeck then acquired, which I joined. Then I started at the bottom again and invested in Golden Goose. This series of events was important for me to understand the logic behind the acquisition of brands, launches and synergies between companies. In a few years I had created 10 brands.

My curiosity has always pushed me to look at 'the best' and to try to understand how they think and act. For me it is the French, and I followed their lead to create a company that would unite all these brands, the 'New Guards' holding company. The name comes from a Business of Fashion article that defined Marcelo Burlon, Virgil Abloh and Shayne Oliver, designer of Hood By Air, the "new guards of street style."

THE VALUE OF THE CONTAMINATION OF THOUGHT AND IDEAS

As I said, curiosity has always been a significant part of my path. I joined OVS because I wanted to learn more about large distribution and fast fashion. At Vintage I was selling T-shirts for $100 instead of $4, everything was different there.

Opening up to new ideas and solutions is fundamental, as is comparing one's thinking with that of others. I cannot fail to mention and thank Remo Ruffini, for example, who inspired me by telling me about his experience with Abercrombie & Fitch. Friends can bring real turning points in a person's life: it happened to me with Marcelo Burlon. It was Marcelo who made me understand that social networks would become the new media, everything would pass through mobile phones and the Facebook Era would apply to business. This has had a huge impact on my business choices; again, at Moncler I met the Art Director Francesco Ragazzi who inspired another brand, Palm Angels. How did it all start? Showing me his photography book, 'Palm Angels,' which I was very impressed with.

I see the importance of contamination in teamwork. Growth with my partners was aided by me being the oldest in my group, because I tried to help them avoid the same mistakes I had made. I made sure they were focused on what they did best, and what I didn't know how to do. For example, I was good at making product, but not at communicating it. On the other hand, they are masters at it, each in their own way. The bulk of it happened thanks to them; I had the intuition of bringing them together.

The fourth Industrial Revolution has led to a new way of doing business (especially in the COVID-19 era). I remember during the pandemic when we made our first 3D digital collection and the team was made up of people living in Australia, New Zealand, China, Africa ... I will never know them, but I have worked with them. And that's what I find fascinating. I think we live in the fourth Industrial Revolution. It is very interesting to explore these worlds, even if we basically do 'rags,' as some call them. But the fact of contaminating, taking, reworking and giving again allows you to explore through cinema, music, arts, and this is what the company continues to do.

New Guards began without its creative directors, intent on touring the world all year round. Ours was an unconventional way of working; we created collections on WhatsApp, the only tool that allowed us to share our ideas. With WhatsApp we also opened the first Off-White store in Hong Kong, only meeting in person at its inauguration. And this is what I mean when I say acceleration.

STRATEGY MEANS CHOOSING

At 35, after having already made a career, I felt old, no longer able to make a product for 15-18 year olds. But I didn't want to make a product 'for old people.' First important choice: with the help of a partner,

Claudio Antonioli, we started selling our product directly, thinking like a big brand. Second choice: we decided to not distribute it across sportswear stores, but in the most premium ones in the world, such as Colette and Antonia Milano, selling T-shirts from €150-€300. We also started 'seeding,' i.e. we sold our product to a small circle of 'friends & family' before launching it. By doing so, we managed to put our T-shirts on Jay-Z, Madonna and many in the entertainment world. It is something that helped us go viral, to become a product that you see but cannot find; thus creating a strong attraction toward the brand. This huge growth was achieved in just three months. Off-White is also a matter of choices. With Virgil Abloh we decided to open the first stores of different brands in cities such as Hong Kong, Manila, Kuala Lumpur, Melbourne. Why? Because we follow our followers, who are searching for us and who are the most active on our social pages. In this way the consumer is rewarded, and this is how 'loyalty' is created. This way of working continues today.

With New Guards we have never worked with any magazine. Another choice. We have always enjoyed using new media, always trying to be innovative. In 2020 we have grown in double digits, despite what the world has gone through in this period. This was possible once again thanks to the ability to adapt and change strategies quickly.

VALUABLE PARTNERSHIPS TO ACHIEVE INTEGRATION

I have a dream: to become the first fully integrated company in the world, a company that does everything in-house and manages the entire process. I find it's fundamental to think about how fast we have to be to keep up with the times and adapt as much as possible to better penetrate the market. That's why I joined Farfetch.

With them we started a new way of creating a product. We conduct interviews with our consumers, we take the inputs that arrive and we reintroduce them, reworked, into the market. We often say that ours is always a dialogue and never a monologue. All this was possible thanks to our industrial partners with whom we created 'companies within companies,' going from a lead time of 2-3 months for each type, to building a product in just three weeks. In 2020 New Guards created around 200 collections across all brands, focusing on making small collections rather than collections of 2,000 pieces that we knew would not hit the spot.

A STIMULATING FUTURE AND TECHNOLOGY AT THE SERVICE OF IMPROVEMENT

How do I see the future? I like to think of it a certain way. I look at my two children, who never turn on the television, unlike me who couldn't wait to watch cartoons. They always use the iPad; they use YouTube and those kinds of channels. I see different approaches, which will also take place in fashion.

I see a very interesting, stimulating future. What I can say is that technology, which does not yet have a great impact today, will have it tomorrow in a lot of aspects. Let's take the example of a cotton shirt: no matter what brand it is, it still remains a blue and a white thread, not too different from a 100-year-old product. Within 10 years, however, that shirt will be made from sustainable cotton, with chemical properties that will tell us when it is dirty and how much longer it may be worn. A nanotechnology that will not change our lives, but that will communicate with our devices and always be at our service.

I don't think we're going to have our shoes made in-store. We will go there for the pleasure of living an experience, because our devices will have already scanned our shoes in 3D and sent them to the company to be manufactured. I see personalization as the strongest desire that we can satisfy: we will do everything in our form and likeness, because we do not want to be standardized. We may all want that cotton shirt, but we want to have the chance to bring a personal touch to it. We are moving in this direction, toward something more refined, subtle and complex than sewing a letter to a garment. Today we are studying biocompatible products or super technological and sustainable sneakers that will disappear in a few years without a trace. I don't think, or at least I hope, that technology will only be used to make more profit. I believe it will be put at the service of something cleaner and to help us improve. Working with many young people helps a lot in appreciating this, because they are even more attentive and understanding toward these matters.

LORENZO BERTELLI

HEAD OF MARKETING & HEAD OF CORPORATE SOCIAL RESPONSIBILITY @PRADA S.P.A.

ON DIGITAL TRANSFORMATION

Quite often within companies, the process of digital transformation is managed in a non-strategic way or it's interpreted incorrectly: digitalization is assessed in relation to the new technologies and processes that their use requires. Instead, I consider digital transformation to be a real cultural change, one which I would say is complex. And as such, it requires new logic and processes, particularly for companies that started before this era and who have a harder time dealing with these changes.

Digital transformation concerns individuals first of all and is created through discussion and inclusion. Some companies have made the mistake of creating dedicated teams, designed as independent and vertical nuclei in charge of organizing the change. These teams can help accelerate the transformation process in a first phase, but they have to be integrated into the organization to allow a solid and lasting change to take place. Communication itself was one of the areas that suffered the most from the attempt to graft these vertical nuclei, of course with some difficulty. Digital, a term I don't like, really signifies transversality for me.

In the fashion sector, in particular, some companies that had individuals with entrepreneurial intuition and the ability to interpret societal changes were able – before the digital age – to thrive. But when the talent wasn't there, it was hard to make marketing and strategy choices that aligned with market demands. To a certain extent, today's digital revolution allows us to bridge the gap generated by the inability of managers to perceive trends, thanks to actual market analysis, which lets us understand the actual trends that are going on. I think that in our industry marketing plays a fundamental role: acting as a 'funnel' to collect data on the one hand, and on the other hand as a 'lens', to interpret and analyse it as best as possible.

At Prada, we recognize that we were late in starting the digital transformation process compared to our competitors. And we also created a specific team for the first phase. When I started here, as the manager of this role, I really tried to accelerate its complete integration so that we could reach a real cultural change, of mindset, as I tried to explain previously. In addition, we immediately gave ourselves the goal of making each decision measurable, so we could verify and better understand internally every small strategic step we took. The collection and analysis of data lets us share 'objective' and strategic information with the various departments in the company.

DIGITAL VERSUS CREATIVE VISION

It seems to me that marketing, especially in the fashion sector, must help in a functional way, as a tool to aid in avoiding making mistakes. It doesn't replace or drive creativity. **Every competitor can potentially have access to the same information and data and can develop solutions using them, but then in doing so companies may end up offering very similar products. So then where does innovation reside? You have to give creatives the room to make mistakes and ... create.**

For example, the engagement rate is a highly valued metric as reported by consulting or financial companies, but it's really just an indicator as to whether content is aligned with the demands of the public. In an industry like ours, isn't it more important to dictate the pace, rewrite the rules and from time to time appeal to a new audience?

SOCIAL ISSUES AND SUSTAINABILITY

Fashion and luxury are processes of social influence, generating both a feeling of belonging and exclusion at the same time. They are expressions of individualism and hedonism. Humans seek beauty and affirmation through the expression of the self. I'm convinced that people will always want to feel at ease with others, and their desire for ways that allow them to express a message, to communicate who they are, will always endure.

Will the sector be able to embrace a new paradigm, defined by less production (and lower revenue) as a source for the creation of new value? In my opinion, vintage and second-hand are interesting opportunities, challenges to disrupt the seasonality of fashion. And beyond that, the circular economy will be an important test for companies in the sector, as was digitalization.

MICAELA LE DIVELEC LEMMI

FORMER CEO @SALVATORE FERRAGAMO

GLOBALIZATION AND LOCALIZATION: THE BALANCE BETWEEN BRAND AND MESSAGES

Globalization and the strong acceleration in the spread of social media have led to a general standardization of the various markets in the luxury range. These phenomenon have created leverage for those groups that, having greater resources at their disposal, have been able to make better use of the new channels and tools that the digital world has offered. The consequence has been an even more pronounced polarization of the market's attention toward the global brands.

Ferragamo has moved slightly counter to this trend in the last decade, centralizing the design of collections and delegating strategy implementation at the local level. This has led to a fair degree of autonomy in the various markets, but also to positions not always aligned between the two, with the negative consequence of not being able to fully benefit from the halo of more global initiatives in terms of commercial impact. We need to work toward cohesive images, not by standardizing the offer, but by appearing consistent and unified in terms of the customer's viewpoint.

That is why in the last two years **we've focused on aligning our strategy and positioning around brand values, while maintaining respect for the distinctive local markets: a strong DNA that must then be interpreted to move in sync with the local culture.** Since COVID-19 prevents people from moving freely, it's even more necessary to enhance the geolocalization of messaging and product offerings. I'm referring in particular to Asian markets, such as that of China, which require us to be extremely respectful of the local culture, without losing the brand equity. Chinese consumers, when travelling in Europe and the rest of Asia, have had the opportunity to try diverse customer experiences, and they have been driving pre-COVID product offerings in other regions for years. China is a model that can be followed in other regions when developing initiatives and experimenting with new communication channels.

In general, I see a tendency to revert to geolocalization. It's important to be able to have a dialogue with customers in every market, regardless of the channel. We need to be even more respectful of customers, determining how to engage them in the right way rather than expecting them to come look for us. This forces us to rethink the approach in an even more focused and personalized manner.

SUSTAINABILITY AS A LEGACY AND A NECESSITY

Our sector is known to be one of the most polluting and consequently the sustainable approach is no longer optional. Mobilizing for a better future is imperative. But the world of sustainability is extremely wide-ranging (focusing on the environment, people, biodiversity, etc.) and for this reason companies must take a gradual and well-thought-out path toward it. The company must understand its impact and then establish priorities and a sustainable strategy.

Our founder used recycled materials to make his creations right after the war: basic materials such as leather weren't available on the market, so he invented the cork wedge. This is a reminder that we have an important legacy. Our collections are progressively integrating responsible and innovative materials, focusing on sustainable production processes that pay increasingly more attention to the issue of circularity, whether it's in the choice or reuse of materials or, where possible, in the reuse of products. It's a path that aims to make the production process ever more virtuous and one that can't be separated from the projects that relate to the entire supply chain.

Ferragamo has been active in sustainability issues for years and has a track record of excellence with respect to initiatives launched and milestones achieved, whether in the field of CO_2 reduction or in the social or cultural arena. For example, we've joined the Fashion Pact, but we are well aware that sustainability is much more: it's a process that must be embraced by the entire organization, a way of thinking and acting, that must be fully integrated with the strategy. All luxury brands should make this their aim, possibly through collaboration.

THE CONCEPT OF ARTIFICIAL HUMANITY

The world of luxury makes it possible for dreams to come true. By their definition, dreams have an emotional connotation, which starts with the product but is amplified by the experience and the evocative elements of the brand. At a time when physical accessibility to collections is restricted and yet the time the consumer has available has grown exponentially, the digital experience acquires a specific relevance as a point of contact with the brand and the product. And right now, for practical reasons, it's also fundamental for the conversion of the sale. For a brand, the online store is the world's largest storefront, the most visible store window. **It's a space where a mix of editorial and product content enriches the value system and brand strategy.**

I believe that human contact is and will remain a key point within the luxury experience. In my opinion, technology and digital are meant to unite spaces and facilitate an experience that would otherwise be limited, but I don't see them replacing physical experience. I like to think of it as artificial humanity.

A MORE INCLUSIVE DREAM

We talk about democratization, but I prefer to use the term 'inclusiveness.' **New generations feel a need to evaluate their affinity with brands to decide whether to engage in a shopping experience. I believe the attitude of exclusivity has had its day and is a distancing element; the more inclusive brands can be, the better they will be able to connect with consumers.** This doesn't detract from the fact that the product can and should remain of the highest quality and excellent workmanship. Quality, artisanship and excellence will remain as top-of-mind values for consumers and, in fact, we are seeing these qualities grow in importance in the post-COVID period. More and more they are a distinctive but at the same time unifying element for a brand like Ferragamo.

Brand recognition isn't dependent on approval. After all, the other side of democratization simply means popularity. However, it's crucial to start by defining the purpose, in order to begin projects that facilitate the accessibility of the brand, such as those of co-branding.

THE INFLUENCER AS A TOOL BUT ALSO A MODEL

The way brands communicate has changed and must continue to evolve. Ferragamo is working on moving away from a unidirectional approach toward a more conversational one. We need to move toward less self-referential messages, we need to listen to the audience and understand how they read the brand from the outside, and be ready to react, even if it comes at the cost of receiving criticism.

Influencers are a useful tool for all this. Their role has changed and today they are true editors. **They've become a media in their own right. They obviously influence the audience, but they also guide the brand, interpreting some of the needs that the audience is looking for, but which the brand itself can't grasp. And they play a central role with respect to the geolocalization of the message.** Influencers have taught us the significance of implementing a holistic approach, including communication, sales and customer engagement. Mega, macro, micro and nano influencers all have an effect on the follower base in different ways and, as a result, their actions must be evaluated with respect to the channel as well (for example, Instagram needs a different approach than TikTok, while other social media have local relevance which brings us back to the subject of geolocalization).

Our vision sees communication shifting from just traditional channels (I also consider social media to be within these) toward a multilayer strategy: more channels for more messages aimed at different consumers. It's important to be able to be transversal, in terms of the social media audience, as well as those customers more accustomed to the physical channel. And it's from this point of view that I see the choice of some maisons to remove themselves from social media or to completely reposition their pages: it's a choice to look for the audience in other places, as would happen in the physical world. Therefore, creating a fluid journey that allows us to be truly transversal and capable of acting on multiple levels becomes fundamental.

POST-COVID

COVID-19 has accelerated scenarios that were already on the radar. What should be emphasized is the speed of this event, which requires brands to redefine their priorities and the use of their resources. Some trends will consolidate; others will return. A fluid customer experience (phygital), an increased level of service, the search for convenience in the shopping experience and a more digital and less-traditional way of communicating are all aspects that I'm sure will strengthen as distinctive components, just like sustainability.

We talk about the customer-centric approach as a fundamental element in having a successful strategy and staying in the market. However, the point is that defining the right strategy involves increasingly complex concepts and moving pieces. I believe new professional roles will emerge in the world of high-end, not necessarily sectorial and vertical but instead more transversal. The biggest challenge will be the evolution of companies from traditional organizations and ones that are focused on results, to those that are managing all aspects in sync, with the right skills.

I'm equally sure that people are eager to start travelling again and enjoy the experience of shopping during their trips. This will generate a recovery in travel retail and reward brands' localization choices. Post-COVID is the real challenge for all of us.

GABRIELE MAGGIO

CEO @STELLA MCCARTNEY

DIGITAL AND CULTURAL TRANSFORMATION

We've gone through a period of rapid and radical changes. Digital has spread in a pervasive way, modifying both the external aspects of the brand such as its way of communicating, as well as the internal aspects of the company, such as operations and workflow. Specifically, it has meant companies making significant cultural changes as they move to more collaborative and interactive models. Now, managers in our industry, who are for the most part still tied to pre-digital dynamics, need to demonstrate humility by listening to young talent who really understand these new dynamics. That's because in a very short time we've gone from newspapers to Instagram and from Instagram to Tik-Tok. The era of exclusive runway shows and interviews is over: today's market is global and digital with all the pros and cons that it entails.

THE 90S REVOLUTION

During these years, some prominent brands were able to switch gears and rewrite the rules of the category. The leap forward happened thanks to the adoption of logic that went beyond the sartorial dimension to confirm the industrial one. It's the addition of business dynamics (merchandiser, production chain, etc.) added to that of creative flair, which, thanks to globalization, has allowed these prominent businesses to grow on an international scale. It was a real revolution many businesses weren't able to face and that resulted in their exit from the market.

SPEED AND OFFER OVERLOAD

We've put more products on the market in the last five years than in the previous 50. The consumer is constantly demanding new things, both within the brand offer and outside it. On the one hand, this has led to the creation of new businesses; on the other hand, it's pushed those already working in the industry to broaden their offer. The time it takes to spread a message has shortened and everything is instantaneous now. So the product life, in addition to the constantly changing offer, is worn out by the same communication, which inevitably ends up reaching our audience even before those goods are actually available. Today, the same fashion shows and runway events aren't just for the buyers; now they've become global communication events.

SUSTAINABILITY AND TRANSPARENCY

Today everyone is being asked to have an opinion on sustainability. It's becoming an increasingly important issue because the market is urgently asking for it to be addressed. Consumers today want to hear how companies are paying attention and committing to issues regarding the climate, plastic, the oceans.

The fastest, and shall we say, less strategic initiative that companies can implement is compensation: continuing to operate within the status quo and, for example, planting trees to offset carbon dioxide emissions. But at Stella MCC, we've been pioneers in the field of true sustainability. Back in 2002, we tried designing a more circular and less capitalist model. Incredible work has been done, including with suppliers who've been educated on these issues and pushed to find techniques to develop sustainable products. However, the market is still in a theoretical stage, studying these models, because to be truly sustainable you need suppliers and a network of partners who are also qualified in the same regard. And for that reason, it's not possible to guarantee total transparency in the production process, as no one has complete control over the entire supply chain.

Nowadays the market is fairly aligned in terms of sustainability. It's the new normal. And for this reason, we're trying to set the bar higher, with tangible solutions. We're working on a new model, which might even have a different name, to get away from the industry's standardized information. This 'sustainability 2.0' is an expanded concept that, for example, also affects the rights and wellbeing of workers, a set of rules and principles that we want to promote externally. **We want to foster this culture and make a real impact on the entire sector, industry and governments. We feel that right now there isn't a real spirit of collaboration and we want to overcome this. Now it's time for action, not just more talk.**

NEW MODELS
OF CONSUMPTION

New purchasing models that touch on the theme of sustainability are also emerging. I'm referring to developments like resell or rent. These markets will experience exponential growth in the coming years. The limitation I see, at the moment, is that they can't be implemented directly by businesses.

REDUCTION IN
CONSUMPTION

As a result of the massive limitations caused by the COVID-19 pandemic, consumer habits have changed much faster than expected. Now the aspects of service and convenience have become important ideals for driving sales; hence, the huge growth of the digital channel. **I don't believe that 'degrowth' – described in some scenarios as the only viable solution that won't deplete the planet's resources – is something that companies can ever promote. Instead, it will be the market that will shift demand in that direction.** However, it must be remembered that purchases, especially in our sector, are deeply influenced by an ideal standard or benchmark to which, consciously or not, we aspire. It's only by working on this ideal and resetting it that a rebalancing of consumption can take place.

DIGITAL AND
PHYSICAL

In the future, I see more major changes. We will certainly move toward a consolidation of digital tools and a rebalancing of relationships with the physical ones. In this sense, the store will evolve from a simple vessel for products to a place in which brand experiences are built, a manifestation of the brand's culture, world and ideals. To maintain a perception of high-end one must still be present in particular shopping streets and invest in certain ways.

THE VALUE OF CREATIVITY

It's unrealistic to think that our industry will remain forever in a bubble where the designer's creative idea controls everything. It's necessary to adapt and apply management rules typical of other sectors, such as market research, customer profiling, etc. These terms, which are becoming familiar now, couldn't be mentioned five years ago; they were an anathema. Everyone thought the designer was the marketing. While this could be true if you have very few clients, the market has become global and the logic to remain competitive must change. In the new context of post-COVID, the contribution of creative ideas will be even more important for the success of the brand. With reduced spending power and changing priorities within consumers' lives, the product will have to be constantly more unique and special. In this sense, understanding the big picture of your target audience is increasingly important.

THE ROLE OF THE BRAND

In this scenario of great change and transformation, we're also working very hard on the brand, what it represents for our clients and the values on which it's based. This is essential in order to not be blown away by increasingly rapid purchases and consumption. The brand is always unique and special as long as it represents clear and meaningful values. For this reason, translating these values into products and a communication language is essential for success, as is a coordinated transversal strategy for products, communication and distribution. The company must always speak the same language in every market touchpoint.

DOMENICO
DE SOLE

CHAIRMAN @TOM FORD INTERNATIONAL

DO NOT CONTAMINATE
YOUR DNA BECAUSE OF A TREND

It may sound contrarian, but I just think the last five years reshaped nothing. The factors that really count are still the same. Among these factors are the quality of your product and your DNA. For every brand, DNA is fundamental. You can't change that. At the end of the day, you have to be who you are. People talk about fast fashion; the same companies do fast fashion and they do it very well, but it doesn't mean that companies that have a very clear DNA have to rewrite their history and change themselves to follow a trend. Here's a good example: everybody thinks that everybody wants to be informal now. The reality is that that's not true at all. The trend was already there, and greater informality was some-what accelerated by COVID-19. The United States recovered faster this summer than other countries and people have gone back to buying suits. Ladies are back to buying evening dresses and cocktail dresses. I see people going back to their old habits, so brands can't feel a sense of urgency to change.

Trends can be accelerated but reality is a long-term game. I'm an old man, have been around for a long, long time and I've seen this movie many times before, in which people say: "Oh my God, luxury will never exist again because of something." That is not true. If you go into caves inhabited 10,000 years ago, you see hieroglyphics or paintings of women with earrings and bracelets and necklaces. As is human nature, people want to look better and that's not going to change, ever. It may take different forms, but we are designed to want to look better; to make ourselves more attractive. I've seen this drama unfolding and then immediately luxury brands have picked up and have become stronger and stronger. So, I think there is genuinely a big demand for fast fashion, which is totally fine for some brands. But for a company at that level, with the kind of products we produce, fast fashion is a different business. You can't delegitimize your company. You can't be everything to everybody.

Another example is see now buy now. Certain brands did try to do it. It didn't work. It's hard to change some of the ways the industry works because there is a whole system that exists in terms of design-ing, presenting the show, production, etc. Luxury fashion is a very complex industry. Certainly, there are changes; people tend to ask for things faster, but it also depends on what they ask for. If I want to buy an airplane, I know it's going to take some time to get it out of manufacturing.

COVID: A MANAGEMENT LESSON FOR COMPANIES

Companies survived COVID-19. Every company did business online very successfully; the industry changed its way of working and survived. Look at the reduction in travel and consider the related cost savings. Working in a pandemic-world taught many a lesson about running companies in a very serious way and being thoughtful about actions and costs. Part of the reason Tom Ford did so well is that we are really mindful about spending in a wise way and think seriously about the ROI. The credit goes to Tom. He was a real genius, changing the industry in the 90s when business was dominated by families and there was a totally different view of management. COVID-19 has been a scare for companies because overnight they went to zero-cash. Suddenly, all the stores were closed, and you had huge fixed costs. That was a lesson for everybody in the industry.

I think it's going to take some time for a full recovery because there's still a lot of uncertainty. Europe is the origin of luxury and is a strategic area. People travel from abroad to buy in Europe. When you're going through the Champs-Élysées, normally most of the customers are Chinese. Today, we still don't know when the Chinese are going to be allowed back to travel freely (and shop) in Europe.

DIGITAL TRANSFORMATION WON'T ELIMINATE STORES, BUT IT WILL BE FUNDAMENTAL

Digital transformation is unbelievably important. It is something that changed all our lives. I still vividly remember a presentation made by one senior manager at Gucci saying: "One day, somebody will shop by themself in the middle of the night." We knew it was coming; it was something we talked about for a long time and was in the making, which has been somewhat accelerated. Now, I keep hearing that brick and mortar is dead: this is nonsense. It's just silly. People still like the social part of stores. A lot of people like to go to stores, like to touch the product and be familiar with it. So, are digital and e-commerce going to become more and more important? For sure, but the fact is, now that the worst is over, digital and physical will coexist.

E-commerce is a small piece of business now, but it's growing dramatically. The issue is that you can't just say, "It's a small percentage." Yes, it's small, but you have to consider what has happened in the last five years. I really do believe that e-commerce has become very, very important. I think it's critical for companies to really fund and support their digital space. It's literally an investment, because it's going to take some time. Online commerce shares will grow for every brand, going from being minuscule, almost non-existent, to huge.

Does e-commerce change the way we sell luxury? Amazon can deliver items in one day and that's ok. When you sell groceries, for example, you can't offer a three-day delivery, of course, but our industry is different. In the case of a luxury good, it really depends on the high quality of design, the uniqueness, your own point of view and the fine craftsmanship of the product. People expect that this supreme quality is beautifully made with the benefit of time. People understand that there's a difference between a grocery store purchase and ordering a beautiful dress that costs $20,000.

THE COEXISTENCE BETWEEN CREATIVITY AND MERCHANDISING

In this industry, there's a creative part that is critical. Let me say: it deserves 100% of the credit for success. The critical part of Tom Ford is Tom, not me or anything else. At the same time, everybody knows that every company works on the basis of the so called 'merchandising grid.' The designer shares their message through fashion shows, but then the company has to work within certain parameters: the performance of the products, the needs of the market, and so on. A designer's view and brand DNA are the foundation of collections, but the bulk is done according to the merchandising grid. It means taking into consideration the fact that a region doesn't appreciate the colour of a handbag and so there is a need to recolour it. Creativity is the key driver, but there is still a part which takes a more rational look at business.

SUSTAINABILITY: A COMPLEX AND CRITICAL SUBJECT

Sometimes things become 'religious.' Suddenly, there is a new religion and people talk about it. I think most people don't know what they are talking about when it comes to sustainability. For me, sustainability is a wide concept: it is not just material, but it is also about working conditions, an ethical way of production and so on. At Tom Ford, we do everything in Italy to ensure that people are properly paid, that the working conditions are just, and that workers have proper benefits and holidays. It's not just about using recycled materials; there are a lot of components to sustainability, and we try to comply as much as we possibly can. The issue is that it takes time.

I think that people are going to be more thoughtful about production. Thank God I was born in Italy. I love Italy and I look to it for production because I can't pursue anything less than the best quality for Tom Ford. Companies must protect their sources. Here's a lesson: be very careful to make sure you have adequate supplies.

THE FUTURE OF
TOM FORD

Tom Ford? It's very simple. When we started the company, Tom said: "We want to be the first true luxury brand of the 21st century." We started at the beginning of the century, after we left Gucci, and since then that's what I've been doing, that's our mission. We are still a very young brand. Brands can live 100 years (look at Gucci), they keep going and can last forever, so we are still in a very initial phase. However, we are proud of what we have accomplished in a very limited period of time, even after facing several crises that we survived, such as the collapse of the financial system in 2008 and now COVID-19. Our vision is to continue expanding the company. We already have a presence in Asia, but it is relatively small compared to other brands.

We have an incredibly strong product. And again, we are who we are, and Tom is Tom. We are not going to change: we have to continue doing the best with our designs and offering the best quality. Stay the course. It's really as simple as that, and that's what we plan to do.

This is our belief, and that's why we have great customers. At Tom Ford, we know we have some of the best customers in the world and we are happy about that, because they are our influencers. We don't want to pay people to wear our clothes; at the end of the day, if you start doing that, it's no longer an influence, it's advertising. In my view, the best situation is when your customer comes to your store to buy your product and proudly wears it: for me, that's the most effective way to advertise, the truest format of advertising.

JACOPO VENTURINI

CEO @VALENTINO

CHANGE IN FASHION:
FROM DIKTATS TO IDENTITY

Fashion, by definition, has always been linked to the habits and customs of society, and therefore adaptation to social evolution and historical periods is inherent in its concept. Fashion embodies society in a precise moment of history, reflecting its ways and often anticipating its attitudes.

In the past, the message was decidedly taxing: the series of trends were short, seasonal; each new style cancelled out the one that had preceded it. The glorification of consumption left no margin for the collector; the value of the creation plummeted after six months. Accessibility was limited to a few mono-brand stores in large European and American cities and to department stores. But in Europe, and particularly in Italy, there was also an osmosis and diffusion that found its way into the scattered multi-brand boutiques. In this context, the retailer was not simply a merchant, but a selector, an educator and a persuader, guiding the customer and becoming a fundamental link in the whole chain. Through boutiques, fashion reached even the smallest of towns, facilitating aesthetic modernization. But it was fashion that had been filtered through personal vision and therefore only partially represented a maison's entire line and the full expression of the brand.

The new century, the new millennium and the technological revolution – including the explosion of social media – have made fashion, or at least its aesthetic messages, even more accessible and therefore more useful for a global audience. Now its diffusion is widespread. **Brands are now the publishers and megaphones of their own aesthetic, cultural and corporate values. In this sense, there's the possibility of creating longer waves, unrelated to the season and connected to the brand's own value system. In this new scenario, brand identity becomes more relevant along with a renewed importance of the individual** – it's no coincidence that we talk about the 'me' generation, transgenerational and all-encompassing demographics.

HUMANISM, 'PEOPLE FIRST'

In this context, the customer is no longer the final recipient of messaging that she accepts passively, but rather an active subject, moving through an immense sea of offers as if she were an editor. In light of this, the approach we want to take toward the customer has changed, and is still changing. 'People first' is our belief: the people who approach us, whether they are customers, colleagues or friends, must first feel attracted by a shared vision and virtue. Our goal is to make it so that they feel like individuals and at the same time part of a larger community: the Valentino Community, in which they are reflected, not only for their purchases, but also through the use of the content we produce and will increasingly produce in support of the company's vision.

Intimacy is important: as a maison, Valentino welcomes, embraces, includes. The values on which the brand rests are all encapsulated in the definition 'Maison de Couture,' and the strategy and vision are based on these.

A further layer must be added to this. Given the ever-increasing interconnectedness of the world, **there's a particularly strong necessity to reflect the multiplicity of social and cultural backgrounds for greater awareness and sensitivity. The enhancement of diversity and inclusiveness is one of the most important issues and another driver of change, evolution and growth, along with sustainability and, in particular, the idea of giving back.** The thinking we follow is circular: it comes from the desire to give back, not only to nature, according to what we take, but also to the neighbourhoods where we operate businesses and stores. In this way, we create economic micro-worlds, local but interconnected through Valentino, in keeping with our latest idea: to enhance the identity of the individual while building a community. We work constantly on ethics and sustainability, because today the production of beauty, in every sense, cannot be separated from a responsible attitude toward people or the environment.

AFFINITY
OF VALUES

The centrality of the individual has also led to a reconsideration of the role and rituals of the store as a filter and a meeting point with the customer. Today's customer enters a boutique by choice, not by diktat, attracted by an affinity of values. Then the staff acts as a brand ambassador, accompanying the customer through their client journey, tailoring it to the individual: a unique experience which takes place in the store, and comes with its after-sales service, as befits a maison that has couture – understood as creativity, uniqueness, personal attention, an eye for detail, in products and its manner – among its values. The work we are doing at Valentino is one of criticism and discussion, not a monologue; the distributive intermediation of selected clients has value, and allows a dialogue with a market in continuous evolution and with actors who, having experience with a multitude of brands, are an important resource for this discussion.

INNOVATION IS
TRADITION

The digital world doesn't just offer a space to disseminate the brand's output, be it product or content. Digital is now part of reality and therefore must be included in the business growth statements, thanks to e-commerce and new online and digital business initiatives that are emerging. This in no way implies abandoning stores; quite the opposite. For Valentino, the store will increasingly become a special place to discover the collection and, in general, beauty. It's the place where customer attention will be so high that the customer will feel like a guest of the maison, in a home that offers not just unique shopping experiences, but also entertainment linked to the creative vision.

CREATIVITY AS A CORPORATE EPICENTRE

Creativity, human capital and collaboration are the drivers of Valentino's future. The idea is to make the maison a cultural reference point for the international scene; and not only a fashion culture, because today the barriers between worlds and disciplines are more fluid. Creativity is the source of everything: it must be preserved, protected and enhanced on a daily basis. It must permeate the entire company without losing its magnificent energy, but instead increasing it through the contributions of all the actors who accompany it, through to the final customer. People, internal and external, are the other great asset of the company. We are working on the concept of identity from countless viewpoints, putting people and creativity at the centre. Business ethics, along with the value system, create the culture, and this is the basis for implementing the strategy.

So, fashion continues to be an exercise in the habits and customs of society, and right now, at least in our case, the exercise is more about the future than the present. Here and now, the road to tomorrow is being drawn, without resetting codes and without betraying aesthetics.

JONATHAN
AKEROYD

**FORMER CEO @VERSACE
CURRENT CEO @BURBERRY**

FROM THE BRAND DOMAIN TO THAT OF PRODUCTS

I began my career at Harrods, so I was lucky enough to start in a retail environment, meeting all the different up-and-coming luxury brands when they first started off. Twenty-five years ago, there was a cluster of 'must have' brands. They were the brands that people followed and bought when they introduced themselves to the world of ready-to-wear luxury. And then they became loyal to that brand. In my memory, when I started off, it was a very brand-led business. A world where you followed a brand, or a number of brands, and you stuck to those, and you were proud to wear that label. A world driven by a wholesale model, where department stores shaped the industry and pushed certain products over others.

I suppose the first phase of change this industry had was the explosion of this cluster of luxury brands as they became more important in the global landscape, finally expanding into Asia. And then we witnessed a second phase when the industry became more about being creatively driven, and anything that was fresh and new and exciting the press was happy to promote and push to the fore. So new brands were able to grow. I'd say that in the last 5 to 10 years it's been tougher for the newer more creative brands to build their business from start-ups and grow to the point of competing with big houses like Gucci, Versace, Prada and so on.

For me, the biggest challenge today is to move from a brand-lead communication driven world – where it's very much been about the label and being loyal to the brand – to the world driven by product innovation. Today the product is more important than ever. And it's because of this that marketing has replaced traditional PR in the industry. In the past, it was a lot easier to sell a bag or a suit just because of the label and the loyalty to the brand. It was the era of the so-called 'carryover,' and a product could have a lifespan of about 18 months. Now it's a lot shorter and you have to have new strategies to cover its lifecycle. Brand loyalists have become less important for the business. Think about sneakers: everyone used to buy theirs from the traditional footwear brands. Now there are a number of brands that have built their businesses around that accessory.

From my point of view, this is dangerous because they are overly reliant on one SKU, one style. These changes have happened alongside digitalization. High-end fashion was so traditional in what it did, but today everything that was once considered as tactical now has strategic importance. The world is more complicated, you can't just rely on the product, as I mentioned earlier – you need huge talent in design and merchandising and then again in pushing it to the consumer.

COVID-19, AN ACCELERATION FACTOR

It's been a very interesting, challenging year. We've learned a lot from it after starting to work from home and after the critical stage of closing stores, resetting all the budgets and then figuring out how to go forward. The first thing was how we reacted on our digital channels. We decided to stop any promotions and start thinking about wellbeing and welfare. We decided in the end to focus on Versace Home. And so we shifted it that way, and it was the right thing to do, to be sensitive in communicating to people to stay at home and take care of themselves there. We are a family brand and have a history with home products, and so it was well received. And we had a huge uplift on our home products – particularly dressing gowns and robes – obviously through e-commerce.

Unfortunately, we had to close our retail network, but online sales have been incredible. Going into the last quarter of the year (2020), we are in a better position as far as brick-and-mortar is concerned with sales starting up again. From a retail perspective, we are back to normal and have noticed the postive impact e-commerce has had. COVID-19 has really accelerated our digital business, accounting for 25% of total sales in Q3 (2020), in the countries where we also operate online. This success was a learning curve for us and has pushed us to excel in how we leverage the huge amount of traffic generated by our sites and manage it through CRM. I wouldn't say we are the best in class yet, but we are pretty good at doing business online, and now we'll push ourselves to be the best.

PHYGITAL BALANCE

We're a global brand. Our name is well recognized. All the same, we see there's room for improvement in elevating the brand. Today we have 200 stores, and we think there are still opportunities to open others and expand our physical network. Connecting this to what I said before, you can understand that **while we unite physical retail and digital, I'm strongly convinced that investment in the first is more important and crucial than the second.** I'm speaking for brands like Versace. We're going to continue to develop and invest in our retail infrastructure and talent, especially in Asia. The considerations around physical retail also depend on whether the consumers are predisposed to use digital and the market situations in some countries.

THE INDUSTRY REVOLUTION

Everyone in the industry has been debating, for a while now, about how things are going to change and what has to change, whether it's the calendar that we live with, or how we show the collections in a different way, plan how to go to market and so on. All issues that seem easy to handle in theory or talk about. And what's interesting is that many of the people who were trying to reset were journalists and wholesale clients. A lot of brands are cautious about this; a few are stepping forward with radical changes. The industry will have to make changes and improvements, but ultimately my feeling is that the calendar, the collections and other foundations of fashion aren't going to radically change. In the end, the model is the way it is, for a reason, mainly to do with the industrial and organizational sides of the business. They take time and planning. But from a communications angle, the growth of e-commerce will mean paying more attention to consumers than buyers and retailers, due to the increased direct exposure of the brand.

CONSUMER AWARENESS

I'm totally convinced that consumers are aware and will make increasingly more thoughtful choices in the future. Each of us has started to rethink our way of life and why we consume. For brands, working in terms of sustainability is a necessity. Because of the way things have changed dramatically, we've been pushed to consider the lifespan of the product. Now it will be a lot longer. To be honest, we wouldn't have been brave enough to do this if it hadn't been for COVID-19. We made a decision to start our markdowns six weeks later than we normally would, and we gained from it – in margin – and we didn't lose any sales. And for each brand it's important to be able to extend the full price period. For this reason, I expect to see an extension of the product lifespan and a more conscious management of off-price. Brands will not be led by the wholesale channel any more.

Sustainability will certainly be a driver in the future. Brands like ours enjoy a high level of engagement with a young clientele, so it's super important to be aware of what they demand. They are looking for transparency and fairness within our supply chain. Certainly nobody can question what we stand for; we've always been about things like inclusiveness or women's empowerment, for example. How we source or develop our supply chain is a journey that we're on and we've still got work to do, but it will be fundamental, in fact mandatory, in the future.

CONTROL AND INTERNALIZATION

Let me say another thing about control. I think that for us, and big brands, the management of digital information and change has to be direct. **It's important for us to be driving it because otherwise third parties would end up controlling crucial parts of our business. I think one possible direction for big brands will be to acquire the necessary skills internally.** We're definitely investing in this way for our direct digital business.

FOCUS ON
BRAND STRETCHING

I see a choice on the horizon for luxury brands. They'll focus on their core business or aspire to become a lifestyle. I think we have been 'too lifestyle,' to be honest. We've been too broad. We've had to clean up that area because when you do too many things it's difficult for people to understand what you excel at. I think that expanding this lifestyle concept can be counterproductive for a luxury brand and that's the reason we've abandoned this path.

We're a fashion brand and we need to communicate this clearly. Diversifying too much brings confusion and lack of clarity. So we are focusing more. There are numerous brands that are very strong in accessories, and they should continue that. They don't need to expand into other categories.

I think the concept of 'focus' will be very important in general. Our ambition is to grow our core business in volume. Our business is nicely balanced globally and our reach is incredible; we have over 30 million followers on social channels. So our goal is conversion.

FEDERICO
MARCHETTI

FOUNDER @YOOX NET-A-PORTER
FOUNDER @YOOX

CLIENT-CENTRICITY

There's one thing I am very proud of. All the most important milestones that have brought us this far have been reached thanks to an element within our DNA: client-centricity. Putting people at the centre, understanding them and anticipating their needs has always been our mission. I've always identified with the customer.

The adventure started like this: I wanted to access one big digital store where I could wander around undisturbed, choose, rethink and buy articles from vintage to the most exclusive names, all in one place. I began then, in 1999, imagining there could be a new link between supply and demand, that of digital. Since then, I've helped bring many luxury brands closer to their customers through the internet. In 2006, a year before the iPhone was launched, I had a feeling that mobile would change the world forever. I began thinking how it could become a shopping tool in people's hands. Today, more than half our purchases are made through mobile: my intuition turned out to be true.

SUSTAINABILITY

We also anticipated people's needs with regard to sustainability. We'd already launched YOOXYGEN in 2008–2009. We didn't have a marketing objective; we wanted to develop a company-wide initiative that would take into consideration all our employees, moving away from company cars using gasoline or diesel, adopting recycled material for our packaging (ECOBOX was the first sustainable packaging in fashion e-commerce), and focusing on renewable energy. We also set ourselves goals, publishing a sustainability report starting the first year we went public. When the merger happened, with our wealth of accumulated knowledge, we were able to bring our best practices to Net-a-Porter. Thanks to this, today we not only have YOOXYGEN but now also NET-SUSTAIN, the Net-a-Porter division focused on sustainability.

We were also the first to stop selling furs. Once again, this happened because we were paying attention to customers. After conducting a survey, we realized that the majority of our customers didn't want us to continue selling them, and so we decided to eliminate furs from our sites. These are very delicate choices, of course. **At the beginning, being sustainable costs more than not to be. But we felt it was the right direction for our people, our customers and for the community. You can do it if you're an entrepreneur with strong vision, ethics and morals.** In many other situations companies have complex processes that preclude actions, even virtuous ones, that they would like to make.

SOCIAL ROLE

For us, sustainability isn't just the environment. We're working on The Modern Artisan project with The Prince's Foundation, the charity founded by Prince Charles of England, one of the leading, authoritative and authentic figures in this field. The partnership was designed to provide young designers and artisans with project skills based on data analysis and the tools needed to excel in the contemporary digital scenario. We have created a collection focused on sustainability and the value of artisanship, with the collection simultaneously on sale for the first time on all four sites of the group, with the aim of raising funds for The Prince's Foundation. It's interesting to note that the logic in this case was opposite to the normal route: it's an Italian design and an English production.

We also have some long-term projects in place, such as youth education. Through our Digital Education Program, we inspire new generations, especially girls, to pursue technological career paths, thanks to the support of our partners, including the Fondazione Golinelli in Bologna and Imperial College London. Since 2016, YOOX Net-a-Porter's Digital Education Program has reached over 10,000 children and young people, of whom over 50% were girls. One of the most interesting projects is definitely the one on coding, in which the participants plan a drone shipment from a warehouse in Italy to one in Dubai. We believe that the internet is the new *lingua franca* and that's why we're helping the new generation learn it, with the aim of educating the innovators of tomorrow.

INCLUSIVENESS OBJECTIVE: GENDER EQUALITY

We're also working a lot on gender equality. I'm involved with an Australian project, started in 2010, which today includes more than 200 influential men, CEOs and top managers – Male Champion of Change aims to create widespread gender equality that has a positive impact on the economy and society. Within this, I'm a founding member of the Global Technology Group, working to put these intentions into practice in the field of technology. On Women's Day 2020, part of the MCC program was to launch an internal initiative called Sponsorship Program, which aims to increase the representation of women in senior leadership positions, in an industry where traditionally men are at the top. Some of the group's senior executives will sponsor Women in Tech, helping women advance in their professional careers and develop new skills by sharing their expertise.

HUMANKIND AND TECHNOLOGY IN THE COMPANY'S DNA

In my opinion, the foundation for the future rests on the collaboration of humans and robots. In the last 20 years, we've always tried to find a fair balance, asking ourselves how much it made sense to push innovation, robots, algorithms, automation, or instead, how much to try to improve and safeguard the talent of human beings. This vision is already summed up by our name. **YOOX is the DNA of humanity, expressed by the male and female chromosomes, which both encompass and govern the DNA of technology, expressed by the binary code.** In general, I think that AI and big data analysis will help us to build increasingly personalized customer services and perfect the shopping experience.

Let me give you some examples. The first is AI Stylist. We asked ourselves: is it possible to teach taste to machines? The answer was yes. We started from our greatest asset, our images. We were the first to digitalize fashion, establishing ourselves as one of the largest production studios in the world. For us, product photos are not just product; they are data to be analysed. From here we began to teach style to a neural network, incorporating our 20 years of experience in curating and styling, supported by our extensive visual database. We were then able to develop AI Stylist, combining customer insights, the talent of stylists, the climate, the calendar and countless other elements to create a curated selection of products and content. Our personal shoppers use this tool to propose clothes to EIP, our best customers. Used in this way, AI doesn't replace the human touch, but it does improve the ability of our people to do their work.

The second example is 8 by YOOX, our proprietary brand 'powered by data, designed by humans,' which we use to arrive at product development starting from data and not from intuition. By doing so, we don't compete with our customers' designers.

The third and last is YOOXMIRROR, a project that has changed the way customers try on products. With this solution, people can try on garments virtually, mixing and matching while using an avatar. The system uses sophisticated algorithms to detect visual elements (colour, pattern and shape) within a product image while the deep learning network extracts product characteristics to select alternative items, showing which ones work best with each other. Finally, virtual reality technology can adapt to selected items on a 3D model that combines AI with the unrivalled knowledge and experience of YOOX's merchandising team.

As far as visual recognition is concerned, we are the most advanced hub in Italy. We have many agreements in place with Italian universities. We just recently signed one with the research centre of l'Università di Modena e Reggio Emilia to work together on an AI and computer vision program for the fashion world.

Research, innovation and technology will be the pillars for the future development of our industry. **But when everything has been done with data, 3D printing and then delivered by drones, I'm convinced (and also glad) that the most luxurious label will be 'Made by Humans': real luxury will be those things that are handmade by people.** Even if it's delivered by a self-driving flying car.

Let me finish with a quote, even though I don't usually love them, from the philosopher Luciano Floridi: "The computer plays chess better than we do, but knowing how to play chess is not the reason that makes us exceptional, perhaps it is because of the desire to play it, the fact that we would like to win, or that I play worse because I'm playing with my niece, and I want her to win."

THE MODUS OPERANDI OF YOOX NET-A-PORTER

To best describe our work philosophy we've created a formula: $C2C + O2O = EC^2$.

C2C stands for Content to Commerce. Content has been fundamental since our sites were created, but now it's essential. You can't connect with the client if you don't engage them. With YOOX we do this by focusing on our most innovative aspects such as the smart mirror, while at Net-a-Porter we have a more editorial slant. Some brands are just starting to talk about content; we were created with it in mind and that's why it's a fundamental asset for us: we've never been a product catalogue, we're a platform to inspire customers. And numbers in hand, we're the best at it.

O2O signifies Online to Offline. In this case, we're referring to the integration of the online shopping experience with the physical retail space. In 2006, again way ahead of its time, we launched the Online Flagship Stores division to establish e-commerce for many of the leading fashion brands and subsequently all the omnichannel services, which then evolved into the Next Era model. The first to implement Next Era was Valentino and it was a great success, particularly in Europe and the United States. Armani joined in July.

How does it work? We connect the principal stores in a region to the warehouses. This way, customers all over the world can access more products and can choose where and how to shop.

Product availability has increased by more than 300%, the possibility of being sold-out is rare and more than a third of the customers have received products they couldn't have purchased in the past. As a result, the customers are very satisfied and purchase frequency has greatly increased. **C2C and O2O added together create the shopping experience that customers are calling for now, and deliver what we call e-commerce squared.**

FRANCESCA BELLETTINI

CEO @YVES SAINT LAURENT

ELEMENTS OF CHANGE

Fashion always plays a part in the natural evolution of the world around us. Sometimes it reflects changes, but oftentimes it anticipates or provokes them, driven by the creative tension that characterizes it. Among all the factors, digitalization has made the biggest impact in the last 10 years, as it's no longer confined to just the e-commerce business but has permeated every area of the company, both in relationships with the employees and operations, and also in how we communicate externally.

Compared to 10 years ago, operating in a sustainable manner, trying to reduce the impact on the environment, has become a fundamental issue and has created a strong push for change; equally important are the focus on people and the building of experiences instead of simply selling products. Then there are always unpredictable economic and political factors, temporary or lasting, that force us to remain alert in our thoughts and agile in our actions so as not to lose sight of our long-term goal or compromise the brand position. All of this is often uncontrollable.

That's why we focus so much on the factors that we can control in any given scenario, so that we can deal with things as best as possible. **What has not changed, and must not change, is the role our sector plays in creating emotions, and giving people the chance to dream. Consequently, creativity remains central. If it were to vanish, fashion would no longer have a reason to exist.**

AGILITY AS A
BASIC REQUIREMENT

Our approach to development is balanced, aimed at maintaining an equilibrium with product category, geographical area and distribution channel. **The results are the consequence of a coherent vision that is embodied at every customer contact point, from the product to the stores to the communication strategy.**

Particular attention is paid to local clientele in every country, because this allows us to be less affected by changes in tourist traffic, and to speak to every customer first of all on a local level and then stay relevant globally. This strategy has proven to be particularly suitable in an era where circumstances are encouraging domestic purchases. It's essential to be agile while maintaining a broad awareness of the medium- and long-term objectives, flexibility and execution speed. We've worked hard to build a solid foundation on which to base our future. I strongly believe in creating a clear organizational structure that can evolve over time in order to facilitate change rather than hinder it, always conveying the brand's values.

THE HUMAN FACTOR

We have focused a great deal on people (employees, customers, stakeholders) to create a fitting emotional brand experience for each point of contact: in the company, in the store, in the way we communicate, and to do it authentically. Because of this, we are paying particular attention to our employees, providing them with the appropriate tools so that they can do their jobs to the best of their ability, in all areas of the company, so our customers can then participate in the unique experience that Saint Laurent offers. To achieve our objectives, it was essential to create a corporate culture that supports creativity, building an organization that places it at the centre of every process and the entire brand strategy.

At Saint Laurent, our starting point is creativity when developing strategy, and not vice versa. This is possible when you have the privilege of working with a team that understands the importance of this principle and supports it, and respects the values of the company; a team made up of people with passion and determination, evolving, growing and not limiting themselves with a fear of change, with Anthony Vaccarello (Creative Director) leading the way.

FUTURE PERSPECTIVES

We're always attentive to what's going on around us, without letting this create panic or fear, instead working to anticipate as much as possible what could compromise the success of our strategy. At Saint Laurent, the primary objective is to remain relevant by continuing to express the brand's values in an authentic way through innovation and incomparable quality and style.

Thanks to the implementation of a coherent strategy in terms of product, distribution and communication, the brand has built a solid foundation on which to continue its development. The execution of the strategy will continue to focus on growth that is balanced within the various product categories, markets and distribution channels, increasing control over the supply chain in order to preserve the relationship with the consumer.

Of course, what remains key is to continue to ensure the highest level of customer service through unique and desirable experiences. Above all, we will always strive to create desirability, without which luxury becomes a commodity. To do this, the competitive advantage will be the ability to hire and retain talent. Taking for granted the value of the brand, and that it must never be diluted and should be protected without compromise, people are and will remain the factor that makes the difference.

Conclusion

"It is not enough to be born.
It is to be born again that we were born."

———

PABLO NERUDA

In the first part of this book, we focused on five forces that originated well before the COVID-19 pandemic and that have contributed to redesigning the fundamentals of the high-end fashion industry. The **acceleration** produced by the technological and digital transformation, which over the years has become increasingly pervasive to the point of creating a process of **hybridization** between the physical and digital worlds that we have defined with Luciano Floridi as *onlife*. The expansion of the phenomenon known as **disintermediation** (with the dream of the internet's founding fathers becoming a reality in many sectors) has generated forms of neo-intermediation and new concentrations of power that raise important questions. The rise of environmental and social **sustainability** as essential parameters for the actions of fashion companies, on par with traditional metrics relating to economic sustainability. And finally, the process of **democratization** of the desire for high-end products, the result of the combined effect of factors such as globalization, the rapid spread of trends characteristic to the infosphere in which we are immersed, and the need for companies in the sector – often listed on the stock exchange or part of international financial holding companies that are themselves listed – to increase their customer base and therefore their profits.

The global pandemic that has afflicted us has caused an unexpected intensification of all these trends. It has pushed people and businesses into forced digitalization, suddenly making urgent a series of actions that had long been possible but for various reasons (in some cases legitimate) had been subject to procrastination, as if they had to do with a future that remained permanently near. This enormous wave of migration toward digital is not so much relevant in itself but part of a wider process that leads people and businesses to overcome a series of psychological barriers in the use of technology-enabled tools. It means that there will be many more customers ready to buy clothing and accessories without actually touching them, accustomed to electronic payments and conditioned to postponing the gratification of the purchase given the wait necessary to receive them.

This will prompt many more companies to make critical decisions with respect to their online presence, direct and/or brokered by multi-brand sites. And this will produce further effects on the afore-mentioned five forces. Questions about the role of actors between brands and customers, the environmental and social impact of the system, and the dynamics of democratization, whereby products lose desirability if they are too accessible, but gain value if they are desired by a wider audience, will become even more compelling.

Ultimately, the dimensions of space and time will be increasingly disconnected from the parameters with which we have traditionally associated them and will be even more subjugated to the logic of the global infosphere that openly favours the *hic et nunc*.

And it was precisely this intensification of the five forces that led us to define the new scenario as a 'world without rules' on the one hand, and then on the other hand, to make an effort to crystallize 10 rules that could inspire the actions of companies in the high-end fashion sector. Those who have read this far will notice that we have a rather cautious approach to the concept of 'rules.' We are convinced that the uniqueness of the situation makes it imperative to adopt an attitude aimed at experimentation and continuous improvement through successive iterations, avoiding the search for simple solutions that claim to be valid for all companies in all markets. **The arduous task of those governing fashion companies in these times is really that of having to manage an epochal paradigm shift, with the awareness that many of the processes and skills of the recent past have suddenly become obsolete.** And this was exactly the difficult objective we had set ourselves: to provide the sector's professionals with the necessary tools to define the new compass points of an industry that – like many others in this period – has been forced to reinvent itself from the ground up.

As for the near future, we expect acceleration to at least remain constant and to cause brands in the high-end segment to reflect on how they may calibrate the speed of change while managing the tension between the desire for topicality and the loss of relevance. As we've seen, the risk to avoid is that of ending up in a danger-ous spiral leading to a rapid process of commoditization. In this regard, we believe it is wise to capitalize on the observations within Be Inclusive, Be a Vibration and Be Timeless. Without forgetting the need to carefully orchestrate the harmony of contact points between brands and clients as were discussed in Be a Symphony, and the importance of nurturing the dynamic defined in Be Relational as 'branding through the customer.'

The spread of digitalization, and the lowering of cultural barriers that had previously slowed its impact, will inevitably lead to the continued hybridization toward the full attainment of the scenario defined as onlife. This transition will become evermore fluid as we witness the inevitable handover between current generations and digital natives as they helm businesses and institutions. These managers and policymakers will be responsible for regulating the new concentrations of power, for defining the lawfulness of practices and behaviours that are often tolerated today due to a lack of viable solutions, and for drawing the ethical boundaries of the relationship between humans and computers.

What forms will the hybridization of human skills with those of robotics and AI take? How will the role of a sales assistant or a personal stylist evolve in a near future in which, thanks to 5G bandwidth, we will be constantly connected to each other and objects, regardless of space-time barriers? What skills will designers and creative directors need to develop if AI reaches such predictive capabilities as to challenge their ability to anticipate or influence a trend? We hope the thinking offered in Be Inspired provides useful guidance for these difficult choices.

Hybridization will increasingly mean the exploration of new business models, as a result of integrating companies with complementary skills along the value chain. We are referring to companies that are very different from each other and that temporarily (or permanently) ally themselves by pursuing the paradigm of open innovation, as we've previously described. The assumption that will continue to drive these choices is that in such a VUCA context, it is no longer possible to pursue business innovation by leveraging only one's own strengths. This will likely lead to a network of alliances at different stages of the value chain, with objectives ranging from improving production efficiency to finding new competitive advantages by sharing business risks. For end customers, this will mean having access to end-to-end offerings that seamlessly integrate product, service and experience, all under the umbrella of one or more brands that act as a linchpin in the construction of the value ecosystem they offer to the public, and which consequently translates into an exponentially richer value proposition than that which individual brands could offer alone. It is from this perspective that we have to look at the industrial partnerships between the historical maisons of the high-end segment and the pure digital e-commerce players or digital native start-ups specializing in the building of global marketplaces for vintage or pre-owned products. For traditional fashion companies, these alliances with e-commerce players specialized in their sector are also a way of accelerating their own digital transformation process, while at the same time limiting the risks associated with a possible expansion in the range of actions of other pure digital players. In fact, many are keeping a close eye on the actions of companies such as Amazon, Alibaba and JingDong. In Be a Service, we discussed these logics, emphasizing the need to constantly observe the evolution of the customer journey and purchasing behaviour, even in sectors remote from the reference one.

On the disintermediation front – or, as we have more aptly defined it, neo-intermediation – we believe that the role of influencers, who address huge swathes of the public through social media, will reach its full maturity in all advanced markets. It will be requested of these figures – and probably required by new laws – to have more professionalism and a greater sense of responsibility, precisely because of their ability to influence the behaviour of large numbers of people. As is the case with advertising regulations around the world, new conditions will likely be put in place to limit the possibility of the public being deceived by confusing personal and sponsored content. There are even those who suggest that a type of certification is necessary, obtained by following a specific training course. We believe that despite audiences being increasingly savvy and accustomed to the commercial dynamics related to influencers, it is important to set even stricter rules that protect people and allow fair competition between market players.

Furthermore, the maturity we allude to is likely to lead the public to want an ever-greater consistency in the behaviour of influencers, just as it happens for brands that are expected to make well-considered choices in a distinct semantic area. Therefore, they will be expected to take responsibility for their actions and take a stand on issues such as environmental and social sustainability, customer/consumer health protection, minority rights, respect for diversity, etc. **Given the characteristics of social media and the onlife infosphere, and the resulting intermingling of private and public life, influencers will increasingly be required to carefully calibrate their marketing mix and brand portfolio.**

Ultimately, these neo-intermediaries will have a role as a true sales and communication channel in the ecosystem of fashion companies, just like multi-brand stores or social channels. Inevitably, this channel will need to integrate harmoniously in order to enrich the overall brand equity and avoid creating dangerous distortions in the perception of the public. Yet another challenge linked to omnichannel will be that of optimizing touchpoints, which will also need to include the role of these figures, who will be able to operate both online and offline, by combining 'Content to Commerce' techniques (for example, when launching new products with sponsored posts that invite purchases through the brands e-commerce) to proximity marketing techniques (such as generating traffic for a new store). We trust the guidance provided in Be a Vibration, Be Relational and Be Collaborative will prove to be invaluable for those who are confronted with this complex management task.

With regard to the evolution of sustainability, there is no doubt that the greatest challenge in the years ahead lies in the collaboration between companies and institutions. It is certainly up to the institutions to regulate by imposing compliance with higher standards in terms of environmental and social impact, but there is no doubt that in order for companies to comply with these standards, they will have to make significant structural investments, equip themselves with innovative technologies to monitor the supply chain and acquire specific skills. This will have a major impact on the cost structure. In such a complex moment in history, aggravated by the aftermath of the pandemic, it will be fundamental that those who govern establish a precise plan in order to prevent sustainability taking second place while the very survival of the company is at stake, and instead, exploit this phase to restart with a new plan.

We believe it will be necessary to focus on incentives aimed at stimulating the cultivation of eco-friendly raw materials and to calm the financial crisis that would otherwise be caused with the urge to penalize working conditions in countries where legislation is less binding. Incentivizing the virtuous behaviour of companies that embrace the new standards will be necessary to mitigate the investments they will inevitably need to make. All of this goes hand-in-hand with the enactment of new laws that must be applied on the widest possible scale and respected by all market players, including suppliers and sub-suppliers who are often located in areas of the world where less virtuous behaviour is tolerated.

Every crisis offers the opportunity to redefine the balance between institutions, individuals and businesses. The next five years will be crucial in this sense: we must accept that the digital world is a 'common environment' in which people work, study, buy and sell products and services, produce and use content, and interact with each other, exactly how the world was when it was completely analogue. Therefore, even in this new common environment that we have defined as the 'infosphere,' we need rules for this hybrid world that are the same for everyone, written by nonpartisan bodies. These rules will need to be flexible enough to adapt to constant developments, while at the same time not overly generic in order to be truly binding. The fairness and effectiveness they need requires that they be written by supranational public entities, which will have the arduous task of satisfying the needs of the market while ensuring the environmental and social wellbeing of the entire planet.

We hope that institutions such as the European Union – which has already shown itself to be attentive to the impact of globalization on people's lives, for example, with laws such as the GDPR that protect citizens with respect to the use of their data – will require companies that intend to do business in their territory to comply with new standards in the field of sustainability. This would undoubtedly trigger a domino effect that, if the previously mentioned incentives were well thought out, could generate an important virtuous cycle. As we have said, the time is past when it was sufficient to simply compensate or reduce the impact of one's own business on society and the planet. Now it is time to think in terms of regeneration and building the future according to different principles.

In terms of purchasing and consumption habits, in the coming years we expect an evolution in the name of 'less but better' and a continuation of well-established trends such as mix & match. People around the world will tend to embrace more modest lifestyles and, given the complex economic situation, even those who can afford to buy more expensive clothes or accessories will find themselves feeling a certain discomfort in routinely flaunting their own wellbeing. It is quite probable therefore that we will see a general contraction in overall sales volumes, accompanied by a certain stability for the most iconic and representative products of a brand's style. This will make it possible to gratify aspects of hedonism and at the same time convey an image of oneself that is consistent with the historical moment the world is going through. The alignment between this attitude in consumers and the phase of reconstruction that the world will face leads us to sustain that this is a unique opportunity to redefine the logic of the fashion system. In this regard, we refer to the April 2020 letter Giorgio Armani addressed to all the operators in the sector, some passages of which we have included in Acceleration and have considered in Be Purposeful.

The last of the five forces described and examined is democratization, or the phenomenon resulting from the encounter between the founding spirit of the web – under the banner of simplification, accessibility and gamification – with that of the exclusivity characterizing fashion previously. As we have stated, it is more accurate to speak of the democratization of the desire for high-end products, as in many cases the actual accessibility of these products remains the prerogative of a relatively few wealthy customers.

At the same time, the mechanism that leads to the desirability of high-end goods is easily formed and continuously amplified through the labyrinth of opportunities for visibility inherent in the contemporary infosphere. We expect this dynamic to escalate as connections become even faster and more ubiquitous. More and more people on a global scale will want to buy high-end products, whose iconic power will be acclaimed by influencers and celebrities on social media.

This will not generate standardization but instead an infinite multitude of niches, within which there will be room for completely individual choices. **The mix & match we spoke of, amplified by the economic situation and the increased awareness of the dynamics of imitation-differentiation typical of fashion, will generate a strong desire for individuality on the part of global consumers.** We are referring to the desire to assert one's own independence, freed from standards suggested by the media, even if also emphasizing the culture of belonging, in a mix that is novel each time because it is being continually redefined; just like the fluid and multiform daily life in which we are immersed. In Be Inclusive, we proposed several interpretations for this phenomenon. We consider the reflections in Be Purposeful to be useful in this regard, since so many people's choices will be dictated by their affinity with the stance brands take on issues relevant to the public, along with those in Be a Service, given the growing need for convenience and the increasingly evident demand for onlife experiences that involve people in a holistic way.

The last of the 10 rules presented was Be Antifragile. More than a guiding principle, it is an invitation to adopt a flexible mental approach, which allows one to live with a certain level of ambiguity and to tolerate high levels of uncertainty and volatility. The only constant is change. This makes particularly relevant the premise that in an uncertain scenario the *planning* phase is often more important than the *plan* itself. **If we assume that the future will become the present at the speed of an algorithm, we must accept the idea that we will often have to improvise, to act without being aware of all the potential variables.** And there is no way to improvise effectively without careful preparation beforehand, by considering a series of possible scenarios. Only at that point will we be able to act 'by instinct,' guided by previous simulations, even when reality will not conform precisely to predictions.

The antifragile attitude we recommend is this: maintaining the ability to thrive in chaos, like those who accept ambiguity and react initially with resilience, motivated by the desire not to succumb in the face of complexity, but to take a breath and press forward, inspired by the systematic search for new opportunities. This exploration may lead brands that the public associates as operating within a specific symbolic sphere, to enter sectors remote from their own core business, in search of forms of monetization that could possibly represent a considerable portion of company revenues in the future.

In the last few pages, we presented readers with the viewpoints of many leading managers in the global high-end fashion industry. While each of them has their own idea regarding the evolution of the situation and the steps that need to be taken, they agree with the definitive need to confront the opportunities offered by the hybridization of the physical and digital worlds, and that the coming years will be crucial. **We will be collectively called upon to rewrite the rules of one of the most important industries in the world.**

Aware of this great challenge, we take our leave with the hope that we have contributed to this open discussion, and have offered entrepreneurs, managers, consultants and students an interpretive framework useful in understanding the state of the art and in governing the evolution of high-end fashion.

Bibliography

BOOKS AND REPORTS

Aaker D. A. 1996. 'Measuring brand equity across products and markets.' *California Management Review*. Berkeley.

Altagamma, BCG. 2020. 'True-Luxury Global Consumer Insights: 7th edition.' Boston.

Amatulli C., De Angelis M., Costabile M. and Guido G. 2017. *Sustainable Luxury Brands: Evidence from Research and Implications for Managers*. London: Palgrave Macmillan.

Amatulli C., De Angelis M., Pichierri M. and Guido G. 2018. 'The Importance of Dream in Advertising: Luxury Versus Mass Market.' *International Journal of Marketing Studies*, 10:1, 71.

Bain & Company, Fondazione Altagamma. 2018. 'Altagamma Worldwide Luxury Market Monitor 2018.' Wellesley.

Bain & Company, Fondazione Altagamma. 2020. 'Altagamma Worldwide Luxury Market Monitor 2020.' Wellesley.

Bain & Company, Fondazione Altagamma. 2020. 'Bain & Company Luxury Study 2020 Spring Update.' Wellesley.

Bauman Z. 2000. *Liquid Modernity*. Great Britain: Polity Press.

BCG, Fondazione Altagamma. 2019. 'True-Luxury Global Consumer Insight.' Boston.

Braungart M. and McDonough W. 2012. *Cradle to Cradle: Remaking the Way We Make Things*. New York: North Point Press.

Camilleri M. A. 2013. *Corporate Sustainability, Social Responsibility and Environmental Management: An Introduction to Theory and Practice with Case Studies*. Berlin: Springer.

Castaldo S. and Mauri. C. (2007). Innovazione, Experience, Partnership. Casi di Innovazione nel Retail. Milan: FrancoAngeli.

Cline E. 2013. *Overdressed: The Shockingly High Cost of Cheap Fashion*. New York: Penguin Group.

Codeluppi V. 2003. *Che cos'è la moda*. Roma: Carocci.

Codeluppi V. 1994. 'Verso il Marketing della Moda,' in *Micro e Macro Marketing* a.III, n.3. Bologna: Il Mulino.

Collins E. 2017. 'How Consumers Really Feel about Loyalty Programs.' *Forrester*.

Corbellini E., Saviolo S. 2016. *Managing Fashion & Luxury Companies* (2nd ed.). Milan: Rizzoli Etas.

Crick J. M. and Crick D. 2020. 'Coopetition and COVID-19: Collaborative Business-to-Business Marketing Strategies in a Pandemic Crisis.' (University of Ottawa: Telfer School of Management).

Deloitte University. 2017. 'Global Powers of Luxury Goods 2017: The New Luxury Consumer.' Diegem.

Deloitte, Google. 2014. 'The Collaborative Economy.' Sidney.

Deloitte. 2017. '2030 Purpose: Good Business and a Better Future Connecting Sustainable Development with Enduring Commercial Success.' London.

Demirbag-Kaplan M., Yildirim C., Gulden S. and Aktan D. 2015. 'I Love to Hate You: Loyalty for Disliked Brands and the Role of Nostalgia.' *Journal of Brand Management*. 22: 2.

Derval D. 2018. *Designing Luxury Brands: The Science of Pleasing Customers' Senses*. Berlin: Springer International.

Edelman Intelligence. 2020. 'Edelman Trust Barometer 2020 Global Report.' New York.

Erdogmus I. E., Akgun I. and Arda E. 2018. 'Drivers of Successful Luxury Fashion Brand Extensions: Cases of Complement and Transfer Extensions.' *Journal of Fashion Marketing and Management*, 22:1.

Euromonitor International. 2017. 'New Concepts in Fashion Retailing.'

Facebook IQ. 2019. 'Zero Friction Future.'

Freeman R.E. 1984. *Strategic Management: A Stakeholder Approach*. Cambridge: Cambridge University Press.

Fuchs C., Prandelli E. and Schreier M. 2010. 'The Psychological Effects of Empowerment Strategies on Consumers' Product Demand.' *Journal of Marketing*, Vol. 74.

Fuchs C., Prandelli E., Schreier M. and Dahl D.W. 2013. 'All That is Users Might Not be Gold: How Labeling Products as User-designed Backfires in the Context of Luxury Fashion Brands,' *Journal of Marketing*, 77:5.

GlobalWebIndex. 'Influencer Marketing.' 2019.

Kantar. 2019. 'BrandZ Top 100 global brands 2019.' London.

Kapferer J.N. (2017). *Lusso. Nuove Sfide, Nuovi Sfidanti*. Milan: FrancoAngeli.

Kapferer J.N. 2016. "The Challenges of Luxury Branding," in *The Routledge Companion to Contemporary Brand Management*. Edited by Singh J., Dall'Olmo Riley F. and Blankson C. (London: Taylor & Francis Group). Pages 473-491.

Kotler P. and Sarkar C. (2020). *Brand Activism: From Purpose to Action*. Milan: Hoepli.

Kotler P., Kartajaya H. and Setiawan I. (2017). *Marketing 4.0. Dal Tradizionale al Digitale*. Milan: Hoepli.

Kotler P. and Stigliano G. (2018). *Retail 4.0. 10 Regole per l'Era Digitale*. Verona: Mondadori Electa.

Lull J. (2000). *Media, Communication, Culture: A Global Approach*. Great Britain: Polity Press.

McKinsey & Co. 2019. 'Global Sustainability Report: Sustainability Matters, But Does it Sell?' New York.

McKinsey & Company/Business of Fashion. 2017. 'State of Fashion 2018.'

McKinsey & Company/Business of Fashion. 2018. 'State of Fashion 2019.'

McKinsey & Company/Business of Fashion. 2019. 'State of Fashion 2020.'

McKinsey & Company/Business of Fashion. 2020. 'State of Fashion 2021.'

McKinsey & Company. 2018. 'The Age of Digital Darwinism.'

Polhemus T. (1996). *Style Surfing: What To Wear in The Third Millenium*. London: Thames & Hudson.

Radclyffe-Thomas N. 2018. 'Profit and Purpose: The Case for Sustainable Luxury Fashion.' London College of Fashion. London.

Rinaldi F.R. (2019). *Fashion Industry 2030: Reshaping the Future Through Sustainability and Responsible Innovation*. Milan: EGEA Bocconi University Press.

Rinaldi F.R. and Testa S. (2014). *The Responsible Fashion Company: Integrating Ethics and Aesthetics in the Value Chain*. London: Taylor & Francis.

Schwartz B. (2004). *The Paradox of Choice. Why More is Less*. United States: Ecco Press.

Tapscott D. and Williams A.D. (2010). *Wikinomics: How Mass Collaboration Changes Everything*. New York: Penguin Group.

Thomas D. (2019). *Fashionopolis: Why What We Wear Matters*. New York: Penguin Books.

Trend Watching. A Post-Corona World. 10 Emerging Consumer Trends That Have Been Radically Accelerated by the Crisis. 2020.

UN General Assembly's Open Working Group Press Release. 2014. 'Sustainable Development Goals.' New York, July 22.

Unity Marketing. 2016. 'How to Create Brand Loyalty Programs to Attract Affluents: Designing Loyalty Programs for Luxury Brands.' United States.

WEB REFERENCES

Abrams M. (March 13, 2020). 'Why Luxury Fashion Houses Still Open Restaurants.' *Vogue Business*. Last modified 13 March, 2020. https://www.voguebusiness.com/consumers/luxury-fashion-houses-restaurants-louis-vuitton-tiffany-bergdorf-goodman-browns.

Achille A. and Zipser D. 'A Perspective for the Luxury-Goods Industry During– and After–Coronavirus.' *McKinsey & Company*. Last modified 1 April, 2020. https://www.mckinsey.com/industries/retail/our-insights/a-perspective-for-the-luxury-goods-industry-during-and-after-coronavirus.

Achim A. L. 'The Art of Luxury Brand Licensing.' *Jing Daily*. Last modified 19 September, 2019. https://jingdaily.com/the-art-of-luxury-brand-licensing/

Agrawal S., De Smet A., Lacroix S. and Reich A. 'To Emerge Stronger from the COVID-19 Crisis, Companies Should Start Reskilling their Workforces Now.' *McKinsey & Company*. Last modified 7 May, 2020. https://www.mckinsey.com/business-functions/people-and-organizational-performance/our-insights/to-emerge-stronger-from-the-covid-19-crisis-companies-should-start-reskilling-their-workforces-now.

Aubertin C. 'From Product to Product-as-a-Service. A New Business Model Shaping the Future of Industries.' *Start It Up*. Last modified 2 July, 2019. https://medium.com/swlh/from-product-to-product-as-a-service-37baed471cd6.

Beghelli C. and Casadei M. 'Lusso, il digitale spinge le vendite globali (anche quelle offline).' *Il Sole 24 Ore*. Last modified 11 June, 2019. https://www.ilsole24ore.com/art/lusso-digitale-spinge-vendite-globali-anche-quelle-offline-ACN569N.

BOF team. 'Marco Bizzarri on How Gucci's Company Culture Fuels Business Success.' *BOF*. Last modified 4 January, 2018. https://www.businessoffashion.com/articles/luxury/ceo-talk-marco-bizzarri.

Bolelli G. (21 April, 2020). 'H&M e C&A in cima al nuovo "Fashion Transparency Index", Gucci primo marchio di lusso.' *Fashion Network*. Last modified 21 April, 2020. https://it.fashionnetwork.com/news/H-m-e-c-a-incima-al-nuovo-fashion-transparency-index-gucci-primo-marchio-dilusso,1209020.html.

Bonchek M. 'Why the Problem with Learning is Unlearning.' *Harvard Business Review*. Last modified 3 November, 2016. https://hbr.org/2016/11/why-the-problem-with-learning-is-unlearning.

Burney E. 'The History of H&M's Best Designer Collaborations.' *Vogue*. Last modified 27 March, 2019. https://www.vogue.com.au/fashion/news/the-history-of-hampms-best-designer-collaborations/image-gallery/a00e15daae83dbfcdc97f01653b53a2f.

Camurati F. 'Il Lusso Corre Sul Filo Del Web.' *MFfashion*. Last modified 23 October, 2020. https://www.mffashion.com/amp/news/livestage/il-lussocorre-sul-filo-del-web-202010222033127712.

Cantoni L. 'Gli Epicentri di Prada.' *MyWhere*. Last modified 6 March, 2015. https://www.mywhere.it/14240/gli-epicentri-di-prada.html.

Casadei M. 'Gli Influencer? Nella Moda Creano Valore, Ma Non Nel Segmento Lusso.' *Il Sole 24 Ore*. Last modified 11 July, 2019. https://www.ilsole24ore.com/art/gli-influencer-moda-creano-valore-ma-non-segmentolusso-ACkc1tX.

Casadei M. 'La Rivincita Degli Outlet: Aumentano Incassi e Visitatori.' *Il Sole 24 Ore*. Last modified 27 May, 2019. https://st.ilsole24ore.com/art/moda/2019-05-27/la-rivincita-outlet-aumentano-incassi-e-visitatori-100755.shtml.

Charm T., Coggins B., Robinson K. and Wilkie J. (August 4, 2020). 'The Great Consumer Shift: Ten Charts That Show How US Shopping Behavior is Changing.' *McKinsey & Company*. Last modified 4 August, 2020. https://www.mckinsey.com/business-functions/marketing-and-sales/our-insights/the-great-consumer-shift-ten-charts-that-show-how-us-shopping-behavior-is-changing.

Chen C. 'How Open-source Innovation May Transform Fashion.' *BOF*. Last modified 31 October, 2018. https://www.businessoffashion.com/articles/news-analysis/how-open-source-innovation-may-transform-fashion.

Chen V. 'Luxury Brands are Setting Up Their Own Museums to Preserve Heritage and Honour Arts.' *Style*. Last modified 6 August, 2015. https://www.scmp.com/magazines/style/article/1845191/luxury-brands-are-setting-their-own-museums-preserve-heritage-and.

D'Arpizio C. and Levato F. 'The Millennial State of Mind: Generation Y Prefers the Genuine Shopping Experience.' *Bain & Company*. Last modified 18 May, 2017. https://www.bain.com/insights/the-millennial-state-of-mind/.

D'Arpizio C., Levato F., Fenili S., Colacchio F. and Prete F. 'Luxury After Covid-19: Changed for (the) Good?' *Bain & Company*. Last modified 26 March, 2020. www.bain.com/insights/luxury-after-coronavirus/.

Danzinger P.N. 'Luxury Brand Licensing: 5 Keys to Success Revealed in Critical Look at Tiffany-Coty's Fragrance Deal.' *Forbes*. Last modified 19 August, 2017. https://www.forbes.com/sites/pamdanziger/2017/08/19/luxury-brand-licensing-5-keys-to-success-revealed-in-critical-look-at-tiffany-cotys-fragrance-deal/?sh=16e2e27a17319.

Degli Innocenti N. 'Burberry Apre l'era Del "See Now Buy Now" Con Collezioni Eclettiche Per la P-E 2017.' *Il Sole 24 Ore*. Last modified 20 September, 2016. https://st.ilsole24ore.com/art/moda/2016-09-20/burberry-apre-era-see-now-buy-now-collezioni-eclettiche-la-p-e-2017-092259.shtml?uuid=ADmaPnNB.

Distler J., Seara J., Antrup A., Krueger F. and Hohmann-Altmeier J. 'Dressed for Digital: The Next Evolution in Fashion Marketing.' *BCG*. Last modified 6 December, 2018. https://www.bcg.com/it-it/publications/2018/dressed-for-digital-evolution-in-fashion-marketing.

Dornetti L. 'Perché il Nuovo Lusso Sarà Essere Offline.' *Il Sole 24 Ore*. Last modified 15 July, 2019. https://www.ilsole24ore.com/art/perche-nuovolusso-sara-essere-offline-ACGlxuY.

Editorial staff. 'The CNMI Diversity and Inclusion Manifesto.' Last modified 12 April, 2019. https://www.cameramoda.it/en/associazione/news/1588/.

Editorial staff. 'Tmall Apre Primo Outlet per Smaltire l'Invenduto.' *Pambianconews*. Last modified 27 April, 2020. https://www.pambianconews.com/2020/04/27/tmall-apre-primo-outlet-per-smaltirelinvenduto-291888/.

Editorial staff. 'LVMH Launches the "LVMH Innovation Award" at Viva Technology 2017.' *LVMH*. Last modified 21 February, 2017. https://www.lvmh.com/news-documents/press-releases/lvmh-launches-the-lvmh-innovation-award-at-viva-technology-2017/

Editorial staff. 'Armani: «L'Entusiasmo per il See Now-Buy Now è Prematuro».' *Fashion Magazine*. Last modified 26 February, 2016. https://www.fashionmagazine.it/business/Dichiarazioni-Armani-Lentusiasmo-per-il-see-now-buy-now--prematuro-68652.

Editorial staff. 'Number of US Amazon Prime Members Grows Steadily: Study.' *Nasdaq*. Last modified 17 January, 2020. https://www.nasdaq.com/articles/number-of-us-amazon-prime-members-grows-steadily%3Astudy-2020-01-17.

Editorial staff. 'Value of the Outlet Personal Luxury Goods Market Worldwide From 2012 to 2020.' *Statista*. Last modified 26 January, 2021. https://www.statista.com/statistics/503098/value-of-the-global-off-price-personal-luxury-goods-market/.

Editorial staff. 'Corporate Entrepreneurship Nel Luxury: Così LVMH Accoglie le Idee Dei Dipendenti.' *EconomyUP*. Last modified 8 January, 2020. https://www.economyup.it/retail/corporate-entrepreneurship-nel-luxury-cosi-lvmh-accoglie-le-idee-dei-dipendenti/.

Editorial staff. 'Accenture e Microsoft Insieme per la Piattaforma Digitale a Supporto Della Milano Digital Fashion Week di CNMI.' *Microsoft*. Last modified 14 July, 2020. https://news.microsoft.com/it-it/2020/07/14/accenture-e-microsoft-insieme-per-la-piattaforma-digitale-a-supporto-della-milano-digital-fashion-week-di-cnmi/.

Editorial staff. 'Armani, Accordo con Yoox Net-à-Porter Per Sinergia Tra Online e Offline. Intesa Siglata Fino al 2025. Giorgio Armani: "Modello di Business Basato su Fare Meno ma Meglio".' *Youmark*. Last modified 22 July, 2020. https://youmark.it/ym-youmark/armani-accordo-con-yoox-net-a-porter-per-sinergia-tra-online-e-offline-intesa-siglata-fino-al-2025-giorgio-armani-modello-di-business-basato-su-fare-meno-ma-meglio/.

Editorial staff. 'Gucci Off the Grid: La Prima Collezione Sostenibile del Marchio Fiorentino.' *Repubblica*. Last modified 16 June, 2020. https://www.repubblica.it/moda-e-beauty/dossier/moda-green/2020/06/16/news/gucci_alessandro_michele_collezione_sostenibile_off_the_grid_jane_fonda_campagna_pubblicitaria_gucci_equilibrium-291091664/.

Editorial staff. 'Farfetch sFonda Sulla Sostenibilità. Lancia Tool Che Misura Impatto Acquisti.' *Pambianconews*. Last modified 18 June, 2020. https://www.pambianconews.com/2020/06/18/farfetch-sfonda-sullasostenibilita-lancia-tool-che-misura-impatto-acquisti-295717/.

Editorial staff. 'Banking is Only the Beginning: 58 Big Industries Blockchain Could Transform.' *CBInsights*. Last modified 3 March, 2021. https://www.cbinsights.com/research/industries-disrupted-blockchain/.

Editorial staff. 'What is the State of Luxury's Hundred Million Dollar Licensing Deals?' *The Fashion Law*. Last modified 10 May, 2018. https://www.thefashionlaw.com/what-is-the-state-of-luxurys-hundred-million-dollar-licensing-deals/.

Editorial staff. 'Gucci, Addio al "Rito Stanco Della Stagionalità". Sfilerà Coi Tempi di Michele.' *Pambianconews*. Last modified 25 May, 2020. https://www.pambianconews.com/2020/05/25/gucci-addio-al-rito-stanco-della-stagionalita-sfilera-coi-tempi-di-michele-294047/.

Editorial staff. 'The RealReal Offre il B2B per Smaltire Invenduto.' *Pambianconews*. Last modified 27 May, 2020. https://www.pambianconews.com/2020/05/27/the-realreal-offre-il-b2b-per-smaltire-invenduto-294280/.

Editorial staff. 'Accordo Tra YOOX NET-A-PORTER e l'Università di Modena e Reggio Emilia per la Ricerca Sull'Intelligenza Artificiale Nel Lusso.' *YNAP Group*. Last modified 29 May, 2020. https://www.ynap.com/it/news/accordo-tra-yoox-net-a-porter-e-luniversita-di-modena-e-reggio-emilia-per-la-ricerca-sullintelligenza-artificiale-nel-lusso/.

Editorial staff. 'Farfetch Spinge lo Sviluppo del Second Hand.' *Pambianconews*. Last modified 9 October, 2019. https://www.pambianconews.com/2019/10/09/farfetch-spinge-lo-sviluppo-del-second-hand-275277/.

Editorial staff. 'Burberry Trasmetterà su Twitch la Sfilata Della Nuova Collezione PE21.' *Brandnews*. Last modified 15 September, 2020. https://www.brand-news.it/brand/persona/abbigliamento/burberry-trasmettera-su-twitch-la-sfilata-della-nuova-collezione-pe21/.

Editorial staff. 'Valentino Esordisce Nel 'See Now-Buy Now'.' *Pambianconews*. Last modified 30 September, 2019. https://www.pambianconews.com/2019/09/30/valentino-esordisce-nel-see-now-buy-now-274021/.

Editorial staff. 'Boggi Milano: dal Blue Code al Bluetooth.' *Sinesy*. Accessed 30 October, 2021. https://www.sinesy.it/omnichannel-customer-experience-boggi-milano/.

Editorial staff. 'Licensing the Luxury Goods Industry.' *License Global*. Last modified 6 April, 2018. https://www.licenseglobal.com/archive/licensing-luxury-goods-industry.

Foley N. 'Eight Principles of Luxury.' *Landor*. Last modified 1 April, 2013. https://landor.com/eight-principles-of-luxury.

Foncillas P. 'With "Hyperservice" Comes "Servification".' *LinkedIn*. Last modified 26 April, 2016. https://www.linkedin.com/pulse/hyperservice-comes-servification-pablo-foncillas-d%C3%ADaz-plaja/.

Foncillas P. 'New Marketing is Changing Everything: Hyperservice and Servification.' *IESE*. Last modified 30 November, 2016. https://blog.iese.edu/blog/2016/11/30/new-marketing-is-changing-everything-hyperservice-and-servification/.

Friedman V. 'The New Meaning of Fast Fashion.' *The New York Times*. Last modified 20 April, 2017. https://www.nytimes.com/2017/04/20/fashion/farfetch-gucci-designer-delivery.html.

Gargatte E. and Martinelli R. 'Kering Eyewear and the Maison Cartier Partner for the Development of the Eyewear Category.' *Kering*. Last modified 21 March, 2017. https://www.kering.com/cn/news/eyewear-maison-cartier-partner-development-eyewear-category#.

Glueck J. 'The Service Revolution. Manufacturing's Missing Crown Jewel.' *Deloitte*. Last modified 1 August, 2007. https://www2.deloitte.com/us/en/insights/deloitte-review/issue-1/the-service-revolution.html.

Gonzalo A., Harreis H., Sancez Altable C. and Villepelet C. 'Fashion's Digital Transformation: Now or Never.' *McKinsey & Company*. Last modified 6 May, 2020. https://www.mckinsey.com/industries/retail/our-insights/fashions-digital-transformation-now-or-never.

Gregg B., Heller J., Perrey J. and Tsai J. (June 18, 2018). 'The Most Perfect Union: Unlocking the Next Wave of Growth by Unifying Creativity and Analytics.' *McKinsey & Company*. Last modified 18 June, 2018. https://www.mckinsey.com/business-functions/marketing-and-sales/our-insights/the-most-perfect-union.

Gustafson K. 'The Anti-Amazons: Two Brands Shaking Up Retail.' *CNBC*. Last modified 28 March, 2016. https://www.cnbc.com/2016/03/22/the-anti-amazons-two-brands-shaking-up-retail.html.

Houston J. and Kim I.A. 'Prime Day Deals Aren't the Only Way Amazon Gets You to Spend More. Here are 13 of the Company's Sneaky Tricks.' *Insider*. Last modified 13 October, 2020. https://www.businessinsider.com/amazon-prime-members-spend-more-money-sneaky-ways-2019-9?IR=T.

Idacavage S. 'Fashion History Lesson: The Origins of Fast Fashion.' *Fashionista*. Last modified 17 October, 2018. https://fashionista.com/2016/06/what-is-fast-fashion.

Indvik L. 'The Fashion Industry Wants to Slow Down. Can It?' *Financial Times*. Last modifed 29 May, 2020. https://www.ft.com/content/8bd9fe5e-a02e-11ea-b65d-489c67b0d85d.

Jones O. 'Woke-washing: How Brands are Cashing in On the Culture Wars.' *The Guardian*. Last modified 23 March, 2019. https://www.theguardian.com/media/2019/may/23/woke-washing-brands-cashing-in-on-culture-wars-owen-jones.

J. Walter Thompson Intelligence, Snap Inc. 2019. 'Into Z Future: Understanding Generation Z, the Next Generation of "Super Creatives".'

J.Walter Thompson Intelligence. 2018. 'The New Sustainability: Regeneration.'

Kent S. 'Fashion Industry Still Failing on Transparency.' *BOF*. Last modified 24 April, 2019. https://www.businessoffashion.com/articles/sustainability/fashion-industry-still-failing-on-transparency.

Kimani N. 'Brand Stretching: How Luxury Diversifies its Portfolio.' *The Designers Studio*. Last modified 5 February, 2018. https://tdsblog.com/luxury-brand-stretching/.

Kotler P. 'Branding: From Purpose to Beneficence.' *The Marketing Journal*. Last modified 22 March, 2016. https://www.marketingjournal.org/brand-purpose-to-beneficence-philip-kotler/.

Kraaijenbrink J. 'Using Invite-only Marketing as a Winning Strategy in High-end Luxury Branding.' *Forbes*. Last modified 24 September, 2019. https://www.forbes.com/sites/jeroenkraaijenbrink/2019/09/24/usinginvite-only-marketing-as-a-winning-strategy-in-high-end-luxurybranding/?sh=6ebbb8e0743c.

La Ferla R. "'Cheap chic' Draws Crowds on 5th Ave.' *The New York Times*. Last modified 11 April, 2000. https://www.nytimes.com/2000/04/11/style/cheap-chic-draws-crowds-on-5th-ave.html.

Lark K. 'Loyalty Evolves: From Rewards to Recognition.' *Luxury Branding*. Accessed 17 September, 2021. https://www.luxury-branding.com/library/evolution-loyalty-rewards-recognition/.

Lingala A. 'Elitism is Not Cool: Young People Change Cultural Values.' *Kantar*. Last modified 22 May, 2020. https://www.kantar.com/inspiration/brands/elitism-is-not-cool-young-people-change-cultural-values.

Magids S., Zorfas A. and Leemon D. 'The New Science of Customer Emotions.' *Harvard Business Review*. Last modified November, 2015. https://hbr.org/2015/11/the-new-science-of-customer-emotions.

Mantovani S. 'Customer Retention & Loyalty: i Nuovi Trend per i Brand del Lusso (e non).' *Get Connected*. Last modified 18 September, 2018. https://www.getconnected.it/2018/09/18/customer-retention-loyalty-trend/.

Mastrilli P. 'H&M e la Moda del Luxury Co-branding, da Oggi la Collezione Firmata Marni.' *Brand Forum*. Last modified 8 March, 2012. https://www.brandforum.it/paper/h-and-m-e-la-moda-del-luxury-co-branding-da-oggi-la-collezione-firmata-marni/.

Mauri l. 'Giorgio Armani: "La mia sfilata in tv senza gerarchie e privilegi. Perché dobbiamo scoprire un modo più umano per essere connessi".' *Il Fatto Quotidiano*. Last modified 30 September, 2020. https://www.ilfattoquotidiano.it/2020/09/30/giorgio-armani-la-mia-sfilata-in-tv-senzagerarchie-e-privilegi-perche-dobbiamo-scoprire-un-modo-piu-umano-peressere-connessi/5948011/.

McDowell M. 'Burberry's Partnership with The RealReal Signifies a Real Shift.' *Vogue Business*. Last modified 7 October, 2019. https://www.voguebusiness.com/companies/burberrys-partnership-realreal-secondhand.

Oliver R.L. 'Whence Consumer Loyalty?' *Journal of Marketing*. Accessed 30 October, 2021. https://journals.sagepub.com/doi/10.1177/00222429990634s105.

O'Reilly III, C.A. and Tushman M.L. 'The Ambidextrous Organization.' *Harvard Business Review*. Last modified April, 2004. https://hbr.org/2004/04/the-ambidextrous-organization.

Oszi T. 'Loyalty Program ROI - How LuisaViaRoma Made €16M.' *Antavo*. Last modified 25 July, 2019. https://antavo.com/blog/loyalty-program-roi-lvr.

Pan Y. 'Alibaba Unveils Exclusive Luxury Pavilion Courting Super-Wealthy Chinese Shoppers.' *Jing Daily*. Last modified 2 August, 2017. https://jingdaily.com/alibaba-launches-luxury-pavilion/.

Parguel B., Delécolle T. and Mimouni Chaabane A. 'Does Fashionization Impede Luxury Brands' CSR Image?' *Sustainability* 12(1), 2021. https://www.mdpi.com/2071-1050/12/1/428.

Porter M.E. and Kramer M.R. 'Strategy and Society: The Link Between Competitive Advantage and Corporate Social Responsibility.' *Harvard Business Review*. Last modified December, 2006. https://hbr.org/2006/12/strategy-and-society-the-link-between-competitive-advantage-and-corporate-social-responsibility.

Porter M.E. and Kramer M.R. 'Creating Shared Value.' *Harvard Business Review*. Last modified January-February, 2011. https://hbr.org/2011/01/the-big-idea-creating-shared-value.

PSFK, PCH. 'The Art of the Drop.' New York, July 2020

PwC Global. 2017. 'Sizing the Prize. PwC's Global Artificial Intelligence Study: Exploiting the AI Revolution.'

Rakestraw A. 'The 2010s Were the Decade Luxury & Streetwear Became One.' *Highsnobiety*. Accessed 17 September, 2021. https://www.highsnobiety.com/p/luxury-streetwear-2010s/.

Ricifari C. 'La Startup Siciliana Che Trasforma le Bucce d'Arancia in Tessuto.' *Forbes*. Last modified 23 January, 2018. https://forbes.it/2018/01/23/la-startup-siciliana-che-trasforma-le-bucce-darancia-in-tessuto/.

Romagnoli R. 'Co-branding in the Luxury Industry.' *The Drum*. Last modified 1 July, 2020. https://www.thedrum.com/opinion/2020/07/01/co-branding-the-luxury-industry.

Sahli E. 'I Modelli di Gucci, Tra Bellezza e Diversità (Ben Prima di Armine).' *Vanity Fair*. Last modified 3 September, 2020. https://www.vanityfair.it/fashion/news-fashion/2020/09/03/gucci-armine-harutyunyan-modelle-bellezza-diversita-foto-sfilate.

Salenga M. 'Why the Rise of the Purpose Economy Will Change How we Work Forever.' *tbd*. Last modified 1 January, 2018. https://www.tbd.community/en/a/why-rise-purpose-economy-will-change-how-we-work-forever.

Sauza S. 'L'Epoca Dell'Accelerazione. Appunti Sul Tempo Nelle Metropoli.' *Linkiesta*. Last modified 24 March, 2016. https://www.linkiesta.it/blog/2016/03/lepoca-dellaccelerazione-appunti-sul-tempo-nelle-metropoli/.

Schiro A.M. 'Fashion; Two New Stores that Cruise Fashion's Fast Lane.' *The New York Times*. Last modified 31 December, 1989. https://www.nytimes.com/1989/12/31/style/fashion-two-new-stores-that-cruise-fashion-s-fast-lane.html.

Shukla P. 'Luxury Brand Extension: Handle with Care.' *Luxurysociety*. Last modified 16 June, 2011. https://www.luxurysociety.com/en/articles/2011/06/luxury-brand-extension-handle-with-care/.

Stankeviciute R. and Hoffmann J. (2012). 'The Impact of Brand Extension on the Parent Luxury Fashion Brand: The Cases of Giorgio Armani, Calvin Klein and Jimmy Choo.' *Taylor and Francis Online*. Published online 12 December, 2012. https://www.tandfonline.com/doi/abs/10.1080/20932685.2010.10593064.

Stephens D. 'Why Paid Memberships Are the New Loyalty.' *Retail Prophet*. Last modified 7 March, 2018. https://www.retailprophet.com/why-paid-memberships-are-the-new-loyalty/.

Stigliano G. and Gallo P. 'Post-Pandemic Leadership: Come Cambia la Gestione d'Impresa al Tempo del Covid-19?' *Harvard Business Review Italia*. Last modified July, 2020. https://www.hbritalia.it/speciale-gestire-le-crisi/2020/07/17/news/post-pandemic-leadership-come-cambia-la-gestione-dimpresa-al-tempo-del-covid-19-4034/?refresh_ce.

The Associated Press. 'Persson E 85; Founded Clothing Chain.' *The New York Times*. Last modified 1 November, 2002. https://www.nytimes.com/2002/11/01/business/erling-persson-85-founded-clothing-chain.html.

Tochtermann T. and Dauriz L. 'How Luxury Brands Can Create a Sense of Lifestyle.' *McKinsey*. Last modified 1 November, 2012. https://www.mckinsey.com/business-functions/marketing-and-sales/our-insights/how-luxury-brands-can-create-a-sense-of-lifestyle.

Tognini M. 'Il Segreto del Successo Miliardario di Supreme: Il Brand di Streetwear in Italia Spopola con Fedez & Ferragni.' *Business24*. Last modified 3 September, 2018. https://business24tv.it/2018/09/03/il-segreto-del-successo-miliardario-di-supreme/.

Tsang J. 'Axel Dumas, CEO of Hermès, Says True Luxury Does Not Always Have to Depend on Marketing.' *South China Morning Post*. Last modified 4 September, 2014. https://www.scmp.com/magazines/style/article/1581182/axel-dumas-ceo-hermes-says-true-luxury-does-not-always-have-depend.

Valette-Florence P. and Kapferer J.N. (2016). 'Beyond Rarity: The Paths of Luxury Desire. How Luxury Brands Grow Yet Remain Desirable.' *Journal of Product & Brand Management*, 25(2), April 2016. https://www.researchgate.net/publication/301673534_Beyond_rarity_the_paths_of_luxury_desire_How_luxury_brands_grow_yet_remain_desirable.

Warrel M. 'Learn, Unlearn & Relearn: What Got You Here Won't Get You There.' *Forbes*. Last modified 12 June, 2020. https://www.forbes.com/sites/margiewarrell/2020/06/12/learn-unlearn--relearn-what-got-you-here-wont-get-you-there/.

Wollan R., Davis P., De Angelis F. and Quiring K. 2017. 'Seeing Beyond the Loyalty Illusion: It's Time you Invest More Wisely.' Accenture Strategy.

Wunderman Thompson Intelligence. 2020. 'Generation Z: APAC. Connected, Engaged and Coming of Age in Asia Pacific.' London.

Wunderman Thompson. 2020. 'The Future 100: Trends and Change to Watch in 2020.'

Zargani L. 'Giorgio Armani on Slow Fashion Post-Coronavirus.' *WWD*. Last modified 6 April, 2020. https://wwd.com/fashion-news/designer-luxury/giorgio-armani-on-slow-fashion-post-coronavirus-1203554219/.

About the Authors

PHILIP KOTLER

Philip Kotler is known around the world as the 'father of modern marketing.' For over 50 years, he has taught at the Kellogg School of Management at Northwestern University. Originally a PhD economist from MIT, he has become the world's leading marketing authority. His book *Marketing Management* is the most widely used textbook in marketing around the world. He is the author of more than 80 books that have been translated in over 20 languages.

He has received honourary degrees from 22 universities around the world. In 2010, he created the World Marketing Summit with the goal of improving the state of the world by engaging global and community leaders in marketing and business, research and academics, politics and society, and women and gender to ensure sustainable business growth of products and services and thus improve the lives of people across the globe.

GIUSEPPE STIGLIANO

A thought leader and sought-after keynote speaker on marketing, leadership, digital transformation, and corporate innovation, Giuseppe is also the co-author of the best-selling *Retail 4.0: 10 Guiding Principles for the Digital Age*, co-written in 2018 with Philip Kotler, and already translated into six languages.

Giuseppe is an entrepreneurial manager with 20 years of international experience in marketing and communication services. As the Global CEO of Spring Studios, he guides a team of 250 talents in their London, New York, Los Angeles and Milan offices. He has a PhD degree in Marketing and Economics and has founded two startups.

He also mentors young entrepreneurs and serves as an Adjunct Professor of Retail Marketing and Entrepreneurship and Innovation at notable international universities and business schools.

RICCARDO POZZOLI

Riccardo is the Persol Global Brand Director, an Italian entrepreneur, advisor and investor. He has founded and advised a dozen start-ups in the past ten years, innovating within the fashion, media and food industries.

Author of inspirational books regarding marketing and business, Riccardo also has a weekly podcast, in which he shares stories about successful business personalities. He works as a consultant for corporations, helping them develop their brand communications, as well as helping promising new start-up projects take flight.